THE GUINNESS BOOK OF
ANTIQUES

A St Cloud white figure of a Pagod, an idol or image to be placed in a pagoda. 9¾ ins (24·8 cm) high. Courtesy Christie's

THE GUINNESS BOOK OF
ANTIQUES

John FitzMaurice Mills

GUINNESS SUPERLATIVES LIMITED
2 CECIL COURT, LONDON ROAD, ENFIELD, MIDDLESEX

© John FitzMaurice Mills and Guinness Superlatives Ltd, 1979

ISBN 0 900424 68 0

Published in Great Britain by Guinness Superlatives Ltd,
2 Cecil Court, London Road, Enfield, Middlesex

Guinness is a registered trademark of
Guinness Superlatives Limited

Printed and bound in Great Britain by
Bemrose and Sons Limited, Derby

British Library Cataloguing in Publication Data
Mills, John FitzMaurice
   The Guinness Book of Antiques.
   1. Antiques – Dictionaries
   I. Title
   745.1'03   NK28

   ISBN 0-900424-68-0

Title page illustration
Stagshorn study of an owl
Ozaki Kokusai. Asakusa School
Courtesy Sotheby Parke Bernet

CONTENTS

FOREWORD

BY LORD MOYNE

There is a complicated cross-roads between the ways of Aesthetics and Craftsmanship and History and Commerce with a by-lane from Aesthetics into the meanderings of Taste and another into the Domestic Convenience of tea-cups or chairs. These cross-roads are bewildering and can lead into the lost directions of false aesthetic values or misspent cash, or on over the stepping stones of skilful repairs or reproductions into the morass of dishonest faking, forging, or selling. Who could be a better guide at such a bewildering junction than John FitzMaurice Mills whose articles in the press and books on such subjects, whose television appearances and radio talks and whose Guinness Book of Art Facts and Feats have already given so much enlightenment, interest and pleasure.

PREFACE

George III gold Freedom Box presented to Sir
Eyre Coote KB, KC by the Corporation of
Clonmell, Dublin 1802. Courtesy of Christie's

Throughout recorded history there is evidence of those who have surrounded themselves with the precious, the rare; the feats of craftsmen and artists. At the same time those records build up a storehouse of techniques and materials; the facts, from the past, the study of which can bring a fuller appreciation and enjoyment of a collection, large or small, a group of items or just a single object.

Earlier in this century there was a movement towards functionalism amongst certain designers. The tenet being that those things for general use should be constructed with regard to function rather than aesthetic consideration; that an object should be shorn of any unnecessary detail and should have just that about it that was required for it to perform its planned use, whether it was a spoon, a chair, a cup and saucer or whatever. This credo has never really reached a widespread appreciation. Even the most mass-produced item seems to collect some decoration along the way.

Trace the work of the craftsman and designer back several thousand years and yet there seems no real sign of a beginning of man's desire to decorate those things he lives with. Ancient papyri of 1500 years before Christ describe the making of a Tabernacle giving instructions as to the kinds of wood, measurements, ornaments, fastenings (loops and taches), curtains of fine linen and coverings of dried skins. The 25th Chapter of Exodus points to the existence of generations of carpenters, joiners, weavers, dyers, goldsmiths and other craftsmen. Solomon when engaged in building his great temple brought in skilled artificers of many trades from various countries. About 450 BC an apartment in the palace of Ahasuerus is described as having: 'white, green and blue hangings fastened with cords of fine linen and purple, to silver rings and pillars of marble; the beds were of gold and silver, upon a pavement of red and blue and white and black marble'. (Esther 1:6).

The Roman Emperor would seek his treasures from the quality of Greece. The Renaissance noble banker sought the excellence of the past and made his own by cultured patronage of the legions of great craftsmen who plied their minds and hands to creative accomplishment in the centres of Florence and Venice and numerous other places across Europe.

What is the catalyst, the signal that communicates between the talented hand and the collector? Is it perhaps a basic something in the unconscious that feels a link which picks up a connection for the collector with the true craftsman; a part of the enjoyment and satisfaction that is generated as he works, often using complex techniques, with gem-stones, fine woods, precious metals. This dedication and sheer love can release a force of mutual harmony, a new comprehension can be found in the mind of the viewer. Taste, an amalgam of knowledge, understanding and humility, is born; and this can lead to an endless movement of discovery out into the infinite realm of the decorative arts.

A few years ago some purists would define the area of antiques as bounded between the medieval period and 1850. The beginning date to a degree sets itself as most artifacts of wood, textiles and other perishable materials earlier than this have more or less succumbed to time, climate and other destructive agents; notable exceptions being such as the hoards from the tombs of the like of Tutankhamen. The records that remain are largely in paintings from such as those at Pompeii and relief carvings. But the cut-out date of 1850 has now been rather broken through; most would accept that antiques certainly go as far as 1914. The embracing term of 'bygones' brings matters up to around 1939 and perhaps is already invading the post-war years.

The phrase 'taste in collecting' is one that has almost endless connotations. Witness to the fact how matters can go at a large and varied country-house sale. At the end of the catalogue there can be several pages of odd lots that would seem to be a waste of time for the auctioneer to raise his gavel on. But sell they do, and if lots are withdrawn it is seldom for want of a bid but much more likely that the bids have not been strong enough.

Go to the likes of Christie's or Sotheby Parke Bernet when there is an important sale in action and there will be met an atmosphere that seems unique, a compound of almost magical forces. The bidders compete under various cloaks of identity, the seller if present holds his breath as the figure of his reserve is reached, passed and left behind. Supporting it all will be the calm words of the man on the rostrum. Bids may move upwards by fives, tens, hundreds and then into thousands. Apart from the voice up in front there is one of the most intense silences found anywhere. Up into the hundred thousands and then a quite small tap from the gavel and it is over, the tension is released. Someone else is taking that beautiful treasure, is taking a lease on that exquisite piece of craftsmanship that is in fact an item of universal heritage.

A French writer, Jules Fleury-Husson, who used the pseudonym Champfleury, published *Les Petits Mystères de l'Hôtel des Ventes;* and amongst his words of advice were a number of tips for those attending auctions, which included:

A bottle of smelling salts as essential.
Wear plain clothes as rich trimmings will draw attention.
Steady the nerves by washing with cold water in the morning.
Avoid rich spicy foods before a sale.
A bar of chocolate will sustain one for a long session.
If you let yourself be carried along with the tide of bidding you might as well expect to win a fortune at roulette.

Some of these may be a little out of date but there are a few points to ponder. Auctions to many are a chance to give battle, to feel the spur of gain within possible reach. Whether as active participants or just as spectators, the business of the matter infects one and all. So much must be learnt before entering the lists if unhappy errors are to be avoided. The scene of the whole area of antiques is so vast and complex that it would take very many books of the length of this to cover everything. But it is hoped that what follows will be a general guide to the different categories, mentioning some of the leading figures, techniques and materials.

What can be advised for the beginner to collect? Far too dangerous a question to answer right out. But as each of us is individual, so each will very likely be led to that which fascinates and fills a void somewhere and satisfies a need, whether this attraction be for exquisite netsuke, massive early oak furniture, delicate Worcester porcelain, Waterford glass or some 'bygone', musical automata, playing cards or carved wooden butter-prints. All these can have a link with the one who selects them. To him or her their presence within the home gives something that may at first thought seem superficial and just decorative but which can actually go much deeper.

In the following alphabetical section there are some 2000 plus headings that could assist when studying the crisp intellectual paragraphs in the catalogues of a sale of fine things. At the end are listings of some galleries and museums around the world and markets and auction rooms where antiques may be studied.

ANTIQUES AS AN APPRECIATING SECURITY

Fine art and antiques are being sold and bought today on a scale that would have dumbfounded the craftsmen and artists who produced these things of rarity and beauty. The great salerooms of Christie's, Sotheby Parke Bernet, the Dorotheum, Rasmussen and a legion of lesser houses, hundreds of select salons in New York, Paris, London, Munich, Rome, Tokyo and thousands of establishments around the commercial globe are dealing; selling, buying, to a total of somewhere around £1 500 000 000 each year. A growth industry of the first rank.

Many are the collectors who are likely to consider the price tag and probable appreciation first and the beauty second. Even such a body as British Rail pensions fund has laid away a comfortable handful of millions, trusting that the rare and ancient will come up as winners after a carefully judged number of years fruitful hibernation. What have these delicate pieces of porcelain, few square feet of canvas and pigment, old armaments, furniture with signs of time, and other such artifacts of men's skill got? The years since the last war have heavily underlined price increases; figures that still continue up the gradient. Those treasures, that have been accepted by many as household details and exquisite decorations, have probably become the safest repository for money. Can a Ming vase, a prize piece of Louis XV furniture, a silver bowl by one of the Irish mastersmiths really be equated against gilt-edged shares or 'blue chip' stocks? The answer is probably in the affirmative. Glance at the results achieved in the salerooms and the world of the stock dealing does not stand quite so high.

The trick for the beginner is to know when, how or where to join the market. But before launching out on to this quick moving torrent of mesmerising values and bewildering variety, take a careful look. It is just as easy to buy a 'safe' silver mine today as it was when Honoré de Balzac sank his hard earnt cash in such a 'will-o'-the wisp'.

Today the absolute top quality is either securely sitting in public institutions or great private collections. If such articles do come out on the public mart a private bidder, or even the general 'ring' will have slight chance of having the final call. Directors of the great national galleries and museums, backed by often immense funds and even at times by national banks, will overrun the opposition, and in so doing often hike the bids up into the magic area of seven figures sterling. Where does this leave the rest of us? In an area that is rich with possibilities in pretty well every category.

But pause before raising the catalogue or lifting the ticket on the beautifully worked rug. Know what you feel you want to acquire, and then as far as possible know all that can be found out about the object. Seek creditable advice, examine specimens in museums, and compare where possible. These things of the past if genuine are as safe an investment as you will find. But there are in the field a growing number of those who have also digested the good news and who are reaping a fine harvest for themselves. It just would not be possible for Mr Chippendale and company to have made all the huge array that is too often credited to them. Beware of becoming a name-, a signature-, or a mark-buyer, as that way points to possible disaster. Although obviously many of these artists' or craftsmen's signs are quite correct, many, many more have been convenient additions. Such an action requires little skill from the warped one seeking a good multiple mark-up. With him or her is a shadow company of skilled hands hard at it to satisfy the hungry demands that have overtaken the supply of good and truthful things.

'St. Hubert and the Stag' carried out in silver, metal-gilt and hardstone. North Italian. Courtesy Christie's

Catalogues couch carefully the wares on offer. For the peak of the genuine there is an open statement of fact. But then matters can become confusing for the tyro bent on acquisition. He can find something described as 'in the manner of', 'from the workshop of', etc, etc. What do these terms indicate? It can be that the object is from a date contemporary with that of the master artist or craftsman; it can indicate the work of a skilled but not generally known hand. It can also mean a reproduction or copy. It may shield 'fiddling', 'marriage' or outright fakery.

Unfortunately the forger and alterer are not people of any one century. They have been polluting the art market for as long as collectors have sought to bring together objects for their enjoyment and security for the lean times or as safe wealth for theirs to come. These fraudulent items often appear when fashions dry up the good examples. Beware of joining a craze in collecting. The

one in first is generally the winner, whilst those following will probably find that in the end they have picked up the lesser crumbs, which can often be found to have an evaporated value.

In recent years a number of lines have been produced for the fashion collector. Almost illimitable Staffordshire figures have moved around. Many of these with a superficial examination appear to have a satisfactory craquelure. Scientific instruments have become an 'in' category, and several people have found their pounds, francs, marks and dollars have shrunk after purchasing such as 16th-century astrolabes with carefully conjured wear patina, that have probably left some skilled artificer's bench a bare few months previous.

Yet, broadly, the field is open if you take the trouble to find out and know. Not all the lots in the rooms are going to go charging high up the scale. In fact the large majority of objects sold will be in three figures or less.

How long does the period of holding an item have to be before the magic starts to take place? Educated guesses can be made, but the market is as capricious as the turf. It can be affected by many factors; fashion can temporarily throw matters, a glut can slow or stop matters, threatened disasters can bring on off-loading. But if you choose wisely and don't rush in, the general scene is one of a steady and often exciting appreciation.

Examples such as the following give pointers. A George III library bookcase fetched £480 in 1971; sold six years later it brings £2500. A Louis XV painted and gilded screen in 1947 realised £1890; thirty years later it comes in at £15 000. A Gubbio Lustre vase fetched £71 8s in 1942 and in 1976 makes £13 000. A Famille Rose Hunting punch bowl fetched £609 in 1964; add on fifteen years and it makes £1700. A St Louis Grasshopper paperweight brings £440 in 1963; twelve years later it multiplies by nearly ten and brings down the hammer at £4200. From the hand of the master, Carl Fabergé, a pale Rose Quartz Chick made £300 in 1957 and in 1976 tots up £7000.

Where does the most impressive growth show? Surprisingly, not amongst the masses of masterful silver, nor with the gleaming furniture of the 18th century, nor with fine oriental porcelain, nor with the old master paintings; but in the area of old master prints, etchings, aquatints, engravings, woodcuts and wood engravings, here the growth factor is up to a multiple of eighteen or more. Lying second in the appreciation stakes comes Chinese porcelain at fifteen times, and third, Impressionists at ten times; and there is another category, which many a stake placer would class as an outsider; this is old books – with a multiple of about eight. Then the field shows silver, glass, old master paintings at six times and French furniture at about five times. Draw a rough comparison with the stock gamble and the appreciation comes out at around three and a half times.

If a glance is taken back to the antics of the market fifty years ago it can bring an acute heartburn for those who may recall selling at that time. Ming pots were for the having at less than £300. An early 17th-century Spinet by Hitchcock once the property of the Princess Amelia, daughter of George III, brought a paltry £80. A marquetry commode, of the time of Louis XV £74 11s. Silver was at times bringing only 3 shillings and 1 penny an ounce. Even working out tables of

Backgammon board made in Augsburg c. 1600. It is veneered with ebony and horn. Courtesy Sotheby Parke Bernet

comparative values, inflation and the rest, matters have changed.

There is not really a reliable rule book that can be handed out for the beginner. Many are the sugary words of promise that give ephemeral gilt-lined dreams as to what will be the lot of those seating themselves on the gilt saleroom chairs, or grubbying their fingers rustling and digging through the barrows and stalls in that strangely or is it aptly named institution, the flea market. The battle has promise; but the way is strewn with trip-wires, boulders, shadows, enticing whispers. The goals are there and well worth the struggle, none the less it calls for coolness, courage and care, seasoned with an ability to play a poker-faced role at times, a touch of foresight and a mind that can whirl round figures in a way that would leave a computer petrified. Not every category or type within a certain category will pursue its upward trend all the time. The multiplied figures quoted earlier are statements of long term happenings. Within this format there have been a number of occasions when matters have taken on the performance of a switchback car.

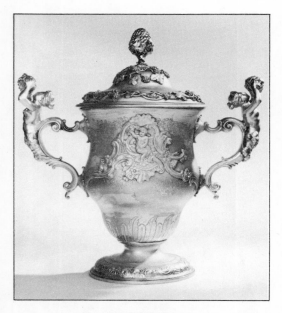

George II two-handled cup and cover. Dublin, 1748. Courtesy of Christie's

In the period between 1950 and 1970, for instance, Chelsea figures fell in 1953, rose in 1956, faltered in mid 1957, rose in 1959, 1960, 1961, bumped down in 1963, rocketed in 1965, hiccupped in 1966 and then continued to go up once more. The overall graph for the period would show a healthy increase of two and a half times. This behaviour is perhaps more marked in the field of old master paintings, which until about 1950 was the most sensitive to fashion or fickle opinions.

The great favourite of the Victorians, George Frederick Watts, gives a clue to period taste. In 1890 his 'Una and the Red Cross Knight' brought £1732 and in 1958 a niggardly £157 10s. Today it would almost certainly be back in four figures. The works of Jean Baptiste Corot have moved at times strangely. In 1914 'Ronde des Nymphes' brought £6830; in 1935, £525; performance here could be affected by the fact that poor Corot has probably been copied, faked more than any other painter. The real rocket class can be represented by such as Thomas Gainsborough with, for example, a portrait bringing £6 in 1797 and £22 050 in 1958 or perhaps even better still by the great Dutchman Jan Vermeer; in 1816 his 'Girl's Head' brought 3 florins, in 1959 around the £400 000 mark.

The shrewd collector the Duke of Hamilton decided in 1882 to put up his collection of

pictures, statues, decorative furniture and so on. An announcement which caused a fair stir in the world of the *cognoscenti* and art marketeers. Christie's were to stage the event of the century. A start was made on Saturday 17 June with Dutch and Flemish paintings, with eighty lots reaching £43 250 11s. Monday 19 June, came Chinese and Japanese porcelain, French and Italian decorative objects, which brought £25 072 19s. 20 June more oriental ware with furniture made by Gouthiere and Riesener for Marie Antoinette totalled £23 485 6s 6d. 24 June Italian pictures added £26 804 18s 6d. 26 June came further far eastern porcelain, as well as Sèvres, and bronzes and bust of Napoleon by Thorvaldsen, in all £30 331 1s 6d. 27 June still more Chinese and Japanese ware, and also silver and armoires by Buhl (Boulle) from the Louvre – £31 500 10s. 1 July more Italian masters £19 785 3s. 3 July Dutch, French and Italian faïence, furniture and antiquities £17 494 5s. 4 July more French faïence, Limoges enamels and other objects of virtu, £29 383 14s 6d. 8 July further Dutch and Flemish paintings £33 562 4s. At this stage after eleven days of watching, waiting and wishing some may have begun to tire but the avalanche of rarities and value still had some way to go.

On 10 July came Japanese lacquer work, Dresden porcelain and more of Marie Antoinette's treasures, which added up to £36 105 19s 6d. 11 July more Japanese work with statues and bronzes £16 079 5s. After this it was the turn of miniatures, on 15 July, £13 348 13s. 17 July more Dresden and Sèvres porcelain £16 996 7s. 18 July small objects of art and virtu with tapestries £14 754 1s 6d. 19 July further Dresden porcelain as well as some English, together with bronzes commissioned by Francis I, total £14 955 12s, and the last day, 20 July, included a fine array of coins and gems, bringing in £4651 9s 6d. The whole totted up to a total of £397 562 0s 6d for 2213 lots. A great figure for those late Victorian days and one to which a certain number of noughts could be added today. The catalogue details present a fascinating insight not only into the taste and wisdom of the collector, but also they give information on what would make a prime collection for a national museum. To the total can be added the Duke's Beckford library sold by Sotheby's for £73 551, and further books and manuscripts, which in all got the Duke his half million; in fact, £554 005.

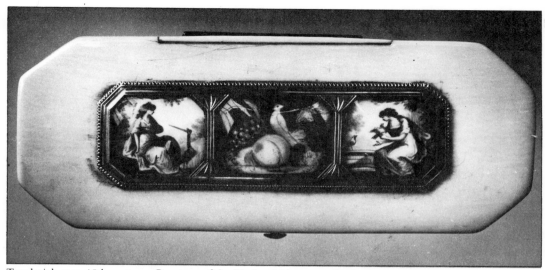

Toothpick case, 18th century. Courtesy of the National Museum of Ireland

The 19th-century estates were in many cases nurtured by the wonderful spending sprees of 18th-century ancestors. Those gentlemen who sped across the channel and then coached at speed or leisure across France or Germany to land up in that treasure land, Italy. There they certainly must have spent large sums of money and sent many a creaking springless waggon piled with the precious, the delicate and the magnificent back to the north French coast, where the suffering objects were subjected to Channel crossings, not always of the kindest. Many are the stories of overladen vessels beset by sudden gales that capsized or foundered. Yet these men of taste pack-filled the great halls and houses all over the land to such an extent that even sales such as that of the Duke of Hamilton and the blood-letting spate today do not seem to have emptied them. Investments the families made have often had to be brought under the gavel to satisfy punitive duties or launch yet another squire on his way; but still the sale-catalogues are filled; during the annual season tens of thousands of lots come and are gobbled up increasingly by the dollar-loaded, the Deutsch-mark-heavy and the yen-lined new collectors or more probably investors following the old thought . . . 'buy and hold if you can afford to'.

Back to a query raised earlier as to how, when or where to start a collection that can not only be enjoyed, but also give the comforting feeling that it is working away for your interest on its capital.

Possibly, if it is necessary to begin with a small outlay, the field that can offer fair promise is that of bygones. But be warned; here some of the values can be ephemeral and to a high degree affected by fashion. Having said that, the things of yesterday can provide an area for a mild gamble and may come up quite high unexpectedly. Another attraction can be that the variety is vast. Purchasing places may be the sale-room, dealers, or perhaps better still small house-auctions, where patience is generally needed because it may be those last lots have the select titbits. Other grounds for hunting can include village fêtes and jumble sales and a number of enthusiasts have even been finding it profitable to prod around on refuse heaps, and dig in ditches.

One of the most prolific producers of articles can be a kitchen or rather generally the pre-1939 kitchen. Items can include such as cork-screws, old fruit-juicers, sieves, food tins, vegetable slicers, ice-cream machines, lard presses, cherry stoners, fly-traps, fruit-parers, sausage stuffers, jelly moulds, family grist mills, Britannia dippers and for those visiting the United States a wary eye can be kept for doughnut cutters and sorghum skimmers. That lot is only a brief selection from just one source. What else around the house? Well, try door furniture: the locks, finger-plates and handles; or out-of-date bell fittings. Old office or study equipment including clips, pen wipers, ink bottles and not least early fountain-pens. Out in the hall might be discovered

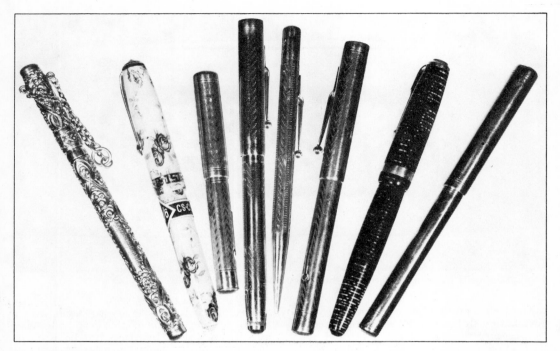

Fountain pens including such as: Waterman, Swan, Conway Stewart and Onoto. Courtesy Christie's, South Kensington

coat and hat hooks and walking sticks. The bottom drawer of a great uncle's roll-top might yield small boxes for vestas, both decorative and commercial examples; and also visiting card and stamp cases. Move upstairs and into the bathroom, surely not! But yes, you could find such a rarity as an American Virginia stool shower which was in use around 1835. This noble device had a revolving seat, a lever to pump water up to the shower-rose, which at the same time moved a scrubbing brush up and down the user's back. Lesser fry include soap dishes and brackets, tooth-brush holders and powder boxes.

The late Victorians, Edwardians and those of the twenties seem in some ways to have been much more imaginative with their choice of gadgets. Jewel boxes ranged from those topped by children lying on toboggans to detailed representations of old wellheads complete with buckets. A boudoir, a name now almost extinct, was a woman's small private room, although the literal French translation could be 'a place to sulk in'; here one could come across a hair crimping and curling set, a ring stand or a bonnet brush, and also delightful instruments such as ear spoons – recognising

one of these might even tax a well-versed connoisseur. Around the boudoir or bedroom could also be what are generally grouped as baubles: vinaigrettes, buckles, pins, buttons, hairpins, lorgnettes and back combs. An old workbox could surrender thimbles, pin-cushions, bodkins, needle-cases and perhaps a 'magic' darning machine.

The nursery, another almost obsolete place, or the schoolroom, now dust-covered too, would have harboured a plethora of those things for play and study that have today been replaced by space-age productions or tank warfare sets. But still examples of 'Magnetic Jack Straws' may be come across or 'Monkey Donation Party', the 'Game of Negoni' or 'Moneta'. Wander down to the fast dis-appearing general store and seek out such as twine boxes, scales, cash registers, tobacco cutters.

Going round a meadow might be what looks like a strand of just barbed wire. But someone somewhere could be looking for just this. In America there is a society that collects barbed wires, and there is even a book devoted to the subject called 'The Wire that Fenced the West' by a husband and wife Henry and Frances

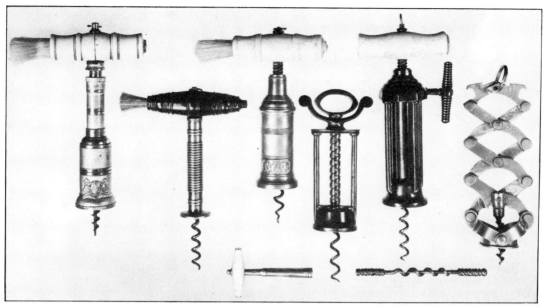

Assorted corkscrews, 19th century. Courtesy Christie's, South Kensington

McCallum. There are a fair number of variations on this prickly theme, including: Four Point, Glidden Pattern, Baker Pattern, Jacob Haish S-wire, Frank Billings and Brotherton Barb.

There is one other factor that includes almost anything collected. This is care. For whether it is a Hepplewhite chair, a leather bound book, an embroidered panel, a piece of earthenware, a bundle of travel pamphlets, a silver salver, a doll or whatever, they can all be de-valued by careless handling, placing or exposure to relevant pests or pollutants.

Central heating and air conditioning can cause havoc with woods, leathers and some papers, if they are set too high or brought in during the autumn too rapidly. Be careful to watch the relative humidity in a room. If it is too high, the atmosphere is too damp and there are stagnant air areas, fungus and moulds can be encouraged. Too dry, cracking can occur and papers made brittle, and also you

will have an arid uncomfortable throat. A small instrument called a hygrometer will keep watch; the ideal is somewhere around 60 per cent.

Insect pests such as woodworm, moths and firebrats should be watched for. Washing china and glass, if the objects are treasured, should always be done one object at a time in a bowl with a piece of soft foam sheet at the bottom. If detergents are used, make the addition small and rinse very well afterwards.

Things that hang on the wall, whether pictures, arms, plates or other items can all too often crash down as high humidity eats into hanging wires and rusty screw eyes rot cords.

Care really means inspecting now and then and if materials are used making sure they are suitable for the object concerned. Just a few moments at intervals can ensure that those antique investments stay as such and do not decrease in value like the oft-times vaunted high per cent stocks.

THE WORLD OF ANTIQUES

ABATTANT
In French cabinetwork; a drop-front or fall-front panel.

ABELLE, LAWRENCE (active 1595)
Recorded as making an early chest of drawers, a 'new cubborde of boxes' for Stratford-upon-Avon; another name used was a 'Nest of Boxes'.

ABRICOTIER
The wood of the apricot tree, *Prunus armeniaca*. It is hard and has a yellowish colour and is favoured by French *ébénistes* for cabinetwork.

ABRUZZI RUGS
These have been woven by the peasants of the Abruzzi highlands in Sardinia. Mostly they are ply or double-cloth weaves or woven with a floated weft pattern. The designs are basically geometric and have been influenced by earlier Renaissance work. Locally, the rugs are used as bed coverings or for carts and chest covers.

ABTSBESSINGEN
A faïence factory believed to have been operating in Thuringia, Germany around 1739 and to have been founded by the Prince of Schwarzburg. Earliest confirming records are for 1753. The faïence produced was of high quality and bore the mark of a pitchfork taken from the arms of the Prince. Motifs were baroque and later rococo with a Chinese influence. Much of the painted decoration was in blue.

ACACIA FAUX WOOD
The timber from the common locust tree, *Robinia pseud-acacia*, which is hard with a fairly pronounced yellow and green stripe. It has been used in cabinetwork.

ACAJOU
The cashew tree, also a term for the mahogany, the Spanish cedar or the marinheiro; and their timber. The woods from these trees are hard, and their colour varies from warm dark reddish brown to yellowish brown.

ACANTHUS
A decorative figure based on a conventionalised rendering of the leaf of the Acanthus plant, *Acanthus spinosus,* which is native to the Mediterranean. The earliest known use of this type of decoration was with the interior columns of the Temple of Apollo at Bassae in Southern Greece and dates from about 420 BC. It has long been a favourite type of carved decoration for furniture, and has been freely used since the Renaissance.

ACINACE
A short straight dagger which was worn on the right side, notably by the Medes, Persians and Scythians. It is seen on the figure of the Persian Prince in the famous Pompeian mosaic of the Battle of Issus.

ACKETON
A quilted leather jacket for wearing under armour to absorb blows. It is likely that it was derived from the Asiatics at the time of the Crusades. The Greek term for the jacket is *ho-kiton* and from this have come numerous corruptions such as *hoketon, hauqueton, hauketon,* and *aketon.*

ACORN
An ornament resembling the fruit of the oak that has been carved since the 16th century; it is often found used as a finial, and also sometimes cast in bronze and gilt.

Pale pink socks, parasol and apron believed to have belonged to Edward VII as a child. Courtesy of Bonhams

ACORN CHAIR
A type of Jacobean oak chair which had a crossrail decorated with acorns.

ACORN CLOCK
Popular in New England from about 1825, this American shelf clock was normally about two feet high and had the top part shaped roughly like an acorn.

ACORN SPOON
An English silver spoon, dating from the 15th century, which had the handle ending with the likeness of an acorn.

ACROTONOMOUS
A term used in the jewellery and gem cutting industry, it applies to the internal structure of a stone and relates to the plane of cleavage running parallel with its base.

ACT OF PARLIAMENT CLOCK
Originally the name was applied to an inexpensive English wall clock, usually weight-driven and having a seconds pendulum and probably an unglazed dial. The story has it that these cheap timepieces were put into inns to help the public who had had to sell their own clocks when Pitt introduced his Act in 1797 which put a levy of an annual five shillings on all clocks and watches. The Act was repealed in 1798.

ADAM, ROBERT (1728–92)
The Scottish architect and furniture designer, the second son of William Adam of Maryburgh. Of his brothers, John, James and William, it was James who was to be the greatest assistance to him. After studying at Edinburgh University he went to Italy in 1854 and spent a lengthy period examining ancient Roman buildings, in particular the ruins of Diocletian's palace at Spolatro.

Among his best known buildings are Lansdowne House, Berkeley Square; the Infirmary at Glasgow; the Register House, Edinburgh; Osterley Park House, Brentford; Kenwood House, Hampstead; and Kedleston,

Derbyshire. He left an enduring mark on interior decoration, not only with ceilings, staircases and chimney-pieces but also, in particular, with furniture. There is a strong Roman influence evident with his use of design features; motifs which he used with great taste and elegance included: drapery swags, radiating fans, festoons of husks, medallions, rosettes, armour, scrolling, classical vases and urns, the lyre, masks, and animal heads such as that of a ram.

He was quite an accomplished landscape painter and with his brothers published a series of engravings of their designs. Robert died in Albemarle Street, London and was buried in Westminster Abbey.

ADAMS, GEORGE (c 1704–73)
Maker of a wide range of scientific instruments who also wrote on their use and on relevant subjects.

ADAMS, WILLIAM
A member of a family of potters working in Staffordshire during the latter part of the 18th century and early years of the 19th. From about 1787 he produced, together with the family, deep-blue jasper ware and cream coloured earthenware. Impressed marks included: 'Adams & Co.', 'Adams B. Adams', 'W. Adams & Co.'. Blue printed wares made for the American market in the 19th century were normally marked with an impressed eagle and a cartouche which contained the title of the subject.

ADDISON, J. (in business 1800)
Globemaker to George IV, also a dealer in scientific instruments. The National Maritime Museum, Greenwich has an elaborate English Orrery sold by him.

ADLERGLAS
Also called Adlerhumpen and Reichsadler-humpen, it is a tall cylindrical German glass with enamelled decoration. The design would include the double eagle of the Holy Roman Empire and armorial bearings of the members of the empire. There would also be the signs of the Pope and the Electors.

ADZE
A cutting tool, with arched blade at right angles to handle, of unknown origin. It was used for trimming large timbers to rough shapes, distinctive marks were left and can be noted on the undersides of boards and the backs of panels.

AEGICRANIA
The heads or skulls of rams, originally used in classic sculpture and then later as carved details with furniture.

AFFLECK, THOMAS
He was born in Scotland and travelled to America in 1763 and settled in Philadelphia, where he had a shop on Second Street. He had considerable influence on other cabinetmakers around him and is credited with producing the finest Chippendale-style furniture made in America.

AFGHAN BOKHARA
A rug woven by the people of northern Afghanistan which has the warp and weft of goat's hair or dark wool. It is often sold as, and confused with, the Khiva Bokhara.

AFSHAR
A rug generally classed as Persian, a poor grade of Shiraz.

AFTABA
A term used in metal crafts to signify a particular shape. It is a type of pitcher with a long spout, found in Central Asia.

AGALLOCH WOOD
An East Indian tree, *Aquilaria agallocha,* popular with French cabinetmaking. It is the aloes of the Bible and is burnt by the Orientals to produce a perfume.

AGATA
An American glass, produced in the late 19th century, that is mottled and shaded from rose to white.

AGATE
A semi-precious stone of variegated chalcedony which can be used in making jewellery. For the craftsmen, especially with gilding, it is used as a burnisher.

AGATE WARE
A type of ceramics made by mixing two or more coloured clays together to produce a marbled effect. In the early part of the 18th century some Staffordshire potters mixed blue, white and brown coloured clays; later the idea was taken up by Wedgwood who made a convincing material looking like agate. It was largely used for ornamental vases.

AGGRAPPES
Hooks and eyes used originally for fastening armour, later with costume.

AGRA
A type of rug made in India. Originally Agra was an important centre of rug-weaving during the reign of Akbar the Great (1556–1605). Early examples were of high quality and were much esteemed during the 17th century. They were generally made with heavy knotting and a thick pile. Present day examples have in general become degraded.

AGRICOLA, GIUSEPPE (1717–1804)
A German, originally called Bauer, who went to Italy in 1739 and changed his name. Working in Rome he was awarded his patent in 1745. His sons Luigi and Vincenzo both trained for and became gem engravers.

AIGRETTE
A jewel clasp that held a feather that would be worn either in a cap, hat, or in the hair, it became a fashion towards the end of the 16th century.

AIKUCHI
A Japanese dagger without a guard carried during the Tokugawa period by important people. The sheath was generally made of metal and was lavishly decorated. It was at times used as a weapon for *hara-kiri*.

AILANTHUS
In the Moluccas known as the 'tree of Heaven', *Simaru ailante*, it is hard and displays a reddish veined appearance. It has been used in cabinetwork.

AILETTES
In medieval armour plates of forged iron or steel worn over the coat of mail to protect the shoulders. In service they were also sometimes of thick leather and carried the Arms of the wearer. Their use more or less ceased during the reign of Edward III (1327–77). In Chartham Church, near Canterbury in Kent, there is a brass of Sir Robert de Septvans which shows the fashion.

AIR TWIST
In glass drinking vessels, a spiral of air in the stem formed during manufacture. The idea was at first probably accidental, with bubbles becoming trapped, but then around the middle of the 18th century it became a popular trick.

AITKIN, ROBERT
Scottish emigrant who was active in the latter part of the 18th century as a publisher and printer in Philadelphia, and was later to prove one of the finest bookbinders. An outstanding work was the three volumes of Blair's 'Lectures', produced in 1784.

AK-HISSAR
A Turkish rug made principally from Mohair.

ALABASTER
A type of gypsum with fine texture which has been used for carving ornaments, tablets and small figures. The colour is generally white, but this may be tinged with yellow if impurities are present; it also has a pleasant translucent appearance. It was first used decoratively in England about 1160. Quarries include sites at Chellaston in Derby and Tutbury, Staffordshire.

ALBARELLO
A majolica jar, more or less cylindrical in form but with concave sides. It appears from the 12th century with Persian and Mesopotamian wares, and with Hispano-Moresque from the 15th century. Principally used for holding drugs.

ALCORA
A faïence produced from a manufactory near Valencia in Spain from around 1726. The founder was the Count of Aranda, and the work was continued by his son. Early craftsmen included Joseph Olerys and Edouard Roux, both of whom had worked for the French Moustiers Centre.

ALCOVE CUPBOARD
An 18th-century fashion where the cupboard was often made of similar wood to that of the panelling in the room.

ALE GLASS
A drinking vessel introduced in the latter part of the 17th century for use with strong ale. It had a tall funnel-shaped bowl with a shortish stem. From about 1740 they were often decorated with engraved hop and barley patterns.

ALENÇON POINT
A needlepoint lace of durable and delicate quality first made in the 17th century in Alençon, France. It is made in small pieces which are later joined together with almost invisible seams. Napoleon was largely res-

ponsible for reviving the making of the lace which had almost died out. Since the middle of the 19th century it has also been made at Burano, Brussels and at Bayeux.

ALEYARD
A long slender glass, with a large bulb at one end and a flared mouth. It is used for drinking demonstrations calling for speed and control during consumption.

ALFORD, LADY MARIAN
A member of the committee of the Royal School of Art Needlework founded in 1872 under the Presidency of HRH the Princess Christian of Schleswig-Holstein. A skilled embroideress and the writer of the comprehensive book *Needlework as Art,* published in 1886.

ALGERIAN EMBROIDERY
A type using flower and palmette (an ornament of radiating petals like a palm leaf) motifs, and colours centred around mauve and warm purple. Typical use was for door hangings; these were generally made in three long panels and joined by lacings of ribbon.

ALICATADOS
Spanish term for cutwork with mosaic tile-work.

ALIDADE
A rule equipped with sights, used in surveying for the determination of direction. It can be employed with an astrolabe or a plane-table.

ALISIER WOOD
The whitebeam or black haw; it is hard and near white in colour and is used in cabinet-making.

ALKANET
A European plant from the root of which is obtained a red dye which was at one time used as a wood finish.

ALLA CASTELLANA WARE
Italian lead-glazed earthenware with a *sgraffito* decoration. It was produced from the 14th century onwards.

ALLA PORCELLANA
A type of majolica decoration practised in Italy which used plant forms in blue in a similar way to the 15th-century Chinese porcelain.

ALLECRET
A light armour used in the 16th century, particularly by Swiss soldiers who are often shown in paintings and prints of this period. It is also spelt *hallecret.*

ALLEN, ROBERT (1744–1835)
A painter working at the Lowestoft porcelain manufactory from 1757. In 1780 he became manager there and when it closed he set up as a freelance enameller of white porcelain.

ALLGOOD
A family of skilled japanners who worked in Wales. The father, Edward, founded the business at Pontypool in about 1730. When he died Thomas the eldest son continued at Pontypool, whilst his brothers set up in opposition at Usk. William succeeded Thomas in 1776 and considerably enlarged the business, but after he died (in 1813) the Pontypool factory closed in 1820.

ALLISON, MICHAEL
Talented American cabinetmaker active around 1800 to 1845 working from Vesey Street, New York.

ALMORRATXA
Spanish glass for rose-water sprinkling. It has a pear-shaped body resting on a high spreading foot. There are four slender spouts for sprinkling. The vessel came into use in the 16th century.

ALMSDISH
A circular dish with a broad flat rim, which may be plain or decorated, for use in a church for the collecting of alms. The early dishes were generally made of base metals such as brass, latten or pewter. Later some were made of silver and gold.

ALPUJARRA
A Spanish peasant hand-loomed rug made in the district that gives it the name, the area is in Granada. Production probably started in the 15th century by the Moors who passed on the technique.

ALTARE
Glassmaking centre started by craftsmen from Normandy in the Middle Ages at this place near Genoa. At one time the products rivalled those from Venice; in fact they became so similar it is difficult to tell them apart.

ALTUN
A gold piece first issued by Mohammed II at Constantinople in 1454. It bore the Sultan's name and mint and date with titles on the reverse. It was patterned on the sequin and florin.

AMANDIER WOOD
The timber from the almond tree, *Amygdalus communis,* which is hard and has a yellowish colour. It has been used particularly by the French cabinetmakers.

AMARANTH WOOD
The *amaranthus* is found in Guiana and is used widely in cabinetwork, having a rich purple-red colour and being hard.

AMASTINI, ANGELO (1754–1815)
A gem engraver born at Fossombrone, he went to work in Rome about 1775. His son Nicolo (1780–1851) followed his father in his craft.

AMBERG
A faïence pottery was founded in the town in Bavaria in 1759 by Simon Hetzendörfer. In 1790 it was producing cream-coloured earthenware and porcelain. The mark was a monogram 'AB'.

AMBERINA
A clear glass coloured with tints of amber and ruby used to make ornamental glass in the late 19th century in America; most objects being mould produced.

AMBO
A large reading desk or pulpit which was used in early Christian and Eastern churches.

AMBOYNA WOOD
The timber of the *Pterospermum indicum,* native of the Molucca or Spice Islands. It is hard with distinctive rose-yellow-brown colours and a mottling with curling much in favour for cabinetwork and particularly veneering.

AMBRY
A chest or cupboard for storing arms. In the ecclesiastical sense it was intended to hold sacramental vessels, vestments and books. In a purely domestic manner it would hold food and drink.

AMEN GLASS
A kind of Jacobite glass brought out to commemorate the 1715 rising when James Stuart, known as the Old Pretender, tried to become James III of England. The glasses have engraved prayers ending with Amen. They usually also have the letters I.R. elaborately scrolled which almost hides a crown and the figure eight; this points to the fact that James also set out to be James VIII of Scotland.

AMERICAN PATCHWORK
Quilts that were worked largely in the 18th and 19th centuries, they displayed amazing invention in design with more than 300 patterns. All kinds of motifs were used; one of the most popular being an eight-pointed star, the so-called 'Star of Bethlehem'.

AMORINO
Infant Cupid often found in Italian 16th-century sculpture which has been incorporated in carved decoration with woodwork, either left plain or gilded.

AMPULLA
A small vessel, generally with a round body and narrow neck, which could be used for wine or more often for precious oils, ointments and perfumes. One of the most famous was the Sainte Ampoule which was used for anointing the kings of France at their coronation. It was kept in the Abbey of St Rémi at Rheims.

AMRITSAR
A rug that comes from the Punjab, India. It is of comparatively recent manufacture and is intended for commercial production.

ANATHEMA CUP
A famous English silver cup made in 1481, so called from the inscription it bore which reads: 'QUI ALIENAVERIT ANATHEMA SIT'. It is quite plain silver-gilt with a bowl with double curved sides in the manner of an inverted bell.

ANATOLIAN
A rug produced in Asia Minor, Turkey, the original ones being small, no more than mat size. The colours are somewhat brash and bright.

ANDIRONS
Fire-dogs, usually of iron, used to support logs on the hearth in an open fireplace.

ANEROID BAROMETER
One that operates from atmospheric pressure bending the thin corrugated top of a closed

and partially exhausted metal box. It was developed around the middle of the 19th century.

ANGE D'OR
A gold coin minted by Philip IV of France in 1341; it showed an elaborate cross, four crowns and St Michael. It was copied in different manners in the Low Countries.

ANGEL
English gold coin issued 1470 to 1634, similar in device to the Anglo-Gallic angelot.

ANGEL BED
With French furniture ,his was a bed that had a flat oblong tester that did not extend for the whole length of the bed. It was fashionable during the reigns of Louis XV and XVI.

ANGERMAIR, CHRISTOF (died c 1632)
Woodcarver noted for his intricate and exquisite details on furniture. The Bayerisches National-museum, Munich has a fine coin cabinet by him which is signed.

ANIMAL CUPS
Drinking cups made in the shape of either natural animals, such as chamois, fox, hare, hound, lion and stag, or mythological beasts like the dragon and griffin. The fashion started at the end of the 16th century and the cups were generally made from silver and originated in Germany.

ANISE WOOD
A timber that is hard with a warm grey colour, favoured by French cabinetmakers. It is the *Illicium anisatum* from China.

ANLACE
A short weapon resembling a sword or dagger, commonly worn by civilians until the end of the 15th century, usually horizontally at the back of the belt. It is also called a *cinquedea*.

ANNEALING
In the glass industry it implies the gradual cooling after manufacture to make the glass less brittle.

ANNULAR CLOCK
A richly decorated clock generally of urn shape on a square pedestal made of marble with bronze mounts. It has an annular or horizontal ring-shaped dial that is usually enamelled white with black roman figures. It was popular during the 18th century.

ANSBACH
A German faïence manufactory, supported by the Margrave Earl Alexander, in production from about 1758. In 1762 it moved to the Margrave's hunting castle at Bruckberg. It survived until 1860. The mark was an 'A', sometimes with an eagle, although much of the ware was not marked.

ANTHEMION
An ornament consisting of floral or foliated forms arranged in a radiating clustre in low relief. It originated with the Greeks. Robert Adam was probably the first Englishman to use the idea. A number of other furniture designers incorporated the motif in many ways on different pieces.

ANTONINIANUS
A double denarius issued in 215 by, and named after, M. Aurelius Antoninus Caracolla. The first examples were in silver, but later it was made of copper with a thin surface of silver.

ANTWERP LACE
Largely concerned with decorative additions to female caps, using potten kant or pot patterns; also varieties of guipure for export to the Spanish Indies. It was a pillow lace worked with a strong thread.

ANTWERP MOQUETTE
A material woven in the same manner as velvet but with coarser materials. It is principally used for upholstery. Antwerp has been one of the main centres of production, but there have also been workshops in Amsterdam, Leyden and in Thuringia, in Germany. It was nick-named 'Brussels Carpet' in England where weavers in places such as Bradford made it. In the 19th century the Jacquard loom was adapted to make it a commercial success.

AOI TSUBA
A Japanese sword mount in use in the 12th century; it has four heart-shaped lobes in the shape of the aoi leaf.

APOSTLE SPOON
A silver or gilt spoon which has the figure of an Apostle on the handle end. During the 15th and 16th centuries it was the custom to give a child at her or his christening such a

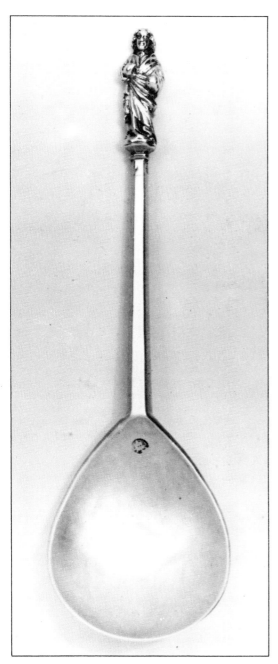

A very important Henry VII Apostle spoon topped with a figure of St John, London, 1498. The maker's mark appears to be a Cypher. The finial is of interest, as it belongs to the rare group of Apostles of the Bishop Foxe's Crosier type, which have great quality in their modelling and presentation of figures. Courtesy Spink

spoon, generally from godparents. A set of twelve is rare, and a set with the Master spoon (depicting the figure of Christ) is even more sought after.

APPLETON, NATHANIEL (1765–1822)
Cabinetmaker working in the Federal Style in Salem, Massachusetts.

APPLE WOOD
Timber from the cultivated and wild tree, *Pyrus malus,* a favourite with American and British cabinetmakers. It is hard with pleasant pink-brown shades, equally usable for veneer, turning or carving.

APPLIED DECORATION
With furniture it means the laying on of decorative pieces of wood or metal and fixing them into place with small pins or glue.

APPLIQUÉ
With needlework it describes the laying on of figures cut from fabric and either sewn or glued in place. It may also be used to describe lacquer designs applied to metal.

APREY
A French faïence manufactory founded by Jacques Lallement de Villehaut, Baron d'Aprey and his brother Joseph in 1744. Best pieces were carried out with a painted coloured enamel decoration in a manner similar to ware from Strasbourg. Marks included 'AP' and 'APR'.

APRON
With furniture it is the downward extension of the frame immediately below a table top, chair seat or the like.

APT
A French ceramic centre established by César Moulin in 1728. Some ware was modelled from silver objects such as ewers and porringers, colours were generally yellow and brown, sometimes with marbling.

AQUAMANILE
An early metal ewer used to hold water for washing the hands of important guests in between courses of a meal.

AQUILINO
A silver coin of the 13th century, in Northern Italy and the Tyrol, with an eagle and a double cross.

ARABESQUE

A type of decoration derived from Graeco-Roman work and found in abundance in the Pompeian villas. It was developed for use with furniture and textiles, and principally uses flower and plant forms in a graceful decorative manner; it can also be completely geometric and abstract.

ARBALEST

A medieval crossbow used to throw arrows, darts and bullets. It consisted of a steel bow set in a shaft of wood with string, trigger and a mechanical device for cocking the bow.

ARCA

A chest that could be adapted for use as an altar; also a large alms box.

ARCANIST

A ceramic worker who claims to have the secret of different ways of making porcelain.

ARCHBANC

In French furniture this is a massive wooden bench with a tall carved back which would seat several people. The seat would lift to disclose a coffer.

ARCHITECTURAL CLOCK

A clock which displays in the top the details of the classical pediment with or without columns, and could use one or other of the orders: Doric, Ionic or Corinthian.

ARDEBIL

A well known Persian rug woven in the latter part of the 16th century which is supposed to have been displayed in the Ardebil mosque. There have been many copies made over the years.

ARGAND LAMP

A lamp with a tubular wick invented in 1782 by a Swiss, Aimé Argand.

ARGENTAN POINT

A needlepoint lace, that rivals that of Alençon, which flourished at its height during the reigns of Louis XV and XVI. Recently it has been imitated at Burano.

ARGYLE

A gravy container roughly cylindrical in shape rather like a small coffee-pot. It has an inner container for the gravy, allowing hot water to be poured around it, or an inner container intended to hold the hot water. They were first made about 1770 in silver, and later also in Sheffield Plate.

ARITA WARE

Japanese porcelain made in the Huzen district from the early years of the 17th century. It was exported from Imari and so took the name of Imari or Imari-Yaki. Yaki is the Japanese for ware.

ARK

A chest, coffer or covered basket.

ARMARIO OR ARMADIO

A large movable cupboard, first made during the Renaissance.

ARMET

A late and perfected type of medieval helmet. It fitted neatly round the head by means of hinged parts, particularly with the visor, cheek and chin pieces.

ARMILLARY SPHERE

An astronomical machine, or skeleton sphere, made up of an assemblage of rings which were designed to represent the positions of important circles of the celestial sphere. The armillary turns on its polar axis within a meridian and horizon.

ARMOIRE

A domestic cupboard, wardrobe or clothes-press of large size; it is often richly decorated.

ARMOUR

Defensive covering for the body. It has generally been of metal although cheaper and lighter materials such as horn, leather, quilted cloth and skins have been used.

ARMPAD

A small cushion padding on the arms of some chairs which would be covered with the same material as the seat and back.

ARMS

Instruments or weapons for defence or offence.

ARMURE

A fabric of silk, wool or cotton made with a fancy weave imitating chain mail.

ARNHEM WARE
A Dutch faïence manufactory founded in 1755 by Johannes van Kerckhoff. Decorations included painting with deep blue. The mark was a cock.

ARQUEBUS
Originally applied to a hand gun with a lug that could be hooked to a firm support so as to absorb the recoil. The name comes from the German word *hackenbusch*. Later the term was applied to a light musket and then a heavy gun. Today it is somewhat freely applied to several early weapons with either match- or wheel-lock.

ARQUETA
A small table-chest or box, primarily for the keeping of jewels.

ARRAS CERAMICS
French soft-paste porcelain from a manufactory founded by Joseph François Boussemaert of Lille. Afterwards it was taken over by four ladies who dealt in faïence. Work ceased in 1790.

ARRASENE EMBROIDERY
A type of chenille work made on canvas, serge, or silk which was intended for curtain or mantel borders. Stitches were various and included crewel, tent and couching.

ARRAS LACE
A coarse bobbin lace supposedly introduced in the 16th century at Arras by the Emperor Charles V. There was also the celebrated Arras gold lace; customers for this included George I for his coronation.

ARROW BACK
A term that mainly applies to American furniture. It implies a Windsor chair which has three or more arrow-shaped spindles at the back.

ARTISANS LIBRES
French craftsmen who chose to work as free-lances outside the control of the Guilds.

ART NOUVEAU
A type of artistic presentation and design that developed about 1895 in Belgium and France. In Germany it was called 'Jugendstil'. It displayed an excessive use of flowing and curved lines based on plant forms; and also motifs of

La Tène. It spread rapidly all over Europe and the United States.

ASH, GILBERT (1717–85)
A talented American craftsman who worked in New York, making amongst other objects some of the best early American Chippendale style.

ASHBURY METAL
A pewter of a hard variety, an alloy of antimony, tin and zinc. Useful for the making of cheaper spoons and snuff-boxes.

ASSAY CUP
A small vessel for assessing wines, generally of silver and gold. Earliest mention seems to be about 1530. It might also be used for the detection of poison.

ASSISI WORK
A type of embroidery where the design is outlined and then the background filled in with long-armed cross-stitches. It was worked with cotton thread, generally blue and scarlet or black and orange. It originated in convents in Italy during the Middle Ages.

ASSOCIATION ITEMS
Those objects that are collected in relation to a particular person or event.

ASTBURY
A family of Staffordshire potters. John (1686–1743) is reputed, somewhat unreliably, to have been the first to use white clay washes and also calcined flint with earthenware. He, with his son Thomas, began production in about 1725. Ware impressed 'Astbury' was made by a later Astbury.

ASTRAL LAMP
A variation of the Argand lamp. The oil reservoir was wide and flat and thus did not obstruct the light.

ASTROLABE
The most important astronomical and observational instrument from early Greek times until the 17th century. It was a compact instrument for observing the positions of the celestial bodies. Today it has been replaced by the sextant.

ASTROLABE CLOCK
One that will point to the phases of the moon, the positions of the sun and the principal planets, as well as tell the time in hours and minutes.

ASTRONOMICAL COMPENDIUM
A small box of varying shape that contains basic instruments such as: compass, nocturnal, sundial, tables, etc. It was mostly used during the 16th and 17th centuries.

ASTRONOMICAL RING
An instrument developed from the armillary sphere which can help with time-telling. It is a great rarity.

ATAUJIA
A type of Moorish inlay work on metal, which uses enamel and gold or other metals.

ATHÉNIENNE
A type of candelabrum which consisted of an urn on an antique tripod. It was derived from early Classic designs.

ATTELET
A small skewer of silver for serving meats to the table, and of iron for kitchen work and cooking. There is a mention of them in use as early as 1473.

AUBUSSON CARPETS
Hand-woven tapestry weave carpets from the place in France that gives them their name. Factories there were in full production from the early part of the 16th century. The carpets are made in exactly the same way as a wall-hanging tapestry.

AUBUSSON TAPESTRIES
The manufactory was active from the early part of the 16th century. Best productions were in the 18th century.

AUMUND
Faïence manufactory founded in 1751 near Vegesack, Bremen. Notable productions included tureens in the Rococo manner with decoration in blue. Marks included: 'Mtt' and 'AvE'.

AUREUS
The most important Roman gold coin.

AURILLAC LACE
Fine gold and silver thread laces which were made in the town of Aurillac probably from the latter part of the 16th century. In 1665, Colbert set up the so-called *Points de France* there.

AVENTURINE
A kind of glass containing particles of copper (for gold aventurine) or particles of chromic oxide (for green aventurine). It was first made in Venice about 1600.

AVRIL, ETIENNE (1748–91)
One of the supreme *ébénistes* of France, a master cabinetmaker from 1774.

AWAJI WARE
Japanese ceramics from the island of that name. First made around 1831 by Kashii Mimpei. A brownish-white clay body with a very smooth surface finish.

AWATA WARE
Japanese pottery from near Kyōto, made from about 1651. A white clay body with deep cream glaze. Distinctive feature is a fine net craquelure.

AXMINSTER CARPETS
Thomas Witty founded the factory for producing hand-knotted pile carpets on the Turkish pattern in the Court House at Axminster in about 1755. Mostly women were employed. In 1835 the factory closed and the looms were taken to Wilton where production continued.

BABY CAGE

A device for teaching a very young child to walk; also termed Baby Pen. Introduced in the 17th century it is a frame which holds the child upright and the whole moves on castors or small swivel mounted wheels.

BABY LACE

English bobbin-lace made in Midland counties, Bedfordshire, Buckinghamshire and Northamptonshire, intended for trimming babies' caps. Dates from the last quarter of the 18th century.

BACCARAT

The centre of fine glass production in France. Here at *La Compagnie des Cristalleries de Baccarat* and at the *Cristalleries de Saint Louis* exquisite examples of crystal glass and the celebrated paperweights were produced. Baccarat was founded in 1788.

BACHELOR CHEST

A low chest of drawers with a folding top, sometimes with candle brackets. It was brought in during the first part of the 18th century, and the top could serve as a form of primitive desk for writing on.

BACHIRU

A method employed in ivory carving, the surface of the ivory is tinted with a colour, and when the design is cut into it the natural ivory shows through.

BACINI

Painted and glazed earthenware plaques, intended to be set in the walls of churches as a complement to the architectural details.

BACKMAN, JACOB

Swiss cabinetmaker who emigrated to America and was working from 1766 in Lancaster County, Pennsylvania.

BACKPLATE

In furniture it is the plain or decorated plate of metal, generally brass or bronze, to which the handle of a drawer or cupboard is attached.

BACKSCRATCHER

A long thin rod of wood, ivory or whalebone, and sometimes ornamented with silver mounts. One end was generally carved into the shape of a human hand, a bird's claw or a miniature rake. Largely intended for back scratching; a secondary use is likely to have been for ladies to adjust their huge wigs and hair-do's in the 18th century.

BACKSWORD

A sword with only one cutting edge, now more usually a broadsword.

BADEN-BADEN

A faïence manufactory established there in 1770 by Zacharias Pfalzer which lasted until 1778. Products carried the Baden coat-of-arms under an Electoral Hat. A second manufactory was founded in 1795 and made faïence in the English manner. Mark was an impressed 'AA'.

BAHUT

A cabinet or chest, often with a rounded top, that was used for travelling.

BAIGNEUSE

A type of upholstered day bed in which the back continues to form the two sides. It came in with the French Empire Style.

BAIL HANDLE

In shape it was a half-circle, generally in brass or bronze. It could be attached to a single or two small back plates.

BAKHTIARI

A rug named after semi-nomads who weave them. Designs include flower and geometric motifs with rich strong colours.

BAKSHAISH

A Persian rug with, generally, angular designs from the place of that name.

BAKU

Caucasian rug taking its name from the town. Materials include cotton, wool, camel and goat hair. Main motif is generally a pear worked into a rectangular area.

Butter prints and pats *c* 1925. Photo by the author

BALANCE WHEEL
A device to balance and regulate motion with a timepiece and also the crown or escape wheel in a verge escapement.

BALDACHIN
A canopy of rich brocade or embroidered material supported on four or more pillars over a throne, seat or altar. Spelling may also be: baldaquin or baldakin. It comes originally from a Spanish term applied to a rich brocade from Baghdad that could include silver and gold threads.

BALL AND CLAW FOOT
Inspiration for this came from the thought of a dragon's claw holding a large pearl. It was introduced about 1700 and is commonly associated with the cabriole leg.

BALL FOOT
A round or spherical foot used with oak and mahogany during the 16th and 17th centuries.

BALLOCK KNIFE
A dagger introduced in the 14th century with a distinctive guard of two lobate shapes, rounded as with a certain type of leaf. Today often referred to as a kidney dagger.

BALLOON CLOCK
A bracket clock deriving its name from the shape of the early balloons. The face is nearly always white enamel, sometimes convex. It became popular in the 18th century.

BALSAMARIA
Small vases of glass, pottery, horn or metal used by the early Greeks and others around their time. They were intended to hold perfumes or unguent oils.

BALUSTER
The upright support for a handrail, either with cabinetwork, stairs or a balcony. They were generally turned into variations of pear-shaped bulges. The fashion became popular with the Late Jacobean style around 1650.

BALUSTER STEM
A term applied to glassware drinking vessels where the stems are given the baluster shape.

BAMBOO TURNING
A method used in cabinetwork where members are turned to give a likeness to bamboo. It was a feature of Chippendale's work in the Chinese Style.

BANC
In French cabinetwork it refers to a simple but extremely heavily made bench.

BANCONE
An Italian variety of writing table with a top that extends over the drawers underneath.

BANDED OR BANDING
A method of inlaying veneers for decorative purposes, the effect being achieved by contrasts with the woods used. Bandings are used mainly

on drawers and table tops, particularly with designs by Hepplewhite and Sheraton.

BANDEROLE
A ribbon or scroll intended to have an inscription or device as decoration. A feature that was in fashion during the Renaissance.

BANISTER
A corruption of baluster.

BANISTER BACKED CHAIR
A tall open-backed chair with split-banisters in the back. It may have been derived from cane-backing. It was popular in America during the 18th century.

BANJO BAROMETER
A type of instrument in which the case was made in the form of a banjo, bulbous end down.

BANJO CLOCK
A form of American wall clock in this shape; probably the first one was made by Simon Willard prior to 1800, the design being patented by him in 1802. The pendulum door was generally decorated with églomisé panels, favourite subjects being Lake Erie and Mount Vernon.

BANKO WARE
A hard Japanese pottery, made during the latter part of the 18th century by Numanami Gozayemon. It showed a brown clay body decorated with enamel in the Chinese manner.

BANQUETTE
A kind of bench-like upholstered seat, probably introduced during the reign of Louis XIV.

BARBERINI TAPESTRIES
A manufactory was set up in Rome about 1630 by the Cardinal Legate Francesco Barberini, a nephew of Pope Urban VIII. Weavers came from the Low Countries and worked under the direction of Giacomo della Riveria.

BARBER'S BASIN
An oval basin with a semi-circular piece cut out on one side to fit the neck whilst being shaved. It was introduced towards the end of the 17th century and could be made of pottery, pewter or silver.

BARBOTINE
A slip or clay paste that was first used with Rhenish pottery from about the 3rd century.

BARBUTE
A 15th century open helmet likely to have been of Italian origin. It had a high pointed crown which was later rounded, it also had flaps to protect the cheeks.

BARCHESTON TAPESTRIES
Those made by Richard Hicks during the 16th century at Barcheston in Warwickshire.

BARGELLO
Another name for the Hungarian stitch in needlework.

BARGUENO
A Spanish cabinet that has a fall-front enclosing drawers.

BARIER, FRANÇOIS-JULES (1680–1746)
The official gem-engraver to Louis XV, one of his specialities being tiny figures in cornelian.

BARLEY SUGAR TURNING
Twist or corkscrew turning, particularly in English cabinetwork.

BAROGRAPH
An automatic instrument for registering variations of atmospheric pressure; a self-registering barometer. The first known example dates from 1765.

BAROMETER
An instrument for determining the pressure of the atmosphere and hence for judging possible changes in the weather or for ascertaining the height of an ascent. It was invented by Torricelli a student of Galileo, at Florence in 1643. In the simplest form it consists of a glass tube 34 ins (86 cm) long filled with mercury and inverted in a bowl of mercury. The column of mercury descends until balanced by the atmospheric pressure. It is also called a Baroscope and Quick-Silver Weather Glass.

BAROVIER, ANGELO
A factory owning craftsman of Murano, Italy, who was lauded in *De Architectura* by Filarete, published 1451–64.

BARREL BACK CHAIR
A high-backed upholstered armchair with a semi-circular back roughly in the shape of a barrel.

BARREL TANG
An anchoring strap attached to the breech of the barrel of a firearm to steady the weapon when firing.

BARTALESI, URBANO (1641–1726)
A Sienese silversmith working in Rome from 1660. He was followed by his son Stefano; both father and son used the same mark, ie a wolf and the Sienese arms.

BARTMANN JUG
A German salt-glazed jug, also called a *Bartmannkrüg*. It was decorated with a bearded mask on the front. At the end of the 16th century it was sometimes called a 'bellarmine'.

BARTOLOTTI, GIUSEPPE (1709–75)
Roman silversmith, active from 1731, using the mark of a fish; he was followed by his son Carlo who slightly changed the mark to a vertical fish between the letters C and B.

BASALT WARE
A black stoneware invented by Josiah Wedgwood around the end of the 18th century. The black colour came from iron and manganese.

BASCINET
A light helmet of the 14th and 15th centuries, at first rounded it was then made conical, the better to deflect sword blows. It also had a skirt of chain mail at the back to protect the neck. At one time it was worn with a sharp protruding nosed visor.

BAS D'ARMOIRE
With French cabinetwork it implies a low cupboard. It was in vogue during the reign of Louis XIV, and was often richly decorated with gilt bronze ornaments; it was also generally given a marble top.

BASILAND
A short dagger or sword carried in the Middle Ages by civilians.

BASKET STITCH
One in which the threads running one way alternately pass under and over cross-threads.

BASSET
A small round or square table very similar to a stool only taller, an innovation of Gothic times.

BASTING SPOON
A long-handled, large-bowled spoon used for basting whilst cooking or for assisting with the serving.

BATAVIAN WARE
Chinese ceramics made during the K'ang Hsi period. The name came from the Dutch East India Company who brought it to Europe.

BATEMAN, HESTER
A determined and illustrious silversmith who when she was widowed in 1760 worked away to expand her husband's small workshop. Assisted by her sons John and Peter her fame soon spread and they produced much fine ware. Hester herself could neither read nor write but had a natural taste. Commissions included a large oval salver for Lancaster Town Hall, a large ogee-shaped punch-bowl of over 71 ounces with the Chester City Arms, and many smaller items that brought fame to the Bunhill Row establishment.

BATIK
A technique for decorating thin fabrics, it consists of putting on a wax resist on the parts not to be dyed. After dipping in the dye the material is boiled to remove the wax.

BAT PRINTING
A type of transfer printed decoration used with some English ceramics; it employs soft gelatinous sheets instead of thin sheets of paper and was brought in at the end of the 18th century.

BAT'S WING FLUTING
A tapered gadrooning used on coffee-pots, teapots, and bowls, principally with silver but also with pottery.

BATTERSEA ENAMEL
A technique started by Stephen Theodore Jannsen in about 1750 at York House in the Battersea district of London. Production only lasted for a few years as Jannsen went bankrupt. Similar enamels were later produced at Bilston and Wednesbury in Staffordshire.

BATTLE-AXE
A short-shafted medieval weapon with a heavy steel blade on one side and generally a sharp point or prong on the other.

BAUDEKIN
A very rich embroidered material, using gold and silk threads. Later the term was used for

This box dates from the 17th century. The decoration includes female allegorical figures in the costume of the period. The faces are worked with coloured silk, and much of the other ornamentation is by the use of beads. Courtesy Christie's

brocades. It probably originated in Baghdad. It was used for processional vestments and robes of state and also for hangings for baldachins.

BAWBEE
A Scottish billon coin issued about 1542 at three half-pence. At first showing the thistle and cross, later a royal portrait on the obverse.

BAYEUX TAPESTRY
The celebrated 11th-century embroidered hanging. Worked on linen it is 231 ft (70·4 m) long and 20 ins (0·5 m) wide. Using just eight colours it shows Harold's visit to Bosham on his way to Normandy, and ends with the Battle of Hastings. Sadly the end of the original work is missing. It is thought that the hanging was made for Odo the Bishop of Bayeux. Originally it was called the Toile de Jean.

BAYONET
A short double- or single-edged dagger or short sword that would clip to the muzzle end of a rifle to make it into a thrusting pike. It began to be used towards the end of the 17th century.

BAYREUTH
An outstanding manufactory established at the town in Bavaria about 1713–14. Main products consisted of exquisite faïence and brown-glazed ware with gilt, silver and engraved decoration. The marks consisted of the initials of the place, the owners, and also the painter's marks.

BEADING
A border ornament used for edges and rims with silver, it consisted of a string of tiny bead shapes.

BEAKER

A large drinking vessel, almost cylindrical with a slight taper. Can be made of pottery, silver, gold, copper, glass or pewter. Often they are richly chased and decorated. They do not have handles.

BEAUVAIS

Tapestries manufactured at the town to the north of Paris. The works were founded in 1664 by Louis Hinart and he then received the help of Colbert. A number of successful hangings were produced in the 18th century from cartoons prepared by François Boucher.

BEAVER

With medieval armour it was a piece that protected the lower half of the face. It was movable and could be attached either to the helmet or breastplate.

BECKER, JOHANN ALBRECHT

A Saxon glass decorator who emigrated to Norway where he worked at Nöstetangen between 1767 and 1773. Afterwards he moved to Drammen to the north-west of Oslo where he set up his own studio.

BED

In the houses of the rich the bed was always looked upon as a very important piece of furniture and often demonstrated the affluence of its owner. One example of this is the elaborately carved oak bedstead of Jeanne d'Albert, mother of Henri IV. This dates from the times of the French Renaissance – 1562 is carved on the lower cornice moulding. King Ludwig II of Bavaria probably took this rich decoration as far as any with his sumptuous glittering beds in his castles.

The iron or brass bedstead came in after the Exhibition of 1851.

BEDDINGTON LOCK

Richly decorated wrought-iron rim lock which carries the arms of Henry VII and VIII.

BEDFORDSHIRE LACE

Work inspired by the skill of lace-workers from Flanders, probably introduced in the 16th century.

BEECH

A hard wood with a pale tone, the tree, *Fagus sylvatica,* is widespread in Europe.

Bellarmine Jar. Courtesy of the Isles of Scilly Museums Association

BEEHIVE CLOCK

An American shelf clock, a type of small Connecticut timepiece; the name is derived from a slight resemblance to the old kind of beehive. It dates from around 1850.

BEILBY, WILLIAM (1740–1819)

A skilled craftsman from Newcastle-upon-Tyne who produced fine enamelled glasswork signed with a butterfly.

BELFAST GLASS

Work produced from about 1781 included enamelled, cut and plain wine glasses. The moving spirit was Benjamin Edwards who continued until 1829.

A 'Skeleton' clock. Enamel dial by Coteau. Revolutionary Period. Courtesy of Ader, Picard, Tajan

18th-century printed Queen's Ware by Wedgwood. Courtesy of the Wedgwood Museum Barlaston

Wedgwood Jasper ware in pale blue, sage green and black. Courtesy of the Wedgwood Museum, Barleston

Fine English Gold Snuff Box. Scene on the lid shows Alexander conversing with Diogenes and is from a print by Salvator Rosa. Inside the lid is a portrait in enamel of a young lady dressed as Mary Stuart by Christian Frederick Zincke. *c* 1740. Courtesy Sotheby Parke Bernet

Horloge astronomique de A. Vérité. Beauvais. Courtesy of SPADEM

BELLARMINE

A large bellied jug that originated in the neighbourhood of Cologne in the 16th century. On one side it bore a bearded face or mask intended to represent Cardinal Bellarmine, a leader of the Roman Catholic Counter Reformation. The jugs were also called 'greybeards' or 'longbeards'.

BELLEEK

A light and delicate parian ware cast in moulds and finished with a pleasant pearl-like glaze. It was invented by William Goss of Stoke, Staffordshire in about 1860 and then improved at the works of McBirney and Armstrong at Belleek, Northern Ireland. One of the first products was the Belleek basket made of woven strands. Early mark was a round tower with a wolfhound to the right and an Irish harp to the left, beneath was a ribbon with the name 'Belleek'.

BELLEVUE

Faïence manufactory founded at the town in France by Lefrançois about 1755. Best works were the figures in chalk-like biscuit. Mark on these was 'Bellevue Ban de Toul'.

BELL FLOWER

An ornament in the shape of open seed-pods that originated in America.

BELLS

These could be table objects for calling servants, generally of silver but also made from copper, brass, steel, bronze and pewter. The handle most often was made with a balustrade shape and could be of the same material as the bell, or of ivory, bone or wood.

BELTER, JOHN HENRY (1804–63)

Skilled New York cabinetmaker active between 1840 and 1860. His work tended to be very ornate.

BELUCHISTAN

A turkoman rug woven by the nomadic tribes of Beluchistan and the Beluches living in Afghanistan. Patterns are geometric, using hexagons and octagons with deep rich colours.

BENCH

A long seat for two or more persons, sometimes with a back.

BENEMAN, JEAN GUILLAUME

A leading French *ébéniste,* active from 1784. A year later he became a *maître-ébéniste* without having to submit to the usual formalities. His finest skill was shown with his marble-topped commodes. He used the stamp 'G. BENEMAN'.

BENNETT POTTERY

A small manufactory started in Baltimore in 1846 by the brothers, Edwin and William Bennett. Distinctive products were pitchers called stag hunt pitcher and wild boar, etc, the names derived from the relief decoration used. Marks included 'E.B.' and 'E & W Bennett'.

BENNINGTON WARE

Earthenware made at Bennington, Vermont, since 1793. The manufactory was started about 1842 by Julius Norton and Christopher Webber Fenton. The wares included Rockingham and Parian. Metallic oxides were applied to the already fired body and the piece was dipped in a clear flint enamel glaze. Results included delightful yellow, orange and blue mottled effects.

BENT-WOOD FURNITURE

Pieces made of pre-bent wood were in fashion in Austria in the middle of the 19th century. The results were called Vienna furniture.

BERETTINO

Decorative designs using opaque white on a light or dark blue tin-glaze ground; especially applicable to Italian ceramics.

BERG, MAGNUS (1666–1739)

A Norwegian ivory carver whose work showed a German influence.

BERGAMO

A Turkish-type rug woven in the village of Pergamo, the name Bergamo being a corruption. The old examples can be very fine, although recent examples have become degraded.

BERGÈRE

A type of upholstered chair or sofa, fashionable in the 18th century; the fashion started during the reign of Louis XVI. Bergères also appeared as confessional chairs.

BERINI, ANTONIO (c 1770–1830)

Born in Rome, he studied with Giovanni Pichler and subsequently became a skilled

A pair of Louis XV bergères made with waxed beechwood frames and upholstered with elaborate needlework.
Courtesy Sotheby Parke Bernet

gem-engraver. Later he was to move to Milan. He was the worker of the famous cameo of Napoleon which by accident or design showed a red vein in the stone, encircling the Emperor's neck. This brought the craftsman a period behind bars.

BERLIN

A porcelain manufactory started in 1751 by Wilhelm Kaspar Wegely with the approval of Frederick the Great. In 1757 the works closed, later to be opened again in 1761 by Johann Gotzkowsky; it then became known as the Royal Berlin Porcelain Manufactory. The best works rank among the finest produced in 18th-century Germany. The later mark was a sceptre with variations.

BERLIN WOOLWORK

A 19th-century fashion for working over ready-printed designs, thought up by a Madame Wittich. The results were chiefly used for chair seats and screens.

BESAGEW OR BESAQUE

A small circular plate in position over each armpit on 14th–16th-century armour. It could

sometimes be square or oval. The plates were kept in position with laces. They were also called motons.

BESHIRE

A Turkoman rug of wool weave and pile. The colour is generally a warm red with Arabic-influenced patterns.

BETTY LAMP

A 17th and 18th century American lamp based on the early European cruzie. Briefly it is a flat pear-shaped vessel of iron or tin with a wick at the small end. It was normally hung on an iron rod and stand or attached to a bar suspended from the ceiling.

BEZANT

A collective name for Byzantine gold coins. In Western Europe the solidus was a gold piece issued by the emperors at Constantinople which circulated from the 6th to the 15th or 16th centuries.

BEZEL

A sloping edge or face on a cutting tool used in joinery and cabinetwork.

BIANCO SOPRA BIANCO

An Italian term which means the application of a decorative pattern in opaque white on a pale bluish-white ground. Italian workers with majolica favoured the method from the 16th century at a number of leading faïence ceramic centres, including Castel Durante and Faenza. In the 18th century, English delftware decorators used a like method.

BIBELOT

A small decorative article, a trinket, a mantel ornament.

BIBERON

A Swiss drinking vessel dating from the 17th century. It is generally made of pewter in the shape of a small kettle. It was lifted by a bail handle which would be attached to a bracket in the dining or living room in a Swiss house. The spout went inside the vessel and down to the bottom so that drinking could be by sucking.

BIBLE-BOX

A small chest or box of the 17th century, or earlier, to hold the treasured family Bible. It was generally made of oak with a flat top.

BIBLIOTHÈQUE

An early 18th century movable bookcase, popular in France. Normally it was longer than it was high and often had a marble top with a fretted metal gallery on three sides.

BIDRI

A type of ware made from a pewter which was composed of tin, zinc and small quantities of copper and lead. After the object had been worked from the pewter, its surface was engraved and into the lines gold and silver were inlaid. After this the surface was wiped with a mixture of saltpetre, ammonia and a little oil; this treatment caused the pewter to blacken. The principal place of manufacture was Bidar, Hyderabad. The ware was also called biddery.

BIGGIN

An early variation of a coffee percolator; it usually had straight sides, a short spout and an inner container for the ground coffee. Invented by Mr. Biggin in about 1800, it often had its own stand and spirit lamp.

BIJAR

A type of Persian rug with coarse heavy yarn and a short wool pile. It is long wearing.

BIJOUTERIE

A term for trinkets or objects of virtu.

BILBAO

A variety of mirror with a marble or marble and mahogany frame, generally ornamented with filigree. It took its name from the port where it was often found by ships' captains who, to a degree, were responsible for importing the mirror into America at the end of the 18th century and the beginning of the 19th.

BILL

A medieval weapon used by the English during the 15th and 16th centuries. It had a long shaft surmounted by a broad blade, with a cutting hook. In all probability it was derived from the hedging-bill which also would have given the bill its name. The name could also refer to a type of broadsword.

BILL, FRANCIS

A west of England chandelier-maker active in 1740 at Dunster, Somerset. He died in 1742.

BILLET

The thumbpiece used to lift the lid of a pewter tankard.

BILLET MOULDING

A type of decoration found in Byzantine and Romanesque architecture. It is composed of cylindrical blocks arranged in a sunken rounded moulding. Some cabinetmakers have adapted the idea for use with wood.

BILSTED

The wood of the sweet gum tree, *Liquidambar styraciflua,* native to America, which was used as a substitute for mahogany.

BILSTON

A centre for japanned ware in Staffordshire from the latter part of the 17th century; one speciality at that time was the snuff-box. Other items in demand included patch-boxes, candlesticks, scent bottles, and animal and bird toys.

BINCHE

A Flemish bobbin lace, one of the earliest of the Flemish laces, was made at Binche. It has a pattern of floral scrolls spreading over the entire width of the lace, no cordonnet or only a very fine one outlining the pattern. The ground is *fond de neige,* sprinkled with tiny discs resembling snowflakes. Later work has become more open and thus lost much of the delicacy.

BINDER'S STAMP

A term used in bookbinding, meaning a design engraved in brass for stamping decoration and titles on covers.

BIRCH

A hard close-grained wood, *Betula alba,* pale in colour that was sometimes stained to imitate mahogany. The north American variety was imported into England during the latter part of the 18th century. The wood was used also for legs, spindles and often for the whole framework of a chair.

BIRD, EDWARD

An artist who for a time decorated japanned trays with scenes from history for the Ryton firm in Wolverhampton during the late 1780s. Later he became an RA and was appointed as Historical Painter to Princess Charlotte of Wales.

BIRKA

A graving tool, with either a triangular or square point, used for carving ivory.

BISCUIT

Earthenware or porcelain that has undergone the first firing, before it is subjected to the glazing. It is also termed *bisque.*

BISCUIT FIGURE

An unglazed modelled figure; the first examples were probably made at Sèvres and Vincennes about 1750–51. The fashion became very popular and the making of them spread to Germany and to England, where they were produced at Derby. The matt surface of these figures has an appealing gentle look. They are best kept behind or under glass, as sooty smoky atmospheres can soon make them grimy, and by their nature they are difficult to clean.

BISETTE

A rather narrow and open bobbin-lace made by peasant women around Paris in the 17th century.

BISMUTH

A metal that can be added to pewter to harden it. The resulting alloy can be called tinglass.

BIZEN

A hard unglazed pottery, usually greyish-white, made at Bizen, Japan. It may have been produced as early as the 14th century. The fired surface sometimes had a bronze-metallic sheen. In the 17th century a bluish-slate coloured variety was made. The method was used for producing vessels for the tea ceremony and also for modelling gods, birds, fish and animals.

BLACKAMOOR

An English name for the candlestand or *guéridon* that came into use in France in the middle of the 17th century. The first mention in English records of a blackamoor being used is about 1679. The carved figures of the moors were shown with brilliantly coloured costumes.

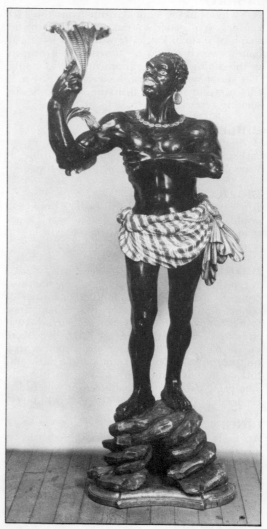

Venetian 18th-century Blackamoor. Courtesy of Sotheby Parke Bernet

BLACK GLASS

A type of glass that is really very dark purple or green which was generally used for bottle-making. For a time, however, it was also employed to make imitation jet buttons.

BLACK JACK

A large vessel for ale or the like, it was originally made of tarred leather. More recently, examples have been fabricated from japanned metal.

BLACK PEWTER

A type of the alloy that consists of around 60 per cent tin and 40 per cent lead. It is thus very soft and was generally used only for candle moulds, and certainly not for making drinking vessels which would have been very dangerous owing to the high lead content.

BLACK WORK

A kind of embroidery first worked during the reign of Henry VIII, which continued to be popular during the reign of Elizabeth I. It may have been introduced by Catherine of Aragon. The technique employed black silk thread on a white ground. It is also termed Spanish work.

BLANC-DE-CHINE

A white variety of Chinese porcelain made at Tê-Hua, Fukien, which is often decorated with embossed ornament, but no colour. It was first manufactured sometime during the Ming dynasty (1368–1644). Favourite pieces were modelled in the likeness of deities and wise men of the Buddhist faith. One such Kwan Yin was made in large numbers. European influence becomes noticeable from the middle of the 17th century.

BLANKET STITCH

A buttonhole stitch worked wide apart on the edge of a material too thick to hem.

BLEEDING BOWL

A vessel about the size and shape of a porringer but with only one handle which was used by a surgeon when drawing blood, a medical custom that by records goes back to at least 1430. The bowl was made of silver, although the earliest examples were probably made of pottery.

BLEU-DE-ROI

The blue used on Sèvres porcelain, it was developed by Jean Hellot about 1755.

BLIND-EARL'S PATTERN

A design used by Worcester from about 1760, it consisted of relief work with birds and rose leaves, and later it took its name from the Earl of Coventry who went blind in 1780.

BLIND-TOOLED WORK

With reference to bookbinding it implies decoration or lettering that is stamped or embossed and left without gilding or applied colour.

BLOCK BOOK

Some of the earliest books were printed with the illustration and the letters and words cut from the same block. The term block books applied to these.

BLOCK FRONT

A type of front, as with some American chests of drawers or with some secrétaires, characterised by a sunken central panel flanked on either side by a raised panel or block. The form may be seen also with chests-on-chests, kneehole dressing tables and short-front desks. It is thought that the idea was developed by an American, John Goddard, of Newport, Rhode Island in about 1770.

BLONDE DE CAEN

A silk bobbin-lace of a startling whiteness that challenged the quality of a similar type from Chantilly. Sadly, when machine-made blondes came in from factories at Calais and Nottingham the lace-makers of Caen gave up the method and turned to a block variety and gold and silver blondes.

BLONDE LACE

A method evolved in France in about 1745 for lace-making with white or pale fair silks, hence the name.

BLONDE MATE

Bobbin-lace that is recognised by rich flower patterns on mesh. It was a favourite with Spanish ladies for mantillas in the 19th century. The laces were made at Bayeux, Caen and Chantilly.

BLOODWOOD

The timber of numerous trees having a red juice or red wood such as the *eucalypti* of Australia, the crape myrtle of the East Indies, and the logwood of the West Indies. The woods have been used in cabinetwork.

BLOWN-MOULDINGS
Articles of glass blown in a mould to give desired shape. Glass made in this way generally retains a slight roughened appearance from the contact with the mould.

BLOWN THREE MOULD
A method of producing cheap decorated glass which was in fashion from about 1815 for some twenty years. The hinged mould held a sunken pattern inside and was normally of three sections. Pieces made in this way can generally be picked up by thin slightly raised lines where the molten glass was forced into the small spaces between the hinged sections by the blowing.

BLUE AND WHITE CHINESE PORCELAIN
The blue employed was obtained from the cobaltiferous ore of manganese. It was found in certain places in China and was imported from the Near East during the T'ang period as well as during the Ming dynasty. The characteristic Chinese blue and white porcelain was achieved by painting decoration on the unglazed body which was then glazed and fired.

BLUE-DASH CHARGERS
Large majolica dishes that came from Bristol and Lambeth during the 17th and 18th centuries. They were intended for decorative purposes to be hung on walls or placed in noticeable positions on furniture. Main motifs for embellishment included fruit, flowers and figures. Later, the painting was very bold and colourful with rich greens, blues, yellows, oranges and reds.

BLUE GLASS
A type made by Irish glass-houses, somewhat similar to the Bristol blue. A recipe for the making was found amongst documents dated 1786 in Waterford, the leading glass centre.

BLUE JOHN
A beautiful variety of Fluorspar found in Derbyshire, which has been used for making vases and other ornamental objects.

BLUE OR LAVENDER GLAZES
Cobalt glazing of the Ming period, later treated with manganese purple in the Ch'ing dynasty to give an exquisite range of tints.

BLUE STEEL
A method of tinting steel by heating on sand, a material used by locksmiths.

BLUNDERBUS
A short gun with a large bore and usually a bell muzzle. It was designed to hold a large number of balls and to scatter the shot for close-quarters work; not intended for accurate aiming. It came to England from the continent in the middle of the 17th century, and its use for protection lasted until well into the 19th century. Some later models included a primitive folding bayonet.

BLUNGER
In ceramics, it means a tank with revolving arms for mixing the clay.

BOAT BED
A French Empire style in which the bed had some resemblance to a boat. In a room it would either be placed in an alcove or length-wise along a wall.

BOBBIN LACE
A type that was made on a pillow with the threads wound round bobbins. The design is pricked through on parchment, pins are stuck through the holes, and the threads plaited about them. It is a slow method with up to 50 bobbins being used to make one square inch of lace. It is also termed pillow lace.

BOBBIN NET
A machine-made lace or netting of cotton, sometimes silk, which has a hexagonal mesh. It was originally intended to imitate bobbin lace. The machine was invented in 1768, probably by a stocking framework knitter of Nottingham. In 1809, John Heathcoat of Longwhatton developed a machine to make bobbin net.

BOBÊCHE
A saucer-shaped dish to catch the drippings from a candle.

BOCAGE
An ornament that was primarily trees, flowers and plants, or that which presents a wooded landscape as seen in tapestries or porcelain.

BOGGLE
A Scotch jug or large pitcher made to look like a man.

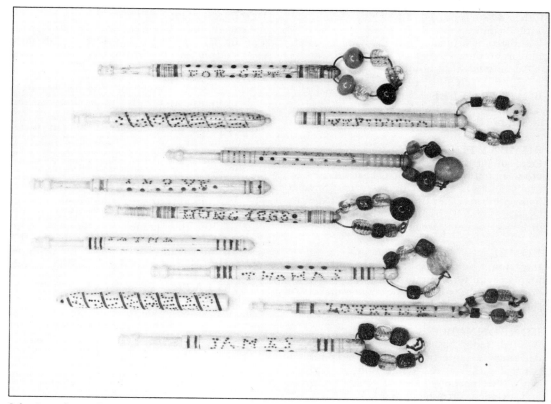

Selection of turned, carved and stained bone Bedfordshire bobbins, *c* 1860–70. Courtesy of Bonhams

BOG WOOD
The wood of trees preserved in peat bogs. It has a shining black ebony colour. Bog oak is the most common, although bog pine and bog deal are also found. It was used for inlay in the time of Elizabeth I, and has also been worked into ornaments.

BOHEMIAN GLASS
A colourless potash-lime glass originally formulated in the late 17th century to emulate Venetian glass. German craftsmen found it worked well for cut and engraved decoration.

BOÎTE À GAUFRE
A small box native to France for holding a honeycomb.

BOÎTE À SEL
A salt box often made as a companion piece to a flour-box and decorated in a naïve but pleasing manner. Both were quite common in France during the time of Louis XV.

BOKHARA
A Turkoman rug in small and large sizes, coming from the region of Bokhara and generally distinguished by very fine knotting and patterns which included octagons, diamonds, cross-stars, angular shrubs and flowers. Colours were rich and ranged over dark blue, vermilion, mulberry red and ivory.

BOLECTION
A portion of a group of mouldings which stands up above the general surface of a panel.

BOLE
A red earth, coloured by oxides, used in preparing an area for gilding. It is painted over the hardened gesso to provide a rich ground for the thin gold-leaf to follow.

BOMBARD
A large drinking vessel usually made of leather, and popular in England during the

17th and 18th centuries. It was bulbous in shape with a handle.

A piece of ordnance for throwing boulders and large stones.

A bomb vessel or bomb.

BOMBARDELLE
A primitive early firearm which consisted of little more than a tube aligned along a staff.

BOMBAY FURNITURE
Pieces made largely in Bombay from black-wood or shisham wood. It is characterised by heavy and somewhat clumsy forms. Smaller items are better and often have quite exquisite lace-carving. It is a hybrid, combining European style with oriental decoration.

BOMBÉ
Implying a puffed-up, blown-out and inflated manner with forms in furniture. It is noticeable with the rich work of the cabinetmakers at the time of Louis XV.

BONBONNIÈRE
A small fancy dish or box for sweetmeats, deriving its name from *bonbon*. In France, in particular, they were often lavishly ornamented with jewels and made of gold or silver, and included tortoiseshell work.

BONE CHINA
One that is made with an admixture of bone ash or calcium phosphate. A patent was taken out in 1748 by Thomas Frye of Bow. Later Worcester and Spode introduced a paste with china clay and bone ash and this was covered with a lead glaze.

BONE GLASS
A type of glass with a milky-white colour due to the presence of bone ash or calcium phosphate.

BONE LACE
Bobbin lace, and so called because the original bobbins were made of bone.

BONHEUR-DU-JOUR
A delicate desk on long graceful legs intended for use by a lady. It was introduced in about 1750 and became a vogue in the time of Louis XVI. It was generally made with a recessed superstructure which contained a series of drawers to hold not only writing materials but also toilet necessities and other personal treasures.

BONNET PIECE
A Scottish gold coin in use from 1539–40 with a profile portrait of James V wearing a bonnet and Scottish arms on the reverse.

BONNET TOP
With cabinet furniture and doorheads a style of broken arch top with the break extending the entire depth of the top. The centre often carried some form of carved or cast metal ornament. The fashion lasted from about 1730 to 1780, and was also known as hooded or the hood.

BONTEMPS, GEORGES (1799–1884)
He was the director of the Choisy-le-Roi factory for 25 years, starting in 1823. It was due to him that France led the way with certain types of coloured glass. Under his directorship advances were made with filigree and opal glass, also stained glass and millefiori.

BOOKPLATE
A label which indicates the owner of a book, generally pasted inside the cover or on one of the front pages. These are often made from engraved wood blocks, and may be highly decorative being built round a fanciful pattern or design connected with the owner of the book. On the other hand, it may simply present the armorial bearings.

BOOK-REST
A support for holding a book or folio whilst studying it; a necessary item in the 18th century library which often contained a number of large volumes.

BOOTLEG PISTOL
An odd type of pistol produced in America, largely in Massachusetts; it had the percussion cap underneath with generally no trigger-guard and the grips set at a right angle.

BORDEAUX
A faïence manufactory started there in 1711 by Jacques Fautier and Jacques Hustin. Most of the ware was imitated from Moustiers and Nevers.

A porcelain manufactory founded there in 1781, according to Jacquemart, by Pierre Verneuille; six years afterwards it changed ownership, and was under the direction of Alluaud and Vanier. The products were decorative and used motifs that included festoons of flowers with bright clean colours. Marks were generally: 'W', 'AV' or two 'V's interlocked.

One of the earliest known English gilt bindings on a manuscript relating to Henry VIII's divorce from Katherine of Aragon, dated 24 March 1530. Courtesy of Christie's

BORE
The diameter and interior of the barrel of a firearm.

BORI
A Japanese sword mount which is often exquisitely decorated by chiselling and engraving.

BORNE
A large round upholstered seat with a padded steep conical back in the centre.

BOSS
A raised circular ornament that may be found in metal work or pottery, and also with furniture. Motifs incorporated could include leaves and flowers.

BOSSUIT, FRANÇOIS VAN (1635–92)
A talented Flemish ivory carver who worked most of his life in Italy. There is a charming example of his work in the Wallace Collection entitled 'Toilet of Bathsheba'.

BOSTON ROCKER
A late modification of the Windsor Chair. It had a wooden seat curved up to meet the spindles of the back; the spindles being held at the top by a flat headrail. It is of American origin and came in around 1840.

BÖTTGER WARE
A distinguished reddish-brown stoneware of German origin, which takes its name from its discoverer, Johann Friedrich Böttger (1682–1719), the famous chemist and ceramist who started the Dresden faïence manufactory. Between 1708 and 1709 he developed the stoneware that was so hard that it could be polished on a lathe. It was somewhat similar to the Chinese buccaro of Yi-hsing. In 1708 he made what was really the first true or hard paste in Europe, and followed this by developing a suitable glaze for use with it. When the Elector of Gascony set up the Meissen manufactory he appointed Böttger as director.

BOTTLE TICKETS
A simpler form of the wine label, they were small plain plaques with the name of the beverage engraved and minimal decoration. They were held round the necks of bottles by thin chains.

BOUFFIOULX
A stoneware that aped the Rhenish. It was made from the late 16th century in various parts of Belgium including the place it took its name from and Namur.

BOUGEOIR
A small candlestick which dates from the 16th century; the name derived from bougie, a wax candle.

BOUGIE BOX
A cylindrical box for a coil of wax taper.

BOUILLOIRE
A tea-kettle mounted on a frame holding a small spirit lamp.

BOUILLOTTE LAMP
A brass or bronze table lamp with a central shaft that supports two or three brackets for

Soap box (or sponge box) which is pierced with shell-and-scroll motifs, and which is by Nicholas Le Fevre of Paris. It is dated 1767 and the hinged lid is engraved at the top with a contemporary coat of arms. It stands 3¾ ins (9·5 cms) high and weighs over seven ounces. Courtesy Spink

candles. It generally has green painted metal shades. A lamp associated with private gaming tables in the 18th century.

BOUILLOTTE TABLE

French card table associated with the game of bouillotte. It came in during the time of Louis XVI. Normally it has a circular white marble top.

BOULLE, ANDRÉ CHARLES

(1642–1732)

The celebrated French *ébéniste,* the son of a carpenter. At the start he led a varied career, moving between architecture, painting and engraving. When he turned to furniture he worked first as a freelance, but in 1672 Colbert appointed him as *ébéniste* to the king. André Charles did not invent the particular type of marquetry associated with his name, but he, with other members of his family, did develop it and bring it to the peak of perfection. No one equalled him in the handling of the combinations of metals and tortoiseshell. He received much of his inspiration for the designs he drew from a collection of master drawings. A difficult point for the collector is that he never signed his work and actual pieces truly from his hand are very rare.

BOULTON, MATTHEW (1728–1809)

A leading maker of objects and mounts in ormolu, he worked from a factory near Birmingham and was in demand for candelabra, clocks and other associated items. He also worked with Sheffield plate.

BOW

A soft-paste porcelain produced possibly from the manufactory working around 1744 with Thomas Frye and Edward Heylyn. Most of the production was with simple domestic ware, although there was some modelling of figures based on inspiration from Meissen.

BOW-BACK

A variation with the Windsor chair where the back is a continuous piece of bent wood.

BOW FRONT

A term for commodes, chest of drawers and similar pieces that have a gentle convex curve in the front from one side to another.

BOW-KNOT

A decorative feature based on bows or knots of ribbons often combined with small sheaves or sprays of flowers.

BOX STRETCHER

A continuous rectangular stretcher, usually set low down, that connects and strengthens the legs of chairs and tables.

BOXWOOD

A very close-grained tough hardwood, the *buxus* is light in colour and useful for inlays and for making musical instruments.

BRACE-BACK CHAIR

A type of chair similar to the Windsor, or a variation of the Windsor, that has part of the back of the seat protruding to take two extra spindles to give extra support.

BRACHIALE

A fence or guard for the upper arm found with ancient armour.

BRACKET CLOCK

One that has a short pendulum and is designed to stand on a shelf or bracket. In many cases such clocks had their own brackets designed especially for them; unfortunately many of these supports have now disappeared.

Bracket or shelf clock by Joseph Knibb, *c* 1690. Courtesy Sotheby Parke Bernet

BRACKET FOOT
A bracket-like foot found on furniture, notably desks, chests of drawers, wardrobes and sideboards. It was mitred at the corner and often scrolled on the free sides.

BRADBURN, JOHN (died 1781)
A skilled carver and cabinetmaker who first worked in Hemmings Row in St Martin's Lane, and later in Long Acre, London. He succeeded William Vile as master cabinetmaker to George III.

BRADSHAW, GEORGE SMITH
Joiner and upholsterer active in 1756, working from Greek Street, Soho.

BRAGUETTE
With 15th century and later armour this is a piece that would correspond to the codpiece; it might be a shaped plate or a skirt of mail.

BRAIDING
A type of embroidery that uses entwining and interlacing of strands, or plaiting together to make long patterns of arabesque form.

BRAMAH LOCK
A type with which the tumblers are thin flat notched bars which receive endwise movement from the key instead of the swinging movement as with the ordinary lock.

BRAMPTON
A manufactory in Derbyshire producing a brown stoneware in the latter part of the 18th and into the 19th century.

BRANDER
An iron pierced plate on a loop handle for suspending close to the fire when making Scottish oatmeal cakes.

BRANDEWIJNKOM
An oval silver bowl associated with the festive season and intended to hold brandy-soaked raisins. Origin was probably Dutch and 17th century.

BRANNAM, C. H.
Director of the Barnstaple pottery which is notable for the production of Barum ware.

BRASS
Originally an alloy of copper with a base metal, usually tin or later zinc. Today an alloy of zinc with the copper, with proportions of around one zinc to two of copper; sometimes small amounts of other metals are added.

BRATINA
A type of Russian drinking cup that could have a spherical shape with a contracted lip. Those for the nobility were made of silver and gold, and for the rest bratinas were made of copper or carved from wood.

BRAZIER
A receptacle for holding burning charcoal for heating or cooking over. They are principally associated with the East and Middle East.

BRAZIL WAX
A hard wax that comes from the Brazilian palm, found as a deposit on the leaves. It has a high melting point, and may be used as a substitute for beeswax. It is also an ingredient of certain lacquers and varnishes.

BREAD OR CAKE BASKET
A silver or Sheffield plate pierced container, generally with a bail handle, frequently richly decorated with chasing and engraving.

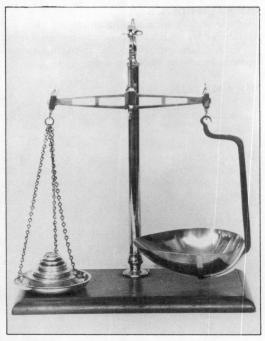

Brass shop scales, Dublin, late 19th century. Courtesy Woburn Abbey Antiques Centre

BREAKFAST TABLE
A small table with hinged leaves that when extended could seat two people. It was introduced about the middle of the 18th century and intended to be used in a bedroom for serving breakfast. After Chippendale's time it was often called a Pembroke.

BREAK-FRONT BOOKCASE
A bookcase or secretary bookcase made with the upper central portion projecting; this would be fitted with glazed doors and adjustable shelves. The lower section, which also had a projecting central section, would have cupboard doors, often with drawers at the sides and in the centre a fall-front fully fitted writing drawer.

BREASTPLATE
A plate of metal covering the breast as defensive armour.

BRECCIA
A kind of marble composed of angular fragments embedded in a stony substance exhibiting a number of colours. It is often sought for table and commode tops.

BREECH
The rear of the barrel of a firearm which receives the cartridge or shellcase.

BRETON WORK
Embroidery that has been developed from peasant costumes. The method is to use coloured silks and gold thread with simple stitches and floral or geometric patterns.

BREWSTER CHAIR
A 17th-century American chair named after William Brewster (1560–1644) of the Plymouth Colony. He is reputed to have brought his own over with him on the *Mayflower*. It is an armchair of turned spindles and posts, with a rush seat. The favoured woods for construction are ash and maple.

BRIATI, GIUSEPPE (1686–1772)
Founder of a glass factory at Murano, later moving his establishment to Venice. His products resembled Bohemian glass, and the range of objects included chandeliers, mirrors, picture frames and grotesque creations.

BRIC-À-BRAC
Curios or antique articles of virtu; miscellaneous objects of an artistic kind, and assembly of knick-knacks.

BRIDE PICOTÉE
A decorative motif consisting of a six-sided buttonhole bar with a row of loops on each side used with Argentan lace.

BRIGANDINE
A late medieval coat of body armour consisting of overlapping metal scales or plates sewn inside leather or linen. Sometimes covered with silk or velvet with rivet heads showing.

BRIGHT-CUT ENGRAVING
A technique for decorating silver, and one that calls for considerable skill. The bright effect is caused by the burnishing of the cuts by the back edges of the graver while the biting edge gouges out the metal. When the cuts are zig-zag a jewel-like effect is produced.

BRISTOL
A centre for delftware with manufactories at Brislington, St Mary Redcliffe and Limekiln Lane. The glaze had a characteristic pale lavender blue tint. Ware produced included puzzle jugs, plates with straight sides sloping down to the bottom, and porringers.

Hard-paste porcelain was produced there from about 1770 when a Plymouth manufactory moved to the city. Wares are skilfully painted with an underglaze blue or printed with overglaze enamel. Some influence from Sèvres is evident. Such figures that were modelled, generally had a rockwork base.

Soft-paste porcelain was made from around 1750 using soapstone as one ingredient. Some of the ware was in imitation of Chinese export porcelain.

Glassmaking in the 18th century was a flourishing industry, with up to 15 works in operation in 1760. Products included cut crystal tableware, decanters and candlesticks, in both clear and coloured glass. The two types of Bristol glass of most interest are the milk and coloured. The milk was in imitation of fine porcelain and was decorated with enamels. Most celebrated from Bristol is the rich blue which was sometimes gilded.

BRITANNIA METAL
An alloy of tin, antimony and copper that was first made commercially by James Vickers of Sheffield around 1770. Early examples can look like pewter. Britannia was intended to ape Sheffield plate.

BROADSWORD
One with a straight wide blade for cutting rather than thrusting. It is a term mainly used for the basket-hilted cavalry swords of the 17th and 18th centuries.

Frederick Gordon Crosby. Bronze model of a racing car at speed with driver and travelling mechanic. Signed and carrying inscription 'To Sammy from his colleagues Premier Award in his Greatest Trial, 1931'. It was presented to S. C. H. Davis whilst convalescing following his accident at the 1931 Brooklands Easter meeting in which he heavily crashed his Invicta. Courtesy of Christie's, South Kensington

BROCADE
A rich fabric with a raised design induced whilst weaving by additional weft threads; these are usually gold, silver or silk.

BROCATELLE
A heavy-figured fabric, usually of linen or silk, widely used up to the 18th century for upholstery.

BRODERIE ANGLAISE
A charming white embroidery characterised by oval and round eyelets with chain, satin and overcast stitches.

BRODERIE DE NANCY
A type of drawnwork sometimes combined with coloured silk embroidery.

BROKEN PEDIMENT
Baroque decorative device where a gap is left in the pediment at the apex.

BRONZE
An alloy of copper and tin, sometimes with small amounts of other metals such as zinc, lead and phosphorus.

Benin Bronze of a Horseman, mid 16th century. Courtesy of Christie's

BRONZE DORÉ
A term for gilt bronze.

BRONZES D'AMEUBLEMENT
A French collective term that cannot truly be translated into English. It draws in all items of furniture, useful and decorative, that employ some form of bronze, either plain or gilt.

BRONZE DISEASE
A surface blemish on a bronze object which consists of greyish-green spots. More prevalent in older pieces; the cause is likely to be the presence of damp and chloride, and the damp could also react with impurities in the alloy. Requires expert treatment.

BRUMMAGEM
A shoddy cheap object of poor manufacture. A counterfeit coin, a fake groat. Mention of the latter in association with Birmingham is found in 17th century records.

BRUNSWICK
The site of a faïence factory founded in 1707 by Duke Anton Ulrich with Johann Philipp Frantz as his manager. Ware included the early 'blue' imitations of the Dutch, then progressing to delicately coloured vases, tureens, pierced baskets and figures. Early marks included: 'VH' 'B & R', 'B' and later crossed 'Cs'.

BRUSSELS CARPET
A type made of various coloured worsted yarns fixed in a foundation web of strong linen thread. The worsted is drawn up into loops to form the pattern. The loops of the ordinary carpet are then left uncut; with the Imperial Brussels carpet the loops are cut to form a pile. Lord Pembroke introduced the ideas at Wilton in about 1740. Later the method was used at Kidderminster.

BRUSSELS LACE
A rather loose term applied to any lace made in the vicinity of the city. More specifically a kind of bobbin lace in which the pattern is made first, the threads following the curves of the pattern, and the ground put in around it afterwards. The ground would have a hexagonal mesh. The so-called *point d'Angleterre* and *point Duchesse* are both Brussels bobbin laces. A more recent development has been the working of the pattern with needles or bobbins, and this is then applied to a machine-made net.

BRUSSELS TAPESTRIES
Records show that the weaving of tapestries here goes back to the early part of the 14th century. A number of leading artists had their designs woven, including: Bernard van Orley and Raphael. These were carried out under the direction of Peter van Aelst, a foremost tapestry maker.

BUCCARO
A Chinese unglazed red stoneware made at Yi-hsing, an everyday-use domestic ware. The manner was successfully imitated by Böttger of Meissen.

BUCCERO WARE
An early Etruscan black ware dating from the 7th to the 5th century BC.

BUCKINGHAMSHIRE LACE
Material produced at Newport Pagnall from the 18th century, a bobbin lace.

BUCKLER
A type of shield of various shapes and sizes worn on the non-sword arm to protect the body. In use from the 13th to the 17th century.

BUCKRAM
A strong durable linen or cotton book-cloth with a coarse open weave, and heavily stiffened with size.

BUEN RETIRO
The most important porcelain manufactory in Spain. It was founded by Charles III, King of Naples, who when he inherited the Spanish crown in 1759, transported potters and artists from Capodimonte to Spain. The site was the garden of the palace of Buen Retiro near Madrid. Much excellent ware with a finish comparable to that of Sèvres was produced, as well as high-quality figures. Until 1804 the mark was a fleur-de-lis, and after that it was a crowned 'M'.

BUFF-COAT
One of thick buff-leather, normally with sleeves and a full splayed skirt. It became a fashion with cavalry from the 17th century onwards as a more comfortable item than armour. The thick leather gave considerable protection from sword slashes.

BUFFET
A sideboard, a cupboard or set of shelves either fixed or movable for the display of china and plate.

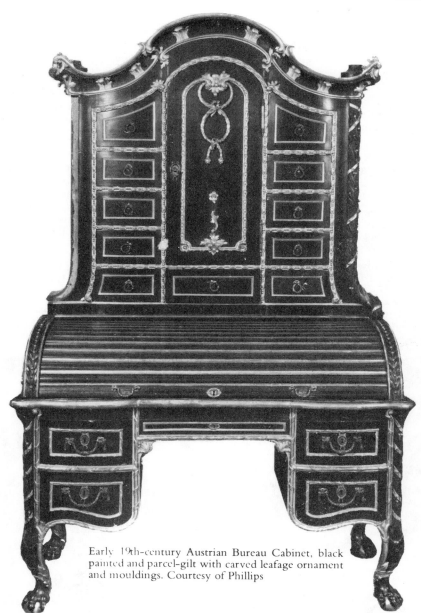

Early 19th-century Austrian Bureau Cabinet, black painted and parcel-gilt with carved leafage ornament and mouldings. Courtesy of Phillips

BUHL
See Boulle, André Charles.

BULL'S EYE LAMP
An early lamp having a thick magnifying glass on each side of the flame.

BULL'S EYE MIRROR
A type of convex mirror produced at Nuremberg and other south German centres from around the end of the 15th century.

BUN FOOT
A round flattened ball-shaped foot used with oak and mahogany cupboards and like pieces from about 1660.

BUNZLAU
A type of salt-glazed stoneware with a clean strong rust-brown colour, that took its name from the town in Silesia where it was made. It was produced chiefly in the 18th and 19th centuries.

BURANO LACE
A material produced on the island of Burano, near Venice. The Burano point is highly esteemed.

BUREAU
A desk or writing table, or a lowish chest of drawers for the bedroom, and again a type of dressing table with a mirror.

BURETTE
A cruet or vase; they are usually made in pairs, in the sacramental sense for wine and water.

BURGONET
An open helmet of the 16th century, somewhat similar to a morion with cheekpieces; also incorporating at times, a chinpiece.

BURL
A tree knot or growth that has induced a pattern in the wood that will show to good effect with a veneer.

BUTLER'S TRAY
A movable tray top for serving food; it has a folding trestle with webbing straps.

BUTTERFLY TABLE
A fashion that came in at the time of William and Mary (late 17th century), it had drop-leaves that were supported when raised by strong swinging brackets.

BYGONES
A group of articles that encompass a large number of categories. Mostly concerned with domestic and everyday objects of comparatively recent times. Things such as butter pats, flat irons, jelly moulds, souvenirs, and the like; all of which are becoming collector's items.

BYRNIE
A coat of linked mail, the name is of medieval Anglo-Saxon origin; it also signifies a chain-mail Scandinavian body armour.

Cast Iron Artillery Bank. American, *c* 1900. Courtesy of Sotheby's, Belgravia

Ornamental turning lathe by Holtzapfell & Co., early 19th century. Courtesy of Christie's, South Kensington

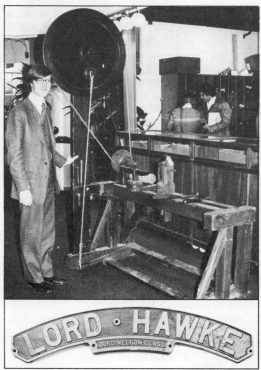

Metal bench vice by Bugatti. Courtesy of Christie's, South Kensington

Railway souvenirs. Engine plate from the Lord Nelson Class. Courtesy of Christie's, South Kensington

CABARET
A small table or tray suitable for holding a matched set of tea or coffee serving utensils; pot creamer, sugar bowl, cups and saucers for one or two people. It can also apply to a travelling case to fit these items.

CABASSET
A small type of morion, a helmet worn by foot-soldiers from the second half of the 16th century and during the 17th.

CABINET
A piece of furniture for holding a collector's smaller treasures. It may be a glass-fronted cupboard for porcelain, glass or objects of vertu, or a set of drawers to hold engraved gems, coins and other small items.

William and Mary oyster-veneered cabinet on stand, c 1690. Courtesy Sotheby Parke Bernet

CABOCHON
A stone cut in a convex form without facets and then highly polished. A decorative motif of similar shape for furniture in vogue during the 16th and 17th centuries on the continent; it appears to have been most popular in England in the middle of the 18th century.

CABRIOLE LEG
A form of leg which curves outwards from the piece which it supports, and then descends in a tapering reverse curve, generally finishing with an ornamental foot. It was much used in the 18th century, particularly by the English and French cabinetmakers. Some credit its origin to China, and there could be some influence from the curved animal legs favoured by the Greeks and Romans.

CACHEPOT
An ornamental container for a flowerpot. Many fine examples were produced by Sèvres.

CADES, ALESSANDRO (1734–1809)
Italian gem-engraver, working in Rome and influenced by Pilcher. He usually signed his full name, occasionally in Greek letters.

'CADOGAN' TEAPOT OR HOT-WATER POT
A strange variety of pot modelled on the Chinese peach-shaped wine jug. It was filled through a hole in the bottom and worked rather on the principle of the spill-proof inkpot. It probably got its name from the Hon. Mrs Cadogan who had brought back one of the Chinese winepots. First examples were likely to have been made in the early part of the 19th century in Staffordshire.

CAEN
A late 18th century porcelain manufactory that produced a distinctive range of domestic ware decorated with landscapes in black and white, with the designs enclosed in small squares combined with wreaths using gold and green.

CAFFAGGIOLA
A centre for some of the finest majolica, this place near Florence produced in the early part

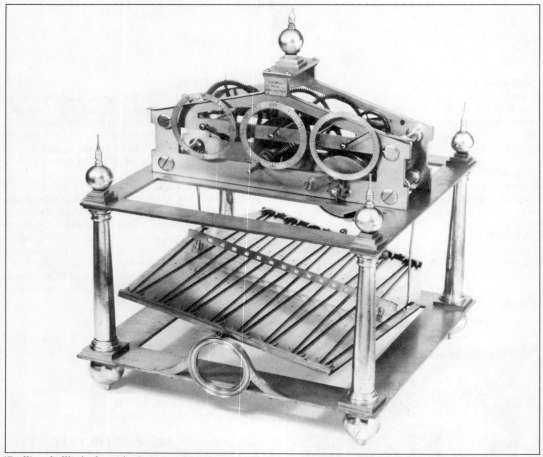

'Rolling ball' clock with Congreve escapement. Designed by G. H. Bell of Winchester. The three 'dial' rings give the hour, the minute and the quarter of a minute. The oscillating table with the channel to take the rolling ball can be seen. Courtesy Christie's

of the 16th century a number of truly beautiful and remarkable pieces. The Fattorini family were active there at this time, and the workshops were in all probability under the patronage of the Medici family as their arms and mottoes appear on some of the wares. Early pieces show influence from nearby Florentine masters, including Botticelli and Donatello. The ware is characterised at times by the bold colour style and rich cherry reds and deep strong blues. A number of large ewers or jugs and large dishes speak for the quality.

CAFFIÉRI, JACQUES (1678–1755) and PHILIPPE (1714–74)
Father and son who were among the leading metal workers of Louis XV's reign. They held

the royal warrants and were skilled as bronze founders and with metal chasing.

CAILLOUTÉ
A decorative ground with a form of pebble-shaped texture sometimes used at Sèvres.

CALAMUS
A reed or cane used as a pen for writing; in ecclesiastical terms it implies a silver tube through which the Communion of the chalice may be received.

CALENDAR CLOCK
One which shows the hour, day, month and year. These timepieces have been popular for a long time and the first seems to have

appeared around 1364 in Italy; various versions have been made since then, and still are.

CALFSKIN
One of the most generally used leathers in bookbinding. It is characterised by its smoothness and lack of grain. It lends itself to dyeing and other manipulation.

CALIATOUR WOOD
An East Indian red dyewood rather similar to sandalwood. Hard and red in colour, it is much used in cabinetmaking.

CALICO
Originally a cotton cloth of any kind imported from the East, the name includes a cotton cloth made in Europe.

CALIVER
A light hand gun, a variety of arquebus, used in the 16th century.

CALLOT FIGURE
A somewhat loose term for a grotesque figure modelled in porcelain. Such figures were produced at Chelsea and Meissen; the inspiration coming from the quaint and imaginative drawings of the French artist Jacques Callot (1592–1635).

CAMAGON WOOD
A tree from the Philippine Islands, *diospyrus discolor* is hard and dark coloured, nearly black at times, with rich warm brown veins. It has been used in cabinetwork.

CAMAIL
A hood or neckguard of chain-mail which can be worn under the helmet. It can also be a protective hooded mantle.

CAMBRIC
A fine linen cloth with a plain weave which takes its name from the French town of Cambrai where it was first manufactured.

CAMEL-BACK CHAIR
A rather free term for a chair, settee or couch with a humped back often in the Hepplewhite style.

CAMEO
A precious stone, such as onyx or agate, which has two layers of different colours, in the upper of which a figure or design is carved in relief. The result is generally set in gold or

Cameo plate made by Villeroy and Boch, *c* 1900. German. Courtesy Kunsthaus am Museum, Cologne

silver, and either worn as a pendant or, if of a large size, stood up as an ornament.

CAMEO GLASS
A kind of glass composed of different coloured layers which can be cut in the same manner as a cameo. Examples of the technique were made as early as Roman times. A notable example is the celebrated Portland vase which was excavated in the late 16th century and is today in the British Museum.

CAMPAGNE
A white bobbin lace produced in narrow strips to be used for either edging other laces or for trimming garments. Its production dates from the 17th century since when gold and coloured silk versions have also been produced.

CAMPÊCHE WOOD
From the tree the *Haematoxylon campechianum,* a kind of mahogany, hard and red-brown in tone, used in cabinetwork. It is also called logwood.

CANADELLA
A type of ewer that is associated with Catalonia. It has a pear-shaped body with a long, wide cylindrical neck, a loop handle and a slender spout. Some 14th century examples still exist.

CANAPÉ
A settee which may be upholstered or caned, it has developed since the period of Louis XV.

Pair of ormolu two armed candelabra with Dresden birds. Louis XV Period. Courtesy of Ader, Picard, Tajan

CANDELABRUM
A lighting device with branches for a number of candles or other light sources. Its manufacture and use go back at least to the Romans. It may range in size from quite small table models up to giants, 6 ft (1·8 m) or more in height.

CANDLE-BEAM
A hanging beam or rail to take candles, or the place to put votive candles. Sometimes they were simple lengths or cross-pieces. It was the medieval way of illuminating their great halls.

CANDLE-BOARD
A small sliding shelf fitted to a desk or table which could be pulled out to take a candle.

CANDLE-BOX
A container of candles that could be rectangular or cylindrical and made of wood, pewter or brass. Some were made so that they could be hung from the wall. In use during the 18th century.

CANDLE-SCREEN
A small mahogany screen that could be adjustable on a vertical rod and tripod legs. It was intended to stand on the table beside the candle to protect the flame from draught. It dates from the middle of the 18th century.

CANDLE-SNUFFER
A small cone-shaped hood on a stem, or with a little handle. It often had a special resting place on the candlestick.

CANDLE-STAND
A light wooden stand or tripod table, popular in the 18th century. It was easily portable and was intended to carry a candle to supplement the light from other sources.

CANDLESTICK
The object that really followed the earlier pricket. An appliance to hold just one candle; it could be made of silver, pewter, brass, iron, ceramics, glass or ormolu. As far as is known, no English candlesticks existed before 1600, but thereafter they proliferated in a great many styles and designs. In the latter part of the 17th century a great number were produced in the then fashionable ormolu.

CANE
Split rattan used for wickerwork, the seats and backs of chairs, and some settees. This type of treatment was popular during the period of Louis XV. An early English use was with the so-called Charles II or Restoration chair.

This pair of candlesticks bear the Royal Arms, and also a presentation inscription, which reads 'At ye launching of his Majesty's Ship the BRISTOL a 4th Rate of 50 guns 1021 tunns the 9th of July 1746. Built by Mr. Ino Holland at Woolwich.' They bear the London date 1723, and the maker was Samuel Margas. Courtesy Spink

CANEPHORA
An ornament in the form of a maiden carrying a basket of offerings on her head. It sometimes appears on furniture from the late Renaissance.

CANISTER
A container for tea.

CANNELLE WOOD
The *Canellaceae alba* from Ceylon and the West Indies; it is hard and near white, and used in cabinetmaking. It is also called canella and cinnamon bark.

CANNON
A gun discharged from a sort of mount or carriage. Early examples were muzzle-loading with a touch-hole.

CANOPY
A covering fixed over a bed, chair, settle or dresser; often this would be made as an integral part of the piece.

CÁNTARO
A Spanish drinking vessel which has two spouts – one for filling and the other for drinking. Some 17th century examples still exist.

CANTEEN
An individual leather case that could hold a personal knife, fork, spoon, small beaker and salt-box which was almost a necessity for travellers during the last part of the 17th century and through the 18th. During the 19th its use widened and a canteen was often carried by officers on campaigns; this would probably include, as well as the foregoing, a bottle and some form of messing plate or food server.

CANTERBURY
An upright stand with divisions for holding music, documents and sundry papers. It often had a drawer and was generally mounted on castors.

CANTON POTTERIES
By repute, Chün-type wares were made there from the Sung period. Other examples such as wares with crackled grey and blue glazes would appear to date from the Ming period. The terms of Canton and Canton china have been somewhat loosely applied to enamelled porcelain which was produced to satisfy the European Market.

CAPODIMONTE
A porcelain manufactory founded by Charles III of Naples in the royal palace in about 1743. Active production continued until 1759 when Charles inherited the Spanish throne and took many of the artists and potters with him to Buen Retiro in Spain. Ferdinand IV re-opened the works in 1771 and moved it to the royal Villa di Portici. Two years later he moved it once more to the royal palace in Naples where it was successfully in production until 1806. The most distinctive work has been the small modelled figures, often based on characters from Italian Comedy; these were marked with a fleur-de-lis. Tableware generally bore a crowned 'N'.

CAPRIMULGUS
A general term for a particular type of subject that frequently occurs in antique gems and in low relief work. It is a goat-milker and it shows a man or a faun milking a goat; sometimes the goat Amalthea, the nurse of the infant Jupiter, is indicated.

CAPUCINE
A collective name for the simple furniture found in monastery cells, derived almost certainly from the order of Capuchins.

CAQUETOIRE

A highly decorative high-backed chair with curved arms. It had a somewhat light and delicate construction. First made in France in the 16th century.

CARBINE

A short light musket or rifle intended for use by the cavalry.

CARD TABLE

It is likely that the first games were played just on chest tops. Those in favour before the 15th century in England included backgammon chess, dice and draughts, closely followed by cards in Elizabeth I's reign. At this time early tables for games had drop leaves supported by sliding bars. As the craze for card games of chance waxed, so the cabinetmakers paid more attention to design and quality. The familiar shape came to be an oblong top, when closed, with rounded corners and a folded leaf; the playing area being covered with green baize. Refinements included places for candles, and shallow wells for coins or counters. Sheraton indulged his clients by designing an oval folding model. There was a triangular shape for the game of ombre.

CARLIER, MICHELE (1665–1741)

A Frenchman who settled in Rome in 1688, he became a skilled metalsmith who was also adept at setting jewels, marking his pieces with a cross on a pedestal; one of the most important patrons was Cardinal Camillo Cybo.

CARLIN, MARTIN (c 1730–85)

French cabinetmaker, a master from 1760. A leading expert in the manner of Louis XVI. He was particularly skilled with marquetry and veneer. One of his leading patrons was Madame du Barry.

CARLTON HOUSE DESK

A large English desk of the latter part of the 18th century, it had a superstructure of small drawers at the back and two sides. The top was panelled in leather and had an adjustable easel rest. It appeared under the given name in Gillows charge book for 1796.

CAROLEAN

A term for the manner of ornament and furniture-making in England for the period 1660 to 1688.

French ormolu carriage clock in the form of a sedan chair. Courtesy of Phillips

CARPET BOWLS

An indoor game popular in England and Scotland during the first half of the 19th century. It was played with heavy pottery balls marked with distinguishing colours and a plain white jack.

CARRIAGE CLOCK

A small clock or large watch with a diameter of around five inches, current in the late 17th and through the 18th century. It was intended to be carried by travellers and generally had a strike to give the time in dark coach interiors.

CARRICKMACROSS LACE

A fairly modern lace made at Carrickmacross, Ireland. The design is cut from muslin and its edges whipped. It is then either applied to net, when it is known as Carrickmacross appliqué, or joined by brides, when it is called Carrickmacross guipure. Earliest examples date from around 1825.

CARTEL

A French wall clock normally made of gilt bronze and often lavishly ornamented with figures and plant forms. The idea came to England in the mid 18th-century.

CARTISANE
A small stick of parchment wound round with gold or silver thread or silks which was formerly used in lace-making and embroidery to produce a raised pattern.

CARTOUCHE
A carved or painted ornament in the form of a scroll intended to be used as a field for inscriptions.

CARVER CHAIR
A heavy turned chair having three vertical and three horizontal spindles in the back. These chairs are generally made from ash, and have rush seats. The name comes from John Carver (1571–1621), first Governor of the Plymouth colony.

CARYATID
An ornament showing a draped female figure supporting an entablature, in the place of a column or pilaster.

CASE
A bookbinding term, it implies the card, or card and linen, or leather cover of a book, apart from the book itself.

CASE BOTTLE
A popular type in the latter part of the 18th century in England. The bottles might be small for scent or drugs or larger for drinks, and they were made in sets for fitted cases.

CASKET
A small box, ornamented and often made of rich materials for jewels.

CASQUE
A loose term for a helmet or military headpiece of any kind.

CASSAPANCA
An Italian heavy and massively constructed combination bench and chest. First examples appeared in Florence about the middle of the 15th century. It often incorporated excellent carving.

CASSEL
A group of four potteries active in Germany during the 18th century, near or at the town. Products included faïence, porcelain and earthenware. They all came under the Landgrave of Hesse-Cassel at various times. Marks included 'HL' and 'HC'.

A glass factory working from the 16th century. One of Germany's leading glass engravers, Franz Gondelach, worked there from about 1695 until around 1716.

CASSOLETTE
A small box with a perforated cover used to diffuse perfumes; and also a vessel in which perfumes might be burnt.

CASSONE
A large Italian chest or coffer with a hinged lid in which it was the fashion for the bride to store her household linen. They were generally six or more feet long and often richly decorated, not only with patterns and sometimes low carving, but also with paintings by such as Botticelli and Uccello.

CASTEL DURANTE
A majolica made there until about 1635 bore its name, but was then termed Urbino. The ware produced is probably one of the finest of its type. Painters of the quality of Giovanni Maria and Nicola Pellipario were involved in the decoration.

CAST IRON
A high carbon iron that is brittle and cannot be worked in a forge, and is shaped by moulding whilst molten. Furniture from this material was made in America from around 1840.

CASTER
A term coined about 1675 for a straight-sided cylinder with a perforated top made of silver. It was intended for use with sugar, pepper or spices. It is also called a dredger.

CASTLEFORD
David Dunderdale made pottery there from about 1790. His ware included the well-known 'Castleford' white stoneware with low relief ornament, also black basalts and creamware.

CASTLE HEDINGHAM
Imitation medieval pottery was produced there around the middle of the 19th century.

CAT
A double tripod for holding a plate which had six legs, on three of which it rests however placed, used mainly in the 18th century.

CATCHPOLE
A medieval lance-like shaft that often had a pronged head, sometimes barbed, intended to be used by foot-soldiers, or mounted, to catch a mounted knight by the throat and drag him from his horse.

CATHEDRAL BINDINGS
A type of decorated binding popular between around 1810 until the middle of the century, it included blind tooling and gilt work using Gothic motifs.

CAUCASIAN RUGS
A collective term for those woven in the Caucasus, the part of Russia that lies between the Black and Caspian Seas. They include examples such as: Circassian, Derbend, Genghis, Kazak, Mosul Kurd, Shirran and Tchichi.

CAUDLE CUP
A silver two-handled cup normally made with a cover to use with caudle, a warm drink made from wine or ale with eggs, bread or gruel, sugar and spices. Existing specimens are now more generally called porringers.

CAUGHLEY
A soft-paste porcelain manufactured in Shropshire from about 1772 by William Turner. In 1799 the Works were bought by John Rose of the Coalport manufactory. Wares included were blue and white, sometimes printed in the Worcester style. Marks used included 'S', 'C' and 'Salopian'.

CAULDRON
One of the most ancient cooking vessels: earliest examples were made of bronze, either with riveted plates or cast; later, cast iron was used. It might or might not have a handle and lid.

CAULIFLOWER WARE
A product of Whieldon-Wedgwood Works, it appeared in sundry shapes, ranging from its namesake to pineapple and such forms. It was an earthenware with distinctive green and yellow glazes.

CAUSEUSE
A small settee or sofa intended for two people. It was introduced in the first part of the 18th century.

CAVETTO
A concave moulding which is nearly a quarter circle in section. It has been used with cornices of chests on chests, china cabinets and the like.

It may also be the centre of a dish or saucer.

CEDAR
There are a number of trees under this name including: the Cedar of Lebanon and other species of *cedrus;* any tree of the genus *juniferus,* notably *virginiana,* the red cedar of eastern North America; the West Indian species *barbadensis;* also any of the genus *chamaecy-paris,* especially *thyoides,* the white cedar; and other varieties from Japan, New Zealand, Australia and Mexico. It is durable and has a pleasant fragrance, making it ideally suitable for chests.

CELADON
A term originally applied to the soft sea-green colour upon pieces of old Oriental porcelain. This was a pigment prepared from green earth, celadonite, a kind of iron silicate. The colour was made to imitate jade. The leading works that produced the ware were at Lung-ch'üan in Chekiang. The work was already well known in the Sung dynasty. The craftsmen applied the decoration by carving with a knife. Menage says the word was capriciously applied by the ladies of the Court of Louis le Grand, after the name of one of the principal characters of the once-famous 'Romance of Astrea'. This term was later applied in France to all tinted porcelain, of whatever colour, when put upon the clay wet, and burnt in at the first firing; this process gives a peculiar softness to the colour.

CELATURE
An embossing; embossed work or figures. A term which may apply to almost any material which has been so treated.

CELLARETTE OR CELLARET
A case for holding a few wine bottles in the dining-room. It was lead-lined, with lock and key, and later castors were added. It may also be that part of a sideboard specially fitted to hold bottles. It was an early 18th century innovation.

CELLINI, BENVENUTO (c 1500–71)
Among the great geniuses with the handling of gold, silver and bronze, also rock crystal. Two of his patrons were Pope Clement VII

and François I. One of the most illuminating accounts of an artist's life during the Renaissance can be found in his autobiography.

CELURE
A canopy or hanging for a bed.

CENSER
A vessel for perfumes, especially incense. The ecclesiastical censer is generally cup-shaped with a pierced cover, and the whole is suspended by chains to facilitate the swinging and so accelerate the combustion. It is also named a thurible.

CERAMICS OR KERAMICS
From the Greek *Keramikos* (earthenware), a general term for the study of pottery. The word 'pottery' in its widest sense includes all objects fashioned from clay and then hardened by fire.

CHAFING-DISH
A dish which can be a kind of brazier with charcoal; it is intended for cooking at the table or keeping food hot. Silver versions became popular in America in the latter part of the 17th century. It could also be heated by a spirit lamp.

CHAIN STITCH
One to imitate the links of a chain.

CHAIR
A movable seat for one person which has a back, sometimes arms, and generally four legs. Earliest versions date back several thousand years. There was the Greek thronos or throne chair, the Roman sella curulis or a folding stool built as an X which became the model for numerous medieval chairs. Most periods have left an individual design.

Dental chair, leather and cast iron, *c* 1910. Courtesy of Sotheby's, Belgravia

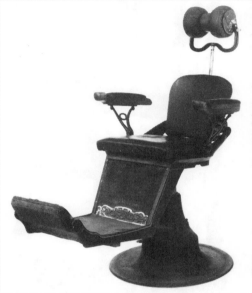

orge II Hall Seat. Courtesy of Sotheby Parke Bernet

Queen Anne Shell-carved walnut armchair. Courtesy of Sotheby Parke Bernet

French Regency armchair upholstered with
authentic Beauvais tapestry of the same period.
Courtesy of Ader, Picard, Tajan

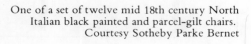

A child's armchair, carried out in walnut, with
caned back and seat. Charles II period. Courtesy
Christie's

One of a set of twelve mid 18th century North
Italian black painted and parcel-gilt chairs.
Courtesy Sotheby Parke Bernet

CHAIR TABLE
A table which is convertible into a chair or settle by raising the hinged top, which could be round or rectangular, to form the back of the chair whose seat would be between the upright supports.

CHAISE LONGUE
An elongated seat or couch, usually having a support for the back at one end only; it could also have eight legs.

CHALCEDONY
A beautiful semi-precious stone that is a translucent substance of rather waxy lustre. In modern jewel-work it is called variously agate, cornelian, onyx and other names. Anciently sometimes called Cassidoine.

CHALICE
A drinking cup or goblet. The cup which is used in the celebration of the Eucharist.

CHAMFER
An edge or angle that has been taken off diagonally, similar to a bevel.

CHAMOIS
A soft leather which is prepared from the skin of the chamois, an antelope that inhabits the highest parts of the Alps, Pyrenees and the Taurus mountains. Today it is often made from the skins of sheep, goats and deer. It is sometimes used in upholstery, but is better known as a fine cleaner for glass, metals and other works of art in the ornamental category.

CHAMPAGNE GLASSES
In England these have had a number of different shapes over the years. In the late 17th and early 18th centuries they had a tall flute with a short stem; this was followed in about 1715, until the early 1730s, by a wide bowl of ogee contour which rested on a baluster or air twist stem and conical-shaped foot. Next came a tall funnel-shaped bowl with a plain, cut or air twist stem which was popular until about 1750, and then a similar glass came into favour which was a little narrower in the bowl and had a longer stem; this in its turn was gradually ousted from popularity in 1830 by one with a more hemispherical bowl.

CHAMPLEVÉ
A process used by early enamellers in producing their plates for the foundation of the work. It consists in so cutting down the copper, that the outline of the ornament, or other subject to be represented, should form a band between the enamel colours and the plate consequently being hollowed out for the reception. It thus took the place of the earlier mode of affixing thin lines of filigree to the plate as a separation to each tint, which might shift or alter in the firing or fusing of the work.

CHANDELIER
A candlestick, lampstand, gas fitting or electric fitting having several branches. It is especially one hanging from the ceiling. It may be made of wood, metal, porcelain or glass. Earliest examples date from the 14th century. Some of the most remarkable and ornate are those made by Meissen and the French gilt bronze examples.

CHANFRON
Protective armour for a horse's head, often with side flaps or cheek-pieces; it was introduced during the 14th century and lasted through until the 17th.

CHANTILLY
A soft-paste porcelain manufactory founded in 1725 by the Prince of Condé and under the direction of Ciquaire Cirou. It lasted until around 1800. The distinctive glaze was made opaque and white by the addition of tin-ashes. The mark most recognised is a hunting horn.

The lace made was a bobbin black silk variety, although blondes were produced.

CHAPBOOK
Any small book containing ballads and tracts, such as were originally carried about by chapmen.

CHAPELLE-DE-FER
The iron flat-topped helmet which was worn by knights in the 12th century and which is frequently shown on their monumental effigies. It was the crudest form of helmet, and went out of use in the following century.

CHARGER
A large, flat dish or plate for carrying meat to the table, made from porcelain or silver.

CHARKA OR CHARKHA
A domestic spinning wheel.

A Russian drinking cup that sometimes had a single handle.

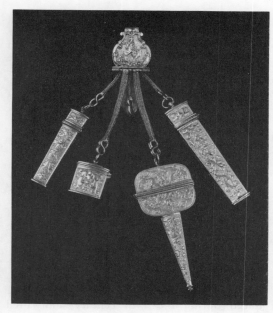

French silver-gilt châtelaine. Courtesy of Corner Antiques, Coltishall

CHASING
When the surface of a metal is textured or given a rough surface by the use of a specially sharpened hammer or punch, it is said to be chased. It is a popular method of decoration with the metalsmith.

CHÂSSE
A box or small coffer of metal or wood which contains the relics of a saint.

CHASUBLE
An ecclesiastical robe; a sleeveless mantle that covers the body and shoulders and has a narrow opening for the head.

CHÂTAIGNER
The wood of the chestnut tree, *Castanea vesca,* hard and palish yellow, and in demand for cabinetwork.

CHÂTELAINE
An ornamental hook, clasp or pin worn at a woman's waist, having a chain or chains to which could be attached keys, a purse, a watch and trinkets.

CHAUFFE-ASSIETTE
In French furniture it is a form of plate-warmer. Inside there was an allowance for some kind of brazier, and the sides and bottom were metal lined.

CHAUSSES
Early medieval armour for the legs.

CHECKERED DIAMOND
A decoration for glass composed of a large diamond with four small diamonds inside.

CHEESE SCOOP
A spoon with a curled shovel shape to deal with large round cheeses. Handles at first were bone, ivory and wood, and later, handles were given the same treatment as the table service.

CHELSEA
One of the leading English manufactories, it was set up in 1745 and lasted until 1784. Charles Gouyn was possibly there in the first years, but later came Nicholas Sprimont. Influences came from Meissen, not only of the German but also the Meissen orientalware including the Japanese Imari and Kakiemon. The modelled figures are considered by many to be the finest ever made in England. The original mark was a triangle and this progressed to a raised anchor, a red anchor, and then a gold anchor. The latter has somewhat prodigally and wilfully been put on many lesser wares by nefarious characters with the intent to improve their value.

CHENILLE
A tufted cord of silk, worsted, wool or cotton, used for embroidery, draperies and upholstery.

CHERRY WOOD
The *Prunus cerasus,* which is quite hard with a warm reddish tint is used for inlay and small pieces of furniture.

CHERUB
A classical figure of a small child used as an ornamental motif.

CHEST
In medieval times it was one of the most important pieces in the house or castle, it acted not only as a store-place for clothes and sundries, but also as a seat and at times as a trunk when travelling.

CHESTERFIELD
A rather large and over-stuffed sofa.

CHEST OF DRAWERS
A case containing drawers standing on short feet or legs. It was established in the late 17th century, with a number of general

18th-century German chest made from pine with some inlay in the two octagonal panels and some fine open carving at the bottom as well as sunk decoration over the body. Courtesy Kunsthaus am Museum, Cologne

Commode in the French Taste by Thomas Chippendale. Courtesy of Sotheby Parke Bernet

Louis XV–XVI Commode by P. F. Guignard
(c 1770) which was once the property of Vladimir
Barjansky. Courtesy Sotheby Parke Bernet

forms including: straight front, bow and
serpentine. The term *commode* is generally
applied to a chest of drawers designed in the
French manner.

CHEST ON CHEST
A double chest of drawers with the lower on
short legs and the upper slightly smaller than
the lower and generally carrying some form of
decoration on top.

CHEVAL GLASS
A full-length mirror swinging in a frame or
from supports. It came in at the end of the
18th century. It was known as a horse dressing
glass. It was sometimes fitted with swinging
candle brackets.

CHIEN WARE
First made during the Sung dynasty in the
Fukien province, most of the ware consisted

One of a pair of Venetian painted small commodes.
Courtesy Christie's

of conical tea-bowls. The glaze of blue-black, streaked with brown, and the fine 'hares' fur was over a coarse black-red stoneware.

CHIFFONIER
An ornamental cabinet with drawers or shelves, a rather high and narrow chest of drawers. During the Regency period the term was applied to a low standing cupboard.

CHIFFONIÈRE
A small decorative table that became fashionable during the Louis XV period. It was intended for the ladies to keep their bits and pieces in, and later acted as a kind of work table.

CHILDREN'S FURNITURE
Scaled down adult furniture for the use of children as opposed to toy furniture for use with dolls.

CHIMING CLOCK
One that sounds-off the quarters on several bells as well as striking the hour.

CHIMNEY GLASS
An overmantel mirror, a fashion that came late in the 17th century.

CHINA CABINET
A rectangular cabinet with shelves and glazed doors for displaying porcelain.

CHINA CLAY
See Kaolin

CHINA TREE WOOD
The timber of the *Melia agedarach* that comes from China and Guiana; it is hard with a black speckled, red-brown colour, much used with cabinetwork. It is also known as chinaberry, pride of India, bead tree, Indian lilac and holy tree.

CHINESE EMBROIDERY
An art form that started very early, and has been done by both men and women. Much of the work is double-sided and this is carried out by painting the design on a piece of thin fabric. This is then put on a wooden frame and stretched. The embroidery is done using a satin stitch backwards and forwards. Floss silk with silver and gold threads is used with a wealth of motifs including: imaginative dragons, monsters, figures, birds, insects and flowers.

A rare clock. The front of the gilt-metal case is signed *Duval Invt. & Fecit a Frevile An 6.* The date An 6 refers to the sixth year of the French Revolutionary Calendar. Courtesy Sotheby Parke Bernet

CHINESE EXPORT PORCELAIN
A loose term for porcelain made in China for export.

CHINESE GLASS
The technique of working glass started in China in the Han dynasty (206 BC to AD 220) and even before. Glass blowing, however, was not used in general until about 1660. Much of the glassware was intended to imitate jade. Cameo glass snuff bottles, aping carved semi-precious stones, achieved success.

CHINESE IMARI
An imitative ware, based on the Japanese which was produced in the late 17th and early 18th centuries.

CHINOISERIE

A broadly-used term in the Arts which signifies anything that is influenced by, or related to, Chinese ornamental design. It appears in architecture, interior decoration, wallpaper, furniture and porcelain. In England, in the 18th century, craftsmen such as Chippendale and others assisted the growth of the fashion. At the height of the vogue even gardening and landscape architecture was influenced – pagodas, temples, and oriental plants abounded in the gardens of the rich.

CHINTZ

Originally painted or stained calico from India that came into England in the early part of the 17th century. Import was banned in 1722 to protect the home country weavers. Later, production started in England, although the import ban continued for some time.

CHIP CARVING

Simple hand carving, generally using a knife or chisel to cut out a formal pattern.

CHIPPENDALE, THOMAS (c 1718–79)

One of the greatest furniture makers, he was born in Worcestershire the son of a cabinet-maker. He went with his father to London in 1727, where a business was set up in Longacre. A move to St Martin's Lane followed in 1753, where Thomas worked until his death.

Thomas drew his inspiration from a number of sources, notably the Louis XV period and Chinese motifs and ideas. At times he also introduced some elements of the Gothic. His furniture is distinguished by excellent and tasteful design plus fine construction and skilled craftsmanship.

His book of designs, *The Gentleman and Cabinetmaker's Director,* was published in 1754 with 160 engraved plates; this was increased to 200 by the third edition. Latterly, much of his career was spent as organising head of a large and thriving business which, even at that date, would take on the job of furnishing a client's whole house.

CHOCOLATE POT

A silver pot brought in from around 1657 when hot chocolate became popular. In shape and design they were similar to the coffee-pots, being made both pear-shaped and cylindrical, sometimes with the spout at right angles to the handle. The main difference was that they had a small lidded aperture in the top cover and it was through this that a stirring rod could be thrust to mix up the contents.

Chippendale card table with cabriole legs. Courtesy Christie's

CHOISY-LE-ROI

A glass-house started in 1821 near Paris and lasting until 1851. During this time much useful work was done with the production of coloured glass.

CHOPIN

A Scottish liquid measure, usually of pewter, that held about one and a half pints.

CHRISMATORY

A case fitted to hold flasks containing the holy oils and Chrism, a consecrated oil mixed with balm and spices. The cases were either quite small for ease of carrying around, or were larger which when not being used were kept in the sacristy.

CHRISTENING GOBLETS

A celebration loving cup, generally with four handles and whistles that could be blown to attract the attention of the man with the bottle or large jug for refilling. Earliest examples probably date from the beginning of the 17th century.

CHRONOGRAPH

A stop watch.

CHRONOMETER

A very accurate timepiece for use at sea and in conjunction with astronomical observations.

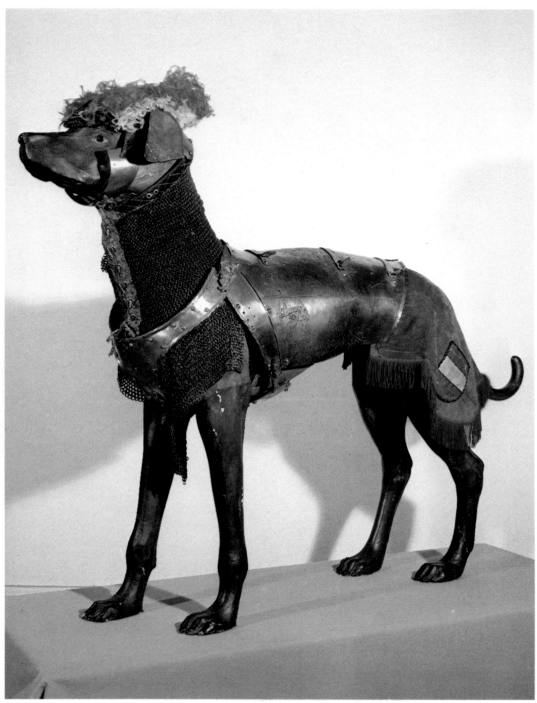

Armour for a hound. Second quarter of the 16th century. Photograph granted and authorised by the 'Patrimonio Nacional', Madrid

Blue and yellow shallow bowl, encircled Yung
Chêng six-character mark and of the period.
Courtesy of Christie's

Unglazed buff pottery figure of a mounted polo
player. T'ang dynasty. Courtesy of Christie's

George II giltwood Wall Mirror in the manner of Matthias Lock. *c* 1750. Courtesy of Sotheby Parke Bernet

CHRYSOLITE
A name which was originally given to various gems of a green colour, including such as zircon, tourmaline and topaz. It is now kept to describe a yellow variety of olivine.

CHÜN WARE
Stoneware produced in the first part of the Sung dynasty. Objects included bulb bowls, two-handled jars and dishes. There was a predominant opalescent glaze varying between lavender and a deep blue.

CIBORIUM
A drinking-cup, generally covered, from the Greek *kiborion* which translated means a cup-shaped seed pod of the Egyptian water lily, the lotus. In art and religious circles, it may also mean a receptacle designed to hold the consecrated bread or a receptacle designed to form a depository for the vessels of the Eucharistic Feast. It was generally of gold and/or silver.

Earlier, a ciborium was a fixed canopy of durable material with supports from which was suspended the receptacle containing the consecrated wafer of the Eucharist.

CINQUEDEA
See Anlace

CIRCASSIAN
An oriental rug grouped with the Caucasian, with foundation and pile of wool.

CIRCASSIAN WALNUT
A light-brown wood with irregular black veining, the *juglans regia,* growing in south eastern Europe and the foothills of the Himalayas, and round parts of the Black Sea.

CIRCUMFERENTOR
A surveying instrument with horizontal compass and a graduated circle of degrees over which moves an alidade. Mainly used from the 16th to the 18th century.

CISELÉ
A type of velvet which was cut and figured and gave the impression of being chased or chiselled. The first were made during the Renaissance.

CISELEUR
A carver or chaser of metals, as with gilt bronze mounts for furniture.

CISELURE
The work of a ciseleur.

CISTA
Chest or box. The so-called mystic chests which were found in the Etruscan Necropolis are bronzed boxes, in which the beautiful bronze mirrors, enriched by engraving, and other ornamental vessels were kept.

CISTERN BAROMETER
The earliest type, one which has the bottom open end of the glass tube below the mercury level in an open bowl.

CISTOPHORUS
A silver coin dating from about 200 BC and issued in Pergamum and other parts of Asia Minor. They bore the sign of the mystic cist.

CITRON WOOD
The timber of the sandarac tree *Tetraclinis articulata;* it is hard and pale with veining and a fragrance; it has been used in cabinetwork.

CLAVICORD
A keyboard musical instrument where the horizontal strings are struck; a forerunner of the piano. Development started in the 13th century.

CLAVIHARP
One that is played by means of a keyboard.

CLAW AND BALL FOOT
A furniture foot shaped like a bird's claw grasping a ball; derivation was from a dragon's claw supposedly holding a pearl. It was used in England from the beginning of the 18th century.

CLAY, CHARLES
English clockmaker active around 1723. His speciality was the making of strange and ingenious musical clocks. Latterly appointed to the Board of Works.

CLAYMORE
A large two-edged and sometimes two-handled sword used by the Scottish Highlanders.

CLAY'S WARE
A kind of papier mâché patented by Henry Clay of Birmingham in 1772. It was used for items such as boxes, trays, tea caddies and panels for coaches, the latter because it was possible to give some slight curve to the material.

CLEPSYDRA

A water clock, a contraption for measuring time by the graduated flow of a liquid through a small aperture.

CLICHÉ

The impression of a die in a mass of fusible tin or melted metal. Medallists or die sinkers use it to make proofs of their work so as to judge the effect and stage of progress before the die is hardened and completed. The term cliché can also be applied to the French stereotyped casts from woodcuts.

CLICHY

A French glass-house founded in 1837 in a suburb of Paris. As well as cheap export glass the factory produced excellent crystal glass and coloured glasses and was noted for its exquisite paperweights.

CLOISONNÉ

An enamelling process which dates back at least to the Byzantine time of the 6th century. The origin may be considerably older. The method means that when the enamel colours were applied, small fences of metal, sometimes gold or silver, were first soldered edgeways on to the base, the interstices thus formed were called cloisons; they were then filled with the vitrified enamel pastes.

CLOSE HELMET

A close-fitting helmet that completely enclosed the head; it had a smallish visor. It dates from around the beginning of the 16th century.

CLOTHESPRESS

A piece of furniture for storing clothes, generally with large drawers; other types had two doors and sliding shelves or trays. It is often referred to as a press, as is also a chest of drawers in some districts.

COACHING GLASS

A small drinking glass without stem or foot, also called a stirrup cup and a fuddling glass. The intention being that the draught proferred should be downed in one – as it would be impossible to put the glass down until empty.

COALPORT

A porcelain manufactory founded in Shropshire by John Rose in about 1796. It obtained moulds and other material from Nantgarw and Swansea in the early 1820s. Distinctive features included ornate flowers, some gilding and a certain green enamel. Marks included: 'CBD' and 'CD'.

COASTER

A stand for a decanter or bottle, generally with a wooden base and a silver wall.

COBB, JOHN

English cabinetmaker who started in partnership with William Vile in St Martin's Lane. He was active around 1750 to 1775.

COBIRON

A support for a spit, an andiron.

COCK

The arm of the flintlock or device which holds the flint and brings it forward to produce the spark.
The gnomon of a sundial.

COCK BEADING

A small projecting moulding often put around the edge of a drawer.

COCONUT CUP

One in which the body is made from a carved coconut shell and is then mounted in silver. Examples date back to the 15th century.

Pear-shaped coffee-pot by John Kerr (Dublin), dated 1768. It has a domed lid with a type of pineapple finial and an ivory scroll handle. The spout is decorated with a dragon's head. Courtesy ROSC

Walnut coffer, South German, early 17th century. Courtesy Christie's

COFFEE-POT
Earliest examples date from about 1680, and designs included tapering cylindrical, baluster and pear-shaped. The spout could be opposite the handle and at right angles to it. Handles were often scroll and of a heat absorbing material such as ivory and bone.

COFFER
A type of box or chest, sometimes covered with leather, or painted and strongly bound with metal bands. Possibly originally intended to store money. The name is often confused with chest.

COFFRET
A small coffer.

COIFFEUSE
A type of 19th-century dressing or toilet table of delicate construction. It was prone to be somewhat lavishly decorated with bronze mounts.

COLICHMARDE
A sword with a blade that is triangular near the hilt and for about a third of its length.

COLT
A hand gun, the first workable repeating pistol with an automatic action. It was patented by Samuel Colt in 1814 and also in 1836. Samuel set up his factory at Paterson, New Jersey under the name of Patent Arms Manufacturing Company.

COMB
In armour, a projecting ridge or crest on a helmet.

COMB-BACK WINDSOR CHAIR
One in which the centre spindles at the back go through the horseshoe arm rail and finish in a crest-shaped rail.

COMMESO DI PIETRE DURE
An Italian term for the inlaying together of semi-precious stones such as: agate, amethyst, cornelian, lapis lazuli and rock crystal. It is also called Florentine mosaic.

COMMODE
See Chest of Drawers

Rare Skaife's Pistolgraph miniature all-brass wet-plate camera, *c* 1863. Courtesy of Christie's, South Kensington

Sliding-box wet-plate camera with Petzval-type lens, *c* 1870. Courtesy of Christie's, South Kensington

Sanderson Roll Film Camera. Courtesy Christie's, South Kensington

C. P. Szirn's waistcoat camera. Courtesy of Christie's, South Kensington

COMPOTIER

A shallow ornamental glass dish in which preserves or cooked fruits are brought to the table.

CONCERTINA MOVEMENT

A folding frame used with card tables for supporting the table top when opened.

CONNECTICUT CHEST

A type of combination chest of drawers and chest which stood on legs.

CONSOLE TABLE

One in which the top is carried by one or more brackets or consoles. It would be fixed against a wall with no legs at the back.

CONSTITUTION CLOCK

A banjo clock with a painting of the naval battle of the Constitution and Guerrière on the pendulum door.

CONSTITUTION MIRROR

A Chippendale-style wall mirror with a frame in mahogany and walnut. Ornaments include strings of flowers and fruit, and a bird at the top with scrolling, all parcel gilt.

CONTORNIATE

A thin Roman bronze medallion having a groove or furrow encircling the flan, and issued about the 4th century AD.

CONVEX MIRROR

An importation to England from France at the end of the 18th century. A circular convex mirror in a gilt cavetto frame with small balls and surmounted by a spreading eagle.

COPAIBA WOOD

The timber of the *copaifera,* from Brazil, red and hard, it has been used extensively with cabinetmaking.

COPLAND, HENRY

English furniture designer. He worked with Lock on a number of books and in 1746 he brought out a series of engraved plates of his own work. Robert Manwaring's *Chair Makers' Guide* of 1766 features some of Copland's designs.

COQUILLAGE

An ornament that features shells.

CORALINE POINT

A type of Venetian lace.

CORDIAL GLASS

A glass of about six to eight inches high with a flute bowl that tapered down to a spreading foot.

CORDONNET

A thread or small cord made of linen or silk to outline the edge of lace.

CORK GLASS-HOUSE

Set up in 1793 to make flint glass and black bottles. Latterly produced quality hard-cut flint glass.

CORNER CHAIR

A square seated chair with an open back on two sides. It dates from the early 18th century.

CORNER CUPBOARD

A triangular cupboard which could stand or hang in the corner of a room. If one was made to fit on the top of another the top doors would generally be glazed. Front shape could be flat or bowed. Some had a legged support.

CORNUCOPIA

An ornament with a twisted horn spouting an abundance of fruit, flowers, corn and vegetables.

CORONA

A suspended round or crossed chandelier of iron or wood to hold a number of candles.

CORSELET

A 16th-century half armour comprised of a helmet, gorget, breast and back plate, tassets, arms and gauntlets.

COSMATI WORK

Medieval Italian glass mosaic inlay work, also decorative stonework and coloured marble inlay. The name was derived from craftsmen called Cosmas. The Cosmati signed their work, which was a departure from the medieval practice of anonymity.

COSTER

A bed hanging dating from the 15th century.

COSTREL

A bottle of leather, earthenware or wood with ears by which it could be hung up.

COTTAGE CLOCKS
A term for a Connecticut spring clock in a wood case, generally rectangular with a decorated panel.

COUCH
A day bed with a raised head and probably one arm.

COUNTERPANE
A coverlet for a bed, frequently stitched, woven or appliquéd with floral, figure and geometric patterns. Early term in the 14th century was counterpoint.

COUNTER TABLE
A table or chest with some divisions often marked with symbols, it was used for counting money.

COURBARIL WOOD
West Indian locust tree, *Hymenaea courbaril,* hard and pale red with veining, it is popular for use with cabinetmaking.

COURTCUPBOARD
An open set of shelves, sometimes with the upper shelves enclosed. It was an American development for the display of china and plate.

COURTING CHAIR
A chair for two with an extra deep seat. The backs were upholstered as well as the seat, though later versions had open backs.

COURTING MIRROR
A gift mirror to one's betrothed; it was quite small being about 18 in (45·7 cm) high, with decorated frame often including glass paintings and perhaps an actual scene. With American examples they date from about 1800.

COUTER
In armour it is an elbow-piece.

COW CREAMER
In English silver and porcelain a small jug, in the shape of a cow, to hold cream.

CRACKLE
In connection with ceramics, a crackle glaze is one that is applied on purpose to give a cracking to the glaze. It is also known as alligator glaze. Interesting effects can be achieved, although accidents play a large part in the finish.

CRADLE
The crib for a baby. These have been made with a great deal of variety, ranging from simple box-like shapes on rockers to suspended ornate miniature draped gilt beds.

CREAMER
Small silver jug for cream which came in about the beginning of the 18th century; baluster and helmet shapes were popular.

CREAMWARE
A type of ware made in Staffordshire around the middle of the 18th century. It was a lead-glazed earthenware with a light body of light clay and generally with calcined flint.

CREDENCE
A small table, shelf or niche beside the Communion table; also a small side table to be placed near the main dining-table for food to be inspected for poisoning.

CREDENZA
A kind of sideboard, or elaborate cupboard or buffet developed during the Renaissance and intended for valuable plate.

CRESSET
An iron vessel or basket for holding burning pitch and oil or other suitable fuel; it is then suspended as a torch.

CRETONNE
A strong white fabric stronger than chintz, it was developed in Normandy about 1850. It has been printed and employed for hangings and upholstery.

CREWEL WORK
A stitch making a line of rope-like appearance, generally worked on plain linen. It is done with a spreading pattern that does not cover all of the ground, the length of the stitches being varied and colours carefully blended.

CRIMPING
An applied decoration of dents and flutes used on glass.

CRINET
Protective plate for a horse's neck, dating from medieval times.

Salt jar, or salt kit. Made by Alexander Spencer, Glasgow, 1856. Courtesy Sotheby Parke Bernet

CRIZZELLING
A fault that can develop in glass, consisting of a network of fine cracks, which may be so intense as to appear like clouding.

CROCHET
A kind of knitting worked with a single hooked needle. The best came from Ireland in the middle of the 19th century, much of it made by poor children under the care of the Ursuline nuns in County Cork.

CROFT
An early type of filing cabinet developed by the Rev. Sir Herbert Croft (1757–1816).

CROSSBOW
A medieval weapon for discharging arrows and other projectiles. It was a bow set crosswise on a stock. It had a trigger mechanism enabling it to be fired rather like a gun.

CROSS GUARD
A sword guard consisting of a short bar which crosses the blade at its junction with the hilt.

CROSS STITCH
An embroidery that uses diagonal stitches in pairs.

CROWN
Originally a gold coin with a value of five shillings, it was struck during the reigns of Henry VIII and Edward VI; early on it had Tudor rose types, and in later reigns up to Charles I it had portrait types. It is also a large silver coin of the same value which was struck during the time of Edward VI with an equestrian portrait.

CROWN GLASS
Windsor glass blown and whirled into a dish in the centre of which is a knot, called the bull's eye, left by the worker's rod. Panes cut from it are brilliant but small and uneven.

CRUET
Correctly a small bottle, but also refers to two bottles for oil and vinegar in a stand of silver or plate, and holders for pepper, salt and mustard of glass or porcelain in some kind of stand or dish with shallow recesses.

CUBITIERE
In medieval armour, an elbow guard.

CUIRASS
An article of armour which was originally of stout leather that covered the body from neck to girdle and consisted of a front and back piece. Leather was fairly soon superseded by steel. It dates from the Middle Ages.

CUISSE
Defensive armour for the thigh, introduced in medieval times.

CUPID'S BOW
Top rail of a Chippendale chair that curls up at the ends and has a dip in the centre.

CURFEW
A utensil for covering a fire. In the Middle Ages there was a regulation that at a certain hour all fires should be covered or extinguished when a bell sounded.

CURRAGH
With Irish lace it implies the making of appliqué flowers in the style of Brussels lace. It was successfully worked around the middle of the 19th century. It is also called Curragh or Irish Point.

CURULE CHAIR OR STOOL
One made with the legs curved and crossed, and it could often be folded up in the manner of a camp chair. It traces its origins back to Early Egyptian times. In ancient Rome it was the seat for the highest dignatories, the senators and praetors. It was sometimes ornamented with gold and ivory.

CUT-CARD WORK
A technique applying to silver, in which pieces of a pattern, such as leaves and petals, are cut from thin silver sheet and then soldered on to bowls, cups and tankards to form a free relief decoration.

CUT GLASS
The decorating of glass by cutting into the surface and thickness with an abrasive wheel; the cuts are then polished by a wheel with a very fine powder.

CUTLASS
A short heavy curved sword with a single cutting edge. It is generally associated with a man-of-war and sailors.

CUTLASS PISTOL
A vicious combination weapon of a single-shot pistol with a fairly broad blade mounted underneath the barrel. It was patented in 1837 by the American, George Elgin.

CUTWORK
An early form of embroidery in which the material was cut away; it is possible that it may have been the origin of lace.

CYLINDER DESK
One that has all the usual drawers and accessories and that is closed by a curved panel or tambour-like cylinder.

CYMA-RECTA
A moulding which is concave above and convex below.

CYMA-REVERSA
A moulding with convex above and concave below.

CYPRESS
A wood from the variety *cupressus* which is valuable in woodworking. It is hard and pale red with warm brown veining. In Persian Art it was continuously used as the emblem for Zoroaster. In Christian and more modern symbolism it occurs in relation to mourning. The wood was much used for statuary by the Ancients.

DACTYLIOGRAPHY
The law or history of gem engraving.

DAG
An obsolete form of pistol. In the latter part of the 16th century and through the 17th the words dag and pistol were interchangeable.

DAGGER
A short weapon for stabbing. It is a general name for such as: anlace, bowie knife, dirk, misericord, poniard and stiletto.

DAGHESTAN
Caucasian rug so named after a particular district. It has a finely-worked wool pile. Patterns have a mosaic look and some simple figures.

DAI-SHŌ
The term for the long and short swords carried by the samurai. The long fighting sword was the katana and the short was the wakizashi.

DAI-SHŌ-NO-SOROIMONO
The complete set of fittings for the two swords.

DAMASCENING
To ornament steel, etc, by inlaying with another metal.

Daguerrotype depicting a large group of Scottish bandsmen, infantry and officers, c 1847. Courtesy of Bonhams

DAMASK

A richly-woven silk fabric with elaborate designs and figures. It derives its name from the city of Damascus. Early 12th century damasks were woven on hand looms, the first specimens being brought to Europe by the Crusaders.

DARNED EMBROIDERY

It consists of elaborate designs formed of lines worked with the stitch used in darning.

DARNED NETTING

An early form of lace-making in which the design was worked on a net ground and the stitching was controlled by counting the meshes of the net. This method naturally produced fairly strict geometric patterns.

DAUM FRÈRES

A French glass house established at Nancy around 1875. Some layered glass was produced with several different colours and from this

cameo-type work evolved. The peculiar soft sheen surface was achieved by carefully applying hydrofluoric acid.

DAVENPORT

A small writing desk more or less square in plan. It had a sloping top, with a writing slide and a small drawer at each side over a set of four graduated drawers. It was mounted on four short legs and castors. The name is supposed to have come from Capt. Davenport who ordered such a desk from Gillow and Barton.

DAVENPORT FAMILY

Potters at Longport, Staffordshire from 1793 to 1882 who produced cream-coloured earthenware and blue-printed porcelain. Marks included 'Davenport' with an anchor.

DAY BED

A type of chaise longue made with a construction similar to a chair, with a head and

stretchers to the legs. It could be upholstered, but was often caned. The origin is supposed to be in Henry VIII's time. Various versions had the style of late Jacobean, William and Mary, Queen Anne, and Chippendale.

DEAL
A board cut from fir or pine to various laid down widths and thicknesses.

DECANTER
A vessel of glass used to decant liquors or for receiving decanted liquors. The purpose was principally to separate the wine from sediment in the original bottles. It was an 18th-century introduction and it had several shapes ranging from almost spherical or pear, to a flat squat body. They were often richly decorated with cutting and engraving.

Decanter and stopper, the base impressed Waterloo Co., Cork, *c* 1820. Courtesy of Sotheby Parke Bernet

Rare glass decanters with gilt decoration and stoppers, *c* 1760. Courtesy Sotheby Parke Bernet

Apothecaries jars in delftware, London, 1684. Courtesy Sotheby Parke Bernet

DELANOIS, LOUIS (1731–92)

A leading French *ébéniste* who worked for Madame du Barry. A master from 1761, his quality attracted a large clientele. He was skilled in the use of gilt bronze mounts.

DELFTWARE

An earthenware coated with an opaque glaze which had had tin ashes added and on which the decoration was painted. It takes its name from the town of Delft in Holland, which became an important centre for the manufacture from the 17th century.

DELLA ROBBIA WARE

Luca della Robbia (1400–82) was born in Florence, where he set up a workshop. First he worked as a goldsmith and then as a sculptor, and finally as a modeller. He discovered a technique for enamelling terracotta, in particular with blue and white glazes which rendered the works extremely durable. Fine examples of this method are the 'Resurrection' and 'Ascension' in the Duomo.

His nephew Andrea (1435–1525), worked in a similar manner, and among his successful works were the decorations for the Loggia dei Innocenti. Andrea had several sons who worked with terracotta not only in Tuscany but also in Naples, Umbria and Sicily. The finest craftsman was Giovanni (1469–1529) who is credited with a fountain at Santa Maria Novella, Florence. Luca's grand-nephew, Girolamo (1488–1566), was an architect and sculptor, and among other matters modelled a figure of Catherine de' Medici.

DEMI GRAND FEU

A French name for medium-fired glazes.

DEMI-LUNE

Crescent or half-moon shape in cabinetwork; often stated as a demi-lune commode.

DEMIRDJI

A comparatively modern Turkish-type rug of coarsish wool which was first woven at the end of the 19th century.

DENARIUS

A Roman coin, originally of silver, dating from 268 BC which was the equivalent of ten bronze asses. Types under the Roman Republic included the helmeted head of Roma. Nero debased the coin until it was little more than a flan of copper washed with silver which soon wore away. It is the penny of the New Testament.

DENIER

A minor coin of France and Western Europe which was derived from the Roman denarius. It continued in circulation until the French Revolution. Under Charlemagne it was of silver, later it was debased to copper with silver wash. In Italy it was called the denario, in Spain the dinero and in Portugal the dinheiro.

DENTELLE

See Lace

DENTELLE À LA VIERGE

A bobbin lace having a double ground made by peasants around Dieppe. Largely it was used for caps, and was probably made first in the 17th century.

DERBEND

A rug of the Caucasian group named after a town in the province of Daghestan. It has a soft pile and the patterns are mostly mosaic-like.

DERBY

A porcelain manufactory was founded there in 1756 under the guiding hand of William Duesbury who was to become the owner. Many modelled figures were made there after Meissen. Later ones were more richly coloured and had some gilding. Tableware was decorated with a distinctive treatment of flowers and birds and moths.

Duesbury secured control of Bow in 1762 and bought Chelsea in 1770. When he died in 1786 he was succeeded by his son and Michael Kean.

The Crown Derby period is from 1786 to 1811. In 1811 Robert Bloor bought the manufactory; sadly he went insane in 1826. Marks include a crowned 'D' with crossed batons and six dots between the crown, and the 'D', and 'D' traversed by an anchor.

DERBYSHIRE CHAIR

A type of Jacobean chair, dating from about 1650, which was characterised by an arcaded top rail and central cross-piece joined with turned spindles. Sometimes there was a grotesque mask carved in the centre of the top rail.

DERBYSHIRE SPAR

Coloured crystalline stone found in caverns at Castleton. It ranges from green to blue, yellow and purple and it has been widely used for decorative objects such as candelabra and vases. Popular name is Blue John.

DERINGER

Henry Deringer was one of the leading American gunsmiths; he was born in 1786 at Easton, Pennsylvania, and died in 1868. Henry was the son of Henry Senior, a gunsmith and the producer of the famous Kentucky rifles. At first Henry made rifles and pistols, but from 1825 he made a speciality of hand guns, some of very small size – about 4 ins (10 cm) long with calibres between 0·33 and 0·51 inches. The small deadly guns were nearly always rifled and fired by a percussion cap. It was with a deringer that John Wilkes Booth assassinated Abraham Lincoln.

DERUTA

One of the most exquisitely painted majolicas, both with polychrome and lustre. It was made between about 1490 and 1550 at the town in Umbria that gives it its name. The decoration came under the influence of the Umbrian School of painters. Potteries still exist to the present day.

DESK

A table, frame or case with a sloping or a flat top for the use of writers. It is commonly supplied with drawers, pigeon-holes and compartments. Early examples were little more than a writing board with a book rest.

DESK BOX

One large enough to write on and with a sloping lid to support a book. In America more often called a Bible Box.

DESSERT TABLE

A small table from which the dessert could be served.

DESSERT KNIFE AND FORK

Usually these would be of silver, set in ivory or bone handles; they came in around the middle of the 18th century.

DEVONSHIRE LACE

A term used for all laces made in the county since about 1500, which, of course, includes the famous Honiton lace.

DEVONSHIRE POTTERY

Simple earthenware with lead-glazing was made around the North Devon area from about the 17th century; principal centres of imaginative work being Fremington and Barnstaple.

Empire style writing-desk made as a gift for Napoleon I. Courtesy Kunsthaus am Museum, Cologne

DIAPER

A repeat pattern of any small quite conventional form, plant form, or geometrical form to completely cover an area. It was also a rich and costly textile woven in the times before the Renaissance.

DIATRETA

A drinking cup made of glass, cut in such a way that the designs or ornaments upon it stand out completely from the body of the vase, and form a tracery which is only united to the vase itself by small ties or pins left for the purpose.

DIE

A metallic stamp used for imprinting a design or letter on a soft surface, such as leather with the cover of a book, or a leather desk top.

DIEPPE LACE

A bobbin-type similar to Valenciennes.

DIMITY

A cotton fabric with raised stripes or cords used for hangings or furniture coverings. It was possibly first woven in the middle of the 16th century in Italy. Hepplewhite makes a mention of white dimity for beds as it will give to them 'elegance and neatness truly agreeable'.

DINANDERIE

Small objects of brass, chiefly for domestic or ecclesiastical use, such as were made at Dinand (now Dinant), near Liege, Belgium, between the 13th and 15th century. Articles such as aquamaniles, jugs and pots and pans may have been simple in design but were of excellent craftsmanship. The Mosan craftwork was at its peak with such larger items as fonts and lecterns, and notably candlesticks.

Unfortunately, Dinand was looted and taken by Philippe le Bon in 1466 and the craftwork centre was dissolved, the skilled hands being dispersed, with some coming to England and others going to France, and other places in Belgium.

DINAR
The principal gold coin of the Moslems, it was first struck in the late 7th century; early examples were imitations of the Byzantine solidi. For several centuries it remained the currency basis for countries under Moslem control. Both obverse and reverse were inscribed with Arabic which gave the date, mint and some religious tenets. It was a Persian coin of account, and also a Serbian and a Yugoslavian coin.

DINING-TABLE
The distinctive English table of the Middle Ages was of oak and of heavy trestle construction. It was not until the time of Elizabeth I that the permanent dining-table appears, with a rectangular top over a carved apron resting on massive legs with bulbous decoration. Towards the end of the 17th century, oval and round tables came into fashion. Walnut began to be used with gate-legs and two drop leaves. The 18th century brought cabriole legs, extension pieces, and later, the pedestal table.

DIRECTOIRE
A style with furniture which is transitional between Louis XVI and Empire, not clearly distinguished from the latter. Much of the design was a continuation of the Louis XVI manner, although a little more aesthetically treated, and there was fairly direct copying of the Graeco-Roman ideas. But slowly the French *ébénistes* sloughed off the unnecessary and fined down the basics of the designs which led to the perfections of the Empire style.

Motifs that were popular included oak and laurel crowns, Phyrgian caps, fasces, lyres, stars and lozenges. Echoes of the Directoire style came to England around 1795 and Sheraton included some details in his 'Cabinet Directory'.

DIRK
A long dagger, probably developed from the ballock, which was formerly much used by the Scottish Highlanders. It is also a short sword or plain dagger worn by junior British naval officers.

DISBROWE, NICHOLAS (1612–83)
Born at Waldon, Essex, he was a cabinetmaker who emigrated to Hartford, Connecticut in 1639. His speciality was oakwork, notably chests.

DISH CROSS
With English silver a stand to put on the table to hold silver and porcelain dishes. It is formed of two rotating arms that are extendable and it has a small spirit lamp at the centre. The majority date from just after the middle of the 18th century, although there may be some Irish ones of an earlier date.

DISHED
A concave depression cut in a surface, as with the seat of a wooden chair.

DISH RING
A decorative silver dish-stand usually thought to be of Irish origin and sometimes called 'potato rings'. Actually the first rings were made in England during the reign of Queen Anne. The Irish rings are generally more elaborately decorated than the English with pierced and repoussé work.

DISTRESS
A term to describe the treatment given to some reproduction furniture to create the impression of age; it can include abrading, bruising, scraping, staining and scorching. Distressing may also be used on other categories such as: silver, brass, copper, pewter, steel, iron, stone, some ceramics, bone, ivory and leather. If it is well and skilfully carried out it can be very difficult to pick up.

DIVAN
A large low couch with no back, ends or sides. It is usually supplied with cushions and probably has its origin in Persia.

DJIJIM
An embroidered Oriental rug that starts from a woven web and it is into this that the needlework is done.

DOBBIN
A small drinking cup which would hold about a gill, and was used in the 18th century.

DOCCIA
A porcelain manufactory which was started about 1735 by the Marquis Carlo Ginori, and which has remained in the family. Imitation Capodimonte was produced, assisted by Capodimonte moulds that were acquired. Some of this ware was also marked with the crowned 'N'. Influences evident with other productions include: Meissen, Vienna and Sèvres. Recent ware is marked 'Ginori'.

DOCUMENT DRAWER
A wide and shallow drawer that is found in some desks.

DOG ARMOUR
This originated as an enlarged collar to protect the neck when fighting or hunting. In the Middle Ages long sharp spikes were added and a body covering of sheets of stiff leather. In the 16th century the armour for dogs emulated that of the knights, the finest of the armourer's skill with steel and decoration by etching and gilding being employed. From a plumed visorless helmet to breastplate and backplate with a chain-mail neck and chest protector the great mastiffs and boarhounds would have stood proudly and somewhat terrifyingly beside their armoured and mounted masters.

For hunting, the hounds, when going after wild boars, would be decked out with a suit of padded leather and linen.

With the advent of the 17th century and the abandonment of full armour for men so the dog lost his and he was left once more with just a collar. These for the next two centuries were often made of brass and were decorated by engraving and piercing and sometimes carried inscribed messages such as this:

I am a poore harmless bitch,
I wander I know not whither,
My master lives in H . . . . . (signs of intentional erasure)
I pray direct my thether.

Thos. Mead. 1699

This example was dug up near Newbury in 1801 with the skeleton of a man. There was no sign of a dog's skeleton, so it would appear that the highway murderer had taken the collar off, scratched away the address, and thrown it in with the body to hide the evidence.

DOGLEGGED STAIRCASE
A type of staircase which has two flights which double back on each other with no well in between them.

DOG OF FO
The Chinese animal that appears again and again in sculpture, ceramics, metalwork, carving and paintings. He has the appearance of lion-featured dog.

DOG'S TOOTH
A moulding which uses ornament of four leaves or petals with spiral fillets.

DOLE CUPBOARD
Originally one kept in a church to hold the bread to be doled out to the poor, a 16th-century introduction.

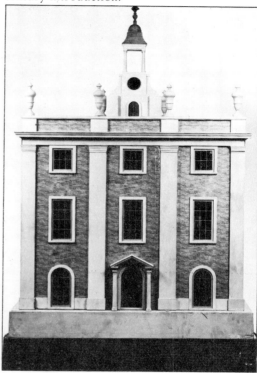

Painted Wooden and Printed Paper on Wood Doll's House designed by Sir Clough Williams Ellis. It is modelled on Orme Court where Rupert Brooke was a frequent visitor. Courtesy of Christie's, South Kensington

DOLL
A child's puppet or play figure, the origin of which goes back far into history. Examples have been found from the time of Early Egypt at about 2000 BC, although with some of these figures it is difficult to be sure whether they were intended for play or for a religious ritual. The crude early dolls were made from clay, bone or wood, whilst those for the rulers' children were of ivory, terracotta, wax and textiles. Jointed terracotta dolls of the Etruscans from about 700 BC have come to light with fashion details modelled on to them.

The dolls of the Greeks and Romans had movable limbs and removable clothes. Plutarch records his little daughter playing with a doll. An excavation showed that a Roman girl had been interred with a chest of her favourite dolls and with them their cosmetics.

Interior of the doll's house 'Titania's Palace'. It shows the Hall of the Fairy Kiss. Courtesy of Christie's

In medieval times dolls appeared carved from wood and made from some material apparently like papier mâché. A fortunate find when paving stones were lifted in Nuremberg included clay dolls of various sizes still in the 14th-century costumes.

A century later evidence comes of professional doll makers; this included the 'Dockenmachers' of Nuremberg. In the 16th century, visual evidence appears in paintings by such as Lucas Cranach. Fully-jointed and carved wooden dolls were around. In the next century the heads began to be made of glazed earthenware. Other materials included pulp and gum which would be a type of papier mâché and alabaster.

Dolls became an industry in the 18th century, with those from Germany in the lead. Clothes in detail and design aped those of the adults; jewellery for dolls appears and also such details as patches and wigs. Dolls cried and moved their eyes from as long ago as 1700. Mass production of papier mâché dolls dates from around 1820. Shops had on offer complete trouseaux for the 'little ladies' that would number such items as: dresses, underwear, stockings, shoes, hats, bags and gloves.

The jointing of the limbs became more and more realistic, with such devices as balljointing of metal and rubber. The heads were produced by some leading porcelain manufactories. Doll types included practically every

Bisque-headed clockwork walking doll, with sleeping brown eyes, pierced ears and blond wig. Courtesy of Christie's, South Kensington

mode of person predominantly female, but also male, from the simplest rag doll to the very expensive 'lady of fashion'.

DOLLAR

A large silver coin first issued in America in 1794. It was modelled on the Spanish milled dollar in which the Continental Congress promised to pay its obligations. Prior to 1873 it was the monetary unit, and since then has been maintained by the government on a parity with the gold dollar.

It is possible the name is derived from the German thaler.

DOLLS' HOUSES

Miniature buildings probably first made on the continent in the 17th century. The most famous and elaborate is Titania's Palace.

DOLPHIN

An ornament in the shape of this creature used in the late Renaissance.

DON POTTERY

Operating from Swinton, Yorkshire, probably from around 1790–1800 it produced creamware and imitations of Leeds-type ware.

DOOR FURNITURE

A collective term for locks, bolts, handles, knobs, knockers and finger plates. Materials used for these have included brass, copper, bronze, steel, iron, glass and porcelain.

DOPPELWANDGLAS

The technique of putting sheets of gold and silver leaf between sheets of glass; it may date back as far as the first century AD.

DOPSKAL

A 17th-century, small Swedish drinking bowl with one or two handles, they were normally made of silver.

DOREURS, CORPORATION DES

The guild in charge of all forms of gilding in France. Towards the end of the 18th century there were some 370 master gilders. The apprenticeship lasted for five years.

DORN, HANS

One of the first makers of scientific instruments to have his name recorded on the ones he produced. He was active around the end of the 15th century.

DOROTHEENTHAL

A faïence manufactory founded in 1715 near Arnstadt, Thuringia by the daughter of the Duke of Brunswick. The ware produced reflected the flamboyance of the baroque and included tankards, two-handled vases and some figures. The mark most used was a monogram of AB.

DORSAL

A hanging, usually of rich stuff, at the back of a throne or an altar, or an apartment wall.

DORSCH, JOHANN CHRISTOPH
(1676–1732)
A gem engraver who had a large production of cameo and intaglio portraits of Popes, Emperors, Kings of France and also copies of noteworthy antique gems. During his time he flooded Germany with these, causing some considerable trouble and confusion for collectors and dealers.

DOS-À-DOS
A back-to-back sofa, or open carriage in which there is seating allowing passengers to sit in the same way.

DOSSAL
An ornamental cloth for the back of a seat.

DOSSIER
The back of a seat, or it may be applied to the head or footboard of a bed; it can also be an anti-macassar.

DOSSIÈRE
In armour, with a cuirass, the backplate; with harness, the back-band.

DOUAI
A faïence manufactory established in 1781 by Staffordshire potters at La Charité-sur-Loire and at Douai. The latter was to produce fine 'stoneware', a soft white ware known by the name of 'English stoneware'. The chief workmen who came from England taught pupils who carried the new process to other centres.

DOUBLE BAROMETER
One that has the mercury divided into two equal parts which stand side by side connected by a tube containing a fluid which is lighter than mercury, such as an oil.

DOUBLE CUP
One that is formed out of two of similar pattern and shape. One is inverted over the other as a cover. Both can serve as drinking vessels. Popular during the Renaissance, and nearly always made from richly-decorated silver.

DOUBLE SPOON
One with a bowl at each end of the handle, of silver. A Dutch innovation of the 18th century for measuring tea.

DOUBLOON
A Spanish gold coin of two escudos, struck in quantity using gold from the New World. Introduced in the late Middle Ages.

DOULTON
A manufactory set up in Lambeth in 1818, at first concentrating on brown ware for industry. Later came salt-glazed stoneware which was decorated by students from the Lambeth School of Art. In the studio also worked the Barlow sisters, George Tinworth and Frank Butler.

Royal Doulton Sung Vase by Arthur Eaton and Cecil Noke, 1923. Courtesy of Sotheby's, Belgravia

DOVETAIL
The joining of two timbers by cutting wedge-shaped openings on the edge of one piece and wedge-shaped projections on the edge of the other. The arrangement locks the two pieces together snugly.

DOWEL
A small round peg of wood that is used to join two or more pieces of wood.

DOWER CHEST
A bridal chest.

DRACHM
A small silver Greek coin struck by a number of centres. The commonest form is the didrachm or double drachm.

It was also a gold coin of the ancient Egyptians under the Ptolemies and a silver coin of the Parthians and the Sassanians.

DRAGON
A short musket carried hooked to a soldier's belt. The barrel was about 16 ins (40·6 cm) and it was either flintlock or snapchance.

DRAM GLASS
A small 17th-century English drinking glass. It is also known as a nip, ginette or joey.

DRAP D'OR
Cloth of gold, the superbly rich cloth used in the 15th and 16th centuries and woven entirely from gold thread.

DRAWN GLASS
Any that is pulled or stretched in the making in contrast with blown, pressed or moulded ware.

DRAWN WORK
Ornamental work made by drawing out threads from cloth, usually linen or silk, and uniting the cross threads into a pattern.

DRAW-TOP TABLE
An extending table first introduced during the Renaissance. It was oblong with the top made in three pieces, two being lower sliding leaves under the centrepiece. By an arrangement of tapered runners the two lower leaves could be pulled out and would then rise level with the centre.

DREDGER
A box with a perforated cover, and also a small straight-sided caster. It could be used for sugar, pepper or spices. It was also called a drudger.

DRESDEN
A faïence manufactory founded in 1708 in Saxony by Johan Böttger a year before he set up the Meissen establishment. The porcelain of Meissen was originally called Saxony porcelain.

Dresden closed in 1784. The ware produced included figures, vases and flower pots and blue and white ware for domestic uses. The mark from 1768 was 'DH'.

DRESDEN LACE
A kind of fine 18th-century drawn-work, also a rather poor imitation of Brussels bobbin lace.

DRESSER
A type of sideboard that may or may not have a fixed or hanging back of shelves and hooked rails. The bottom section may have drawers and a centre ambry. The whole might stand on short bracket feet or short legs. Early ones were generally of oak and later, walnut was used.

DRESSING-TABLE
A low table or stand with a mirror designed for those making their toilet. It could also be a small desk-like object with a swing or triptych mirror.

DRINKING GLASSES AND VESSELS
In history they have been various and often with strange names. In the list below, the material they are most generally made from is indicated and also country, if of special association.

Ale Glass	
Biberon (pewter)	Swiss
Can (silver)	American
Cantir Glass	Spanish
Caudle Cup (silver)	English
Charka (gold)	Russian
Coaching Glass	English
Dandy Glass	
Flute Glass	Dutch
Goblet (silver)	
Jack (leather)	English
Kovsh (gold)	Russian
Milkmaid cup (silver)	English
Muhlenbecher (silver)	Dutch
Nelson Glass	English
Passglas	German
Poro Glass	Spanish
Posset Cup (pottery)	
Quaich (silver)	Scottish
Roemer Glass	German
Rummer Glass	
Schnelle (stoneware)	German
Tankard (silver or pewter)	
Tazza (silver)	
Thistle Glass	Scottish
Thumb Glass	
Trichterbecher (stoneware)	German

Poland. Sigismond III
Wasa: 40 ducats.
Courtesy of Ader,
Picard, Tajan

DROP OR TEARDROP HANDLE

A bulbous handle with back plate, attached
to a drawer front with pins. It is generally
of hollow or solid brass. Other types include
pear-drop, and acorn. They were introduced
in the 17th century.

DROP LEAF

A hinged leaf to a table, one that hangs
vertically downwards when not in use. It may
be supported by extending legs, folding
brackets, draw rails or gate-legs.

DRUM TABLE

A circular top table which rests on a tripod
base, it could be revolved and in the skirt
there could be real or mock drawers. It
became a vogue in the latter part of the 18th
century.

DUBLIN GLASS

The earliest Irish flintglass house was set up
in Dublin at the end of the 17th century by
one Captain Roche. Known as the Round
Glass House, it produced a wide variety of
items as can be noted from an advertisement
in *Faulkner's Dublin Journal* which gave notice
for the following: 'all sorts of the newest
fashioned drinking glasses, water bottles . . .
water glasses with and without feet and saucers
. . . moulded jelly glasses of all sorts and sizes,
sillybub glasses, comfit and sweetmeat glasses
. . . pine and orange glasses, hall lanthorns . . .
glove lamps . . .' (and so on, the full list
covered some 50 plus items, the use of some
of which we can only guess).

DUBLIN TAPESTRY

A small works set up by Robert Baille in
Dublin in about 1728.

DUCAT

A gold coin of several countries of Europe,
it was first coined by Roger II of Sicily in
about 1150. The Venetian ducat, the gold
zecchino, was struck in the 12th century, with
Christ and the kneeling Doge receiving St
Mark's standard.

DUCHESSE LACE

Modern Flemish bobbin lace in which flowers
and flower sprays are made separately and then
united to the ground net with brides.

DUELLING PISTOL

A long barrelled pistol especially made for
duelling, and usually in pairs. It was single
barrel and reasonably accurate up to the
regulation 20 paces.

DUMB-WAITER

A portable serving table or stand, generally
with revolving shelves; intended for both food
and drink. It was an English invention and
came in just before the middle of the 18th
century, and could be tall and stand on the
floor, or there was a simpler one-shelf variety
that could be placed in the middle of a round
table; on the latter could be condiments,
bread, butter, cheese and the like.

DURLACH

A faïence manufactory in Baden started by
Johann Wachenfeld in 1722. It lasted till the
middle of the 18th century. The ware included
pear-shaped jugs and coffee pots decorated with
a distinctive use of contemporary peasant
figures and simple rhyming mottoes.

DUTCH METAL

An alloy of copper and zinc which as a foil
was intended to imitate gold-leaf.

EAGLE

The military standard of the Romans, which was of silver, bronze or gold, displayed with wings extended; some had thunderbolts in their talons. Napoleon's armies had a similar standard. The Holy Roman Empire adopted the Imperial Eagle as an armorial bearing; later it was to be adopted by Austria, Germany, Russia and the United States.

It has been used as a decoration on clocks, mirrors, and also with inlay when it is generally enclosed in a medallion.

It is also the name of an American gold coin, and there are double Eagles, as well as half and quarter Eagles.

EAGLE CONSOLE TABLE

One which is supported on a large spread eagle, generally standing on a rock, itself on a plinth. The top would be marble.

EAR DAGGER

A weapon of the 15th and 16th centuries, popular in Spain and taking its name from the two ear-like plates that formed the pommel.

EARTHENWARE

Vessels and objects made from fired clay, especially the coarser kinds. In England it implies pottery which does not have a vitrified body. Delftware, faïence and majolica are included.

Flemish ebony cabinet, probably dating from the 18th century. Courtesy Sotheby Parke Bernet

EAST, EDWARD
The 'Chief Clockmaker and Keeper of the Privy Clocks' appointed in 1662. Night clocks were one of his specialities, and these had a perforated device for the light from a small lamp to shine through and give the time.

ÉBÉNISTE
A French cabinetmaker, particularly engaged with veneer work. The term is derived from ebony, which wood he would have been preoccupied with in the periods preceding the 18th century.

EBONISE
To treat and stain other woods to imitate ebony. The practice started during the Renaissance.

EBONY
A very hard, heavy and durable wood from the species *dyospyros* of tropical Africa and Asia; the most valued being that wood which is intense black and will take a high polish. Madagascar was a type much sought after by cabinetmakers.

ECHINUS
An 'egg and dart' or 'egg and tongue' ornament used in wood and stonework.

ECKERNFÖRDE
A faïence manufactory set up in Schleswig in 1765 as a takeover from an earlier establishment started in 1759. Most notable ware was probably the flamboyant tureens made in the form of vegetables.

ÉCUELLE
The French version of the shallow porringer with a cover, it would have two flat pierced handles, and also sometimes a salver made in the same style. A 17th-century introduction.

EDKINS, MICHAEL
A painter of glass and pottery from Bristol, he possibly followed his apprenticeship in Birmingham. From records it would appear that he worked as a freelance accepting commissions from a number of firms. Little of his work is signed and this has led to considerable confusion. Distinctive motifs he used included writhing flowers and perched birds. He was active from 1762.

EGGSHELL
Thin-bodied white porcelain made during the Yung Lo time (1403–24). What decoration there was, was done by very shallow incising or thin applications of slip. The ware was highly regarded and sought after, especially the ultra-thin examples. Some Japanese porcelains of the last hundred years are essentially eggshell, but they have not captured the subtle qualities of the earlier Chinese.

EIRAKU WARE
A Japanese porcelain made in Kyoto. The name was derived from Eiraku, a potter whose real name was Zengoro Hozen, who was active in the early 19th century. He was a clever imitator of late Ming and other wares.

ELECTOR GLASS
A large cylindrical beaker decorated with enamel to show the Emperor of the Holy Roman Empire and the Seven Electors. Most glasses of this type date from the end of the 16th century to the early part of the 17th.

ELECTROPLATING
To cover a base metal core with silver by electrolysis. The technique was made commercially viable in about 1845 by the Elkington Brothers. Their work was a development from Volta's work when he gilded silver in 1805 and the laws of electrolysis formulated by Faraday in 1833.

ELECTROTYPING
A method for reproducing complicated decorative metal objects. Much development work was done on this by Jacobi, and by 1838 he had shown how a reproduction of a metal item could be done by depositing a metal in casts taken from the original. This thin layer of a valuable metal could then be backed by a baser one.

ELECTRUM
A natural, rather pale alloy of gold and silver. It can also be German Silver, a silver white alloy of copper, nickel and zinc; today usually called nickel silver.

ELFE, THOMAS (*c* 1719–*c* 1771)
A highly skilled cabinetmaker from Charleston, Carolina. His workshop was largely manned by Negro slaves whom he had trained into craftsmen. He is best recalled for mahogany casework in the Chippendale manner.

ELLIOTT, JOHN (1713–91)
He emigrated from England in 1753 to Philadelphia, and became one of the best

known makers of wall mirrors. He was followed in this craft by his son John and then by two grandsons.

ELM
Any tree of the genus *Ulmus*; the wood is hard and tough and has been used for furniture and domestic implements.

ELSTERMANN, KRISTOFFER
Active around 1700, a German who is credited with introducing glass engraving to Sweden.

EMBOSSING
A general term to indicate raised decoration on metals, leathers, fabrics, cards and papers. This may be done by repoussé, pushing or hammering through from the back, the use of male and female dies, or with engraved rollers; the latter being especially used for wallpapers.

EMBROIDERY
One of the oldest of the ornamental arts, archaeological expeditions continue to throw light on its beginnings. There are existing specimens of ancient Egyptian work. Herodotus mentions the embroidered vestments of the gods in Egypt. The prophet Ezekiel mentions the embroidery of Tyrus (Tyre). Certainly it was the principal domestic occupation of the ladies in Greece, from the days when Penelope embroidered a garment for Ulysses. Later, there was the period of the exquisite work of the Renaissance, right through to our own days when women – and men, too – continue to add their quota of needlework on cloth in all its various aspects.

EMPIRE
The styles, ornaments, design, fashions, developed during the French Empire (1804–15). The revival of the classic ideas of decoration featured in many ways, at first perhaps a little too ebullient, but then fined down. Motifs included: acanthus, winged classical figures, eagles, swans, wreaths, burning torches, trumpets and lyres.

ENAMEL
In enamel painting the colours are vitrified and fired on to a metal surface; and also to the surface of glass or pottery, for the purpose of decoration; with ceramics such an application when transparent is usually called a glaze.

The history of the process goes well back into antiquity; examples have been discovered in the civilisations of the early Greeks and Romans and also the Egyptians. One of the most famous centres during the Renaissance times was at Limoges in France. A strange branch of enamel painting was discovered by Count Chabrol de Volvic; the material he chose consisted of Volvic stone and lava from the mountains of Auvergne; it was said that even a sharp piece of iron might be drawn over the colours without injuring the surface.

With ceramics, painting with enamel appears as early as the 13th century in China. At the same time the Persians were making their Rhages earthenware with enamel decoration. In Europe the method comes in about 1620 with the application to stoneware. On hardpaste the enamel remains more or less a surface layer not being absorbed; with soft-paste it does sink into the lead glaze.

The use of opaque and transparent enamels for decorating glass also dates from the 13th century, and it is thought that the Saracens were the first to achieve the difficult technique, but there had been attempts by the Romans. Two hundred years later the Venetians developed the method, and in the 16th century the Germans imitated them.

ENCAUSTIC PAINTING
One of the oldest methods of painting, being practised from at least 3000 BC. Some of the finest existing examples are the mummy portraits from Fayum executed about the 3rd century AD. The colours are applied to the support with hot beeswax, either with spatulas or brushes, finally being driven in with a hot iron.

ENCAUSTIC TILE
One that is decorated with inlaid clays and then fired. In 1769, Josiah Wedgwood took out a patent for a decorative process allied to this method, the description read: 'The purpose of ornamenting earthen and porcelaine ware with an encaustic gold bronze, together with a peculiar species of encaustic painting in various colours in imitation of the ancient Etruscan and Roman earthenware.'

ENCOIGNURE
A type of low, corner cupboard, popular from the middle of the 18th century. It was often richly embellished, and could have a marble top.

ENDIVE
An ornament inspired by the lace-like leaves of the salad plant.

Pair of Louis XV Black Lacquer Encoignures. Courtesy of Sotheby Parke Bernet

ENDPAPERS

The first and last pages of a book which are stuck to the cover. They are sometimes left plain, but they may also be decorated with illustrations or by such a method as marbling.

ENGHALSKRUG

German 17th-century faïence jug, it was distinguished by its long neck, and sometimes had a pewter mounting.

ENGINE TURNED DECORATION

With ceramics it implies cutting the surface of a dried but unfired object. This is most commonly done on a lathe to produce a form of basket weave appearance. It is possible the method was developed by Wedgwood around 1760.

With metal it means the use of such as a rose engine to produce the same kind of design. It is often applied to flat cases intended for the pocket and constant use. To a degree it hides excessive abrasion and also tends to give a grip for the hand, apart from aesthetic considerations.

ENGOBE

White or coloured slip applied to earthenware, often as a support for a glaze or enamel.

ENGRAVED GLASS

First records point to the decoration of glass by this method during the first half of the 16th century. The two methods are the diamond point, or the rapidly revolving wheel, which could have various abrasive substances added. The diamond may have been first used by the Venetians during the 16th century. The first wheel work was left matt, only later did it receive a higher and higher polish.

ENGRAVED METAL

Decoration of metals using chisels and gravers, a method particularly applicable to door furniture, armour and many other metal objects. It called for considerable skill and control with the tool, a slip could be very difficult to eradicate.

ENTABLATURE

The upper part of any classical order. It is supported by a range of columns or walls, and consists of: the cornice which is on the top, a frieze in the middle and the architrave at the bottom. Features from this have been included with furniture design.

ENVELOPE TABLE

A small table with four flaps that when folded inwards give it the appearance of an

Engraved glass. On one side it shows a bust of William III flanked by the initials WR, Dublin *c* 1720. Courtesy Sotheby Parke Bernet

envelope, hence the name. The legs are generally delicate, with or without castors. It dates from the early part of the 19th century.

EPAULIÈRE
With medieval armour a part protecting the shoulder and connecting the breastplate and the backpiece.

EPERGNE
An elaborate centre-piece for a table, generally a dining-table, which can be composed of a number of different sized dishes, normally displayed on arms from a main trunk or set in basket-work containers from this central feature. The name is derived from the French épargner, to save; the basic idea behind an epergne being somewhat similar to a round wooden table dumb-waiter. It came into vogue from about 1730.

ERFURT
A faïence manufactory active at the town in Thuringia from about 1717. One speciality was cylindrical tankards with pewter mounts. The mark was supposed to be a six-spoked wheel, but it was not often used.

ESCABEAU
A strongly made stool of trestle form; it could be square, rectangular or round.

ESCRITOIRE
A writing table, generally with some drawers and pigeon-holes. The French for it, now, is *écritoire*; the late Latin was *scriptorium,* a place for writing.

ESCUDO
Spanish gold coin at first bearing the Spanish arms and a cross, later a portrait of Charles III.

The gold monetary unit of Portugal and also a silver coin originally equal in value to the gold. A coin of copper, nickel and zinc equal to the depreciated paper escudo.

ESCUTCHEON
The decorative metal plate or shield around a keyhole.

ESPAGNOLETTE
A decorative motif of a young attractive girl's head, inspired perhaps by the work of Watteau, to embellish various pieces of furniture, notably the tops of cabriole legs, in the early 18th century. The word translated from the French actually means a kind of fastening for a French casement which consists of a long rod with hooks at each end, the rod being turned by a handle; another type can be used to fasten a cupboard.

ESTE
A town between Padua and Ferrara in Italy where there was a faïence manufactory. Little is known of its productions, those remaining being rare; some excellent figures, however, were included. Giovanni Battista Brunello, some years before 1765, was working there.

Paul Storr gilt ewer and stand, *c* 1817. Courtesy of Phillips

He later copied the pottery of Wedgwood calling it *le terraglie inglesi*.

ESTOC
A thrusting sword of the Renaissance, although it came in earlier. A nasty weapon with a quadrangular blade. The first examples seldom had scabbards.

ÉTAGÈRE
A set of open hanging shelves, or it could have glazed doors and a couple of small drawers.

ETCHED GLASS
A method of decorating glass rather similar to etching a copper plate in print-making. The whole surface of the glass is covered with a ground of wax and resin. Then the design and decoration is needled through this ground to expose the glass. After that, hydrofluoric acid is applied so that the pattern is eaten into the glass. As with etching it needs considerable skill and practice to be able to judge just how

far the acid has eaten into the glass. It is possible the idea was first put into use by Henry Schwanhardt in Nuremberg in about 1670.

ETCHED SILVER
A similar process to the foregoing which was used on silver in the 19th century to save lengthy periods of time that would be taken up by engraving. The etched line, however, has nothing like the crisp quality of that left by the graver, it appears somewhat weak in comparison.

ÉTUI
A fancy, decorated box for small articles, a box in which toilet articles could be kept. Early records indicate that they were in use in France in the 14th century. In later centuries special étui originated for such items as toothpicks and needles. Craftsmen made these little cylindrical boxes of gold, silver, ivory, bone, tortoiseshell, and they could be enamelled and embellished lavishly.

EVANGELIAR

A type of illuminated manuscript. The best examples show medieval art at its finest. Examples from the 8th century include the celebrated *Book of Kells* which is in Trinity College, Dublin; the Evangeliar from Lindisfarne which is in the British Museum; the Cuthbert Evangeliar in Vienna and the Golden Evangeliar of Henry III which is in the Escorial in Spain.

These manuscripts were worked on vellum, using not only colours, but also gold-leaf and other metals, tiny fragments of precious and semi-precious stones and raising paste.

EWER

A large jug or pitcher originally intended to hold water for ablution purposes from the Middle Ages until the 16th century; it being the custom for important persons to wash their hands between courses, a necessary action owing to the lack of eating utensils, such as forks. Ewers were often of solid silver and most richly decorated. Besides silver they could be made of rock crystal, hard stones and enamelled glass.

EXETER CARPETS

Hand-knotted carpets made in Exeter around the middle of the 18th century under the direction of Claude Passavant who originated from Basel.

Casque-shaped silver ewer with woman's head dominating handle top. French, 1715. Courtesy Ader, Picard, Tajan

FABERGÉ, CARL GUSTAVOVICH
(1846–1920)

The goldsmith and jeweller supreme to the Russian Imperial Court. He took control of his father's establishment in St Petersburg in 1870 and built it up until 1914 when he was employing upwards of 500 craftsmen. His best known works are probably those gorgeous and fantastically expensive fancies, the Easter eggs which were made for the Imperial family, the first being made for the Tsarina in 1884. Although, undoubtedly, he made a quantity of these rich, jewelled articles and other masterpieces himself, it is realised that with much of the production from his business he was the designer and organiser of this almost unequalled flow of skill, value and splendour.

FACET

In cutting precious stones the facet is one of the tiny surfaces that is cut and polished to reflect the light.

Egg rotary clock, by Carl Fabergé, dated 1902.
Courtesy Sotheby Parke Bernet

FAENZA
Probably the most important centre in Italy
for the production of majolica. Work started
there in the latter part of the 15th century and
from then until about 1600 the wares were
the equal of any others from Italy. Examples
still existing include fine vases, drug jars,
dishes, tiles and plaques. Most are notable for
strong rich colouring and talented drawing.

FAGOTING
A process of drawing out horizontal threads
from a fabric, such as linen, and tying the
remaining cross threads into hourglass-shaped
bunches. It is also a decorative stitch to join
two finished edges, as the seams of a garment,
leaving a small space between them.

FAÏENCE
Decorative earthenware with a tin glaze that
has its name derived from Faenza in Italy; it
was used initially from the end of the 16th
century in France to describe such work. Today
it is a term that takes in most kinds of white
pottery.

FALCHION
A broad-bladed sword with a slight curve
that was used in the Middle Ages. It was
single-edged and was broadest nearest the point.

FALCIFORM
Hooked, curved, shaped like a sickle.

FALDSTOOL
A folding stool or chair made in the manner
of a curule or X shape. It would be intended
as the seat for the bishop when not on his
throne, or when officiating outside his own'
cathedral. It dates from the 11th century. It
can be called a Litany stool from which the
litany could be sung or said. It can also be a
desk at which worshippers can kneel.

FALL FRONT
The front of a writing cabinet that is hinged,
allowing it to drop forward. It is also termed
Drop Front.

FALLING CREEK IRONWORKS
One of the early full-scale ironworks that was
being established in Virginia in 1621. Sadly
this never got into full production as it was
destroyed during an Indian massacre the
following year.

FAMILLE NOIR
With Chinese ceramic objects that have been
enamelled in the *famille verte* manner with a
dull black ground which is then given a coating
of a transparent green glaze. This procedure
gives the rich greenish-black colour that is so
highly prized.

FAMILLE ROSE
Enamelled ware produced in the early 18th
century during the reign of Yung-Chêng
(1723–35). The ware was decorated with pink
and carmine made opaque by thickening with
white. The new painting method was used
particularly with 'eggshell' porcelain bowls,
plates and cups.

French fan with carved Mother-of-Pearl guards. Hand painted, c 1820. Courtesy of Corner Antiques, Coltishall

FAMILLE VERTE

A large range of Chinese enamelled porcelain of the K'ang Hsi reign (1662–1722), which was decorated with a rich palette of bright green, red, dark purple, yellow and violet enamels. It was a development of the Wan Li five colour ware. A distinguishing feature is that there is a considerable use of an overglaze of blue. The enamel was painted on the biscuit, which means that there was no intervening glaze. There were many attractive and intimate objects produced, such as figures, brush-rests and waterpots.

FAN

An object of considerable antiquity; it was used by the Assyrians, early Egyptians, and Greeks. These first examples were generally large and mounted on a shaft or long staff. In early Christian times comes the *flabellum* which was used from the 4th to the 14th century to keep flies away from the altar during the Mass.

Since then there have been two principal kinds of fan, the rigid and the folding. Materials used have been diverse – fine fabrics, paper, parchment, feathers from the ostrich, argus pheasant and peacock, grasses and leaves;

the handles have been carved from wood, bone and ivory, and worked from gold and silver. The first folding fans are credited to the Japanese in the second half of the 7th century. Examples, particularly during the 18th century in France, were miniature works of art with decorative treatment, and later with painted scenes.

FAN BACK CHAIR

A chair in which the spindles at the back are arranged in fan-shape; a Windsor Chair.

FANFARE BOOKBINDING

A style from the 14th century, associated with Nicholas and Clovis Eve, the royal binders to Henry III of Spain. It was distinctive with many fine tooled details of flowers, foliage and tracery.

FAN MOTIF

It was popular for use with inlay work, notably with Adam, Hepplewhite and Sheraton.

FARTHINGALE CHAIR
A kind of broad-seated chair without arms that was popular during the reigns of Elizabeth I and James I. It was essentially a lady's chair and so made that she could sit comfortably in her huge hooped skirt or farthingale.

FASCES
An ornamental motif, popular during the French Empire period. It was a bundle of rods from which the head of an axe protruded, the whole being bound with a wide band.

FATHPUR
A rug from the place in India, an early important centre of rug weaving during the time of Akbar the Great (1556–1605).

FATTORINI FAMILY
A group of potters working in the neighbourhood of Caffaggiolo in 1469, and in the centre from 1506.

FAUBOURG ST ANTOINE
A tapestry weaving house was set up there by Henry IV in 1597, and six years later it was moved to the Louvre. One of the leading weavers associated with the project was Maurice Duborg.

FAUBOURG SAINT-DENIS
A hard-paste porcelain manufactory which started in Paris in 1771. Early wares from the time of Pierre-Antoine Hannong were very translucent. After came a range of high quality tableware.

FAUCHARD
A long-handled medieval weapon with a single convex-edged blade.

FAUCHIER, JOSEPH I AND II
Joseph the senior ran a faïence manufactory in Marseilles from 1710, and was followed in 1751 by Joseph II, a nephew. Wares included wall fountains and good figures.

FAUTEUIL
An armchair with open arms. More strictly the chair of a presiding officer; a university professorship, seat or chair in the French Academy.

FAVRILE
Glass made by Louis Comfort Tiffany (1848–1933), it had a distinctive iridescent look.

FEATHER BANDING
Veneering with the grains of two pieces next to each other running diagonally. This with many woods gave a feather like or herringbone appearance.

FEATHER STITCH
A decorative stitch composed of blanket stitches so arranged to give a zigzag look.

FEDELI, STEFANO (1794–1870)
Italian silversmith who received his patent in 1815.

FEDERAL STYLE
A loose term applied to American furniture made between 1785 and 1830.

FENDER
A low metal frame, often ornamented, placed before an open-fireplace as a protective device for the carpet; it can also have small inner rails on which the fire-irons may rest. Fenders came in about the end of the 17th century.

FÊNG-HUANG
A mythical bird of rich plumage and graceful form said to appear in times of peace and prosperity. It can often be seen in Chinese painting and decorating textiles and ceramics, generally in the form of an elaborate pheasant.

FERAGHAN
A Persian rug of high quality with the warp and weft of cotton and the pile of wool.

FERETORY
A movable or fixed shrine which was used in the Middle Ages as a keeping place for the relics of saints. It was often richly decorated.

FERRARA
A manufactory of majolica in North Italy which was established by Alfonso I, with artists imported from Faenza, in about 1495.

There was a tapestry weaving house from the early part of the 15th century in Ferrara but despite the bringing in of Flemish weavers it never really flourished and more or less closed in the reign of Alfonso II.

It is also a broadsword or claymore bearing the name of Ferrara on the blade. During the 16th and 17th centuries these swords were much sought after in England and Scotland. It is thought that they were made by Andrea Ferrara of Italy, and members of his family.

FERRONIÈRE
A type of ceramic decoration and ornament that has the appearance of wrought-iron work.

FERRYBRIDGE POTTERY
A small manufactory near Pontefract in Yorkshire that produced creamware and stoneware in the manner of Wedgwood. Ralph Wedgwood was associated with it from 1796 until about 1806. Mark used for that period was 'Wedgwood & Co'.

FERRUCCI, FRANCESCO
A skilled craftsman with *pietre dure,* active around 1598, when he executed a portrait of Cosimo I de'Medici using a painting by Domenico Cresti for inspiration.

FESTOON
It may also be called a swag, and means a modelled or painted garland of fruit and flowers suspended from its end or ends. A popular device during the Renaissance, the inspiration coming from the early Greeks and Romans. It was a motif also used with the Adam style.

FIDDLE-BACK
An open chair having a solid splat in the shape of a fiddle introduced in about 1700. Ecclesiastically it refers to a type of chasuble.

FIDDLE PATTERN
A term with table silver for forks and spoons that have a handle in this shape which was introduced in the early part of the 19th century.

FIELD BED
A portable and probably folding bed which possibly originated in medieval times. Much later models consisted of a light framework with four posts which carried an arched tester, comparatively high in the middle from the head to the foot.

FIGULINE
Made of earthenware pottery modelled after natural things, such as shells, fish, lizards and plants, in the manner so ably demonstrated by Bernard Palissy. It is also the clay from which they are made.

FIGURE-HEAD
The figure, bust or statue at the bow of the vessel, at the stemhead.

In America in the 19th century there was a large number of figure-head carvers active, and records list more than 700 such craftsmen. Such men as Charles Sampson of Maine who worked the figure-head for the famous Belle of Oregon and John Bellamy also of Maine who created the huge eagle with a spread of 18 ft for the USS *Lancaster,* which latter survives in the Mariners' Museum in Virginia. The origin of figure-heads is almost as ancient as ships themselves, carvings of mythical and strange beasts, fierce heads and more latterly fine ladies have breasted the waves, their conception wrapped in a superstition related to guardianship.

FIGURINE
A small carved or a modelled figure, especially applicable to terracotta.

FILIGREE
Intricate metal craftwork, executed with wires, scrolls and twists, usually of gold, silver or copper to decorate metalwork. Ornamental openwork of delicate or intricate design.

FILLET
A flat strip separating two architectural mouldings. A fillet in a frame is a flat strip either gilded, painted or covered with linen, which separates the main frame from the picture.

FILLEY FAMILY
Active in the Vermont, Philadelphia and New York areas in the early part of the 19th century, making and selling Japanned tin-plate.

FINGER BOWLS
Small vessels introduced into Europe in the 17th century. They were for holding water to rinse the fingers at table and could be made of silver, brass, pewter or glass.

FINIALS
A carved ornament placed on top of bed-posts, mirrors, chair-backs, and also cast ornaments on covers. Motifs used included acorns, flaming torches, plumes and plain turned bulbous and tapering knobs.

FIREARM
Any weapon from which a shot can be discharged by an explosive. The first use of light firearms was in the 14th century. The first hand gun was little more than a tube of brass or iron with a touch-hole and a primitive stock. This was followed by the matchlock and then the wheel-lock and the flint-lock at

the end of the 17th century. The Brown Bess used by the British in the Napoleonic wars was a smooth-bore flint-lock. In 1807, Alexander John Forsyth developed the idea of the percussion cap which brought in the percussion lock.

FIRE-BACK

A moulded cast-iron slab placed at the back of the fire-basket against the stones or bricks to give them some protection. The back was frequently decorated with coats of arms, mythical beasts and often carried dates.

FIRE-DOGS

See Andirons

FIRE-IRONS

Utensils for a fire-place; poker, tongs, shovel. They were made from iron or steel, with or without brass decorative handles.

Brass and steel fire grate, *c* 1900.
Courtesy of Sotheby's, Belgravia

19th-century cast-iron stoves. On the right from Southwell in Nottinghamshire and on the left one from Germany. Courtesy of Lustre Metal Antiques

Fabergé silver-gilt and shaded enamel tea caddy by Feodor Rückert, Moscow, 1896–1908. A Russian silver-gilt and shaded enamel casket, the Eleventh Artel, Moscow, 1908–17. A Russian gilt and shaded enamel strawberry spoon, Moscow, c 1910. A Fabergé silver-gilt and shaded enamel small box, by Feodor Rückert, Moscow, 1908–17. A Fabergé silver-gilt and shaded enamel tumbler cup, Moscow, 1908–17. Courtesy of Sotheby Parke Bernet

A Persian lacquer pen-box with scenes of Heaven and Hell and Napoleon in battle, left unfinished by the Painter Laureate, c 1847, and finished by the artist Jala'ir in 1853, Qatar. Courtesy of Sotheby Parke Bernet

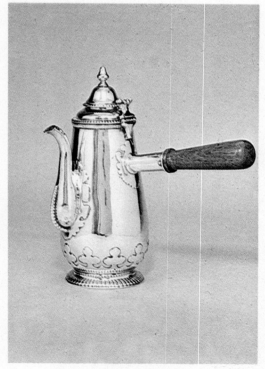

Silver coffee-pot by Thomas Bolton, Dublin, 1696. Courtesy of the National Museum of Ireland

Claret jug, Waterford, c 1810. Courtesy of the National Museum of Ireland

A Louis XIV Savonnerie carpet, third quarter of the 17th century. Courtesy of Sotheby Parke Bernet

Three casters by David King, Dublin, 1699. Courtesy of the National Museum of Ireland

Lead Bulla of Innocent III used for sealing Papal 'bulls'. Courtesy of the National Museum of Ireland

Meissen Celestial Globe. Courtesy of the National Museum of Ireland

Silver mustard pots. From left to right: Mr Punch by Robert Hennell IV, London, 1868; seven-sided vase shaped on pedestal foot by Nicholas Edwards, London, 1799; and a large cylindrical pierced work by Edward Edwards I and II, London 1847. Courtesy of the Colman Collection

Blue cloth frock coat from an important Micmac Chief's Ceremonial Costume. Courtesy of Phillips

A French repeating cylinder watch by Vauchet à Paris. The movement with pierced bridge cock and ruby coqueret, signed Vauchet en la Cité, *c* 1780. Courtesy of Phillips

FIRE MARK

A metal plate, attached to a building to mark it as insured. They were used by the 18th century fire-insurance companies of London to identify buildings that had paid premiums and thus were entitled to fire-fighting efforts.

FIRE-SCREEN

A protection from the heat and also to protect the carpet and nearby furniture from flying sparks and red-hot fragments. The screen could be of meshed or pierced metal or for shielding from heat, as with a pole-screen.

FISH SLICE

A fish server introduced in the latter part of the 18th century; of silver and decorated with pierced designs.

FLABELLUM

See fans

FLAGON

A large vessel for liquors, generally with a spout, lid and handle and with a pear-shaped or bulbous body. Later flagons had a slightly tapered cylindrical body and did not always have spouts.

FLAG SEAT

A term for a rush seat. They were popular in America for plain chairs.

FLAIL

An unpleasant medieval weapon made like the common threshing flail.

FLAMBÉ GLAZE

Variegated effects with the colours that come from firing conditions. At first these were accidental but later they were deliberately mastered and included with certain wares. The flambé method is mainly associated with Chinese ceramics. It can also be the technique of applying the glaze irregularly by splashing.

FLASH

When pottery is discoloured because it has been in direct contact with the flames during firing.

FLAT CHASING

A low-relief surface decoration for silver made by hammering with small blunt instruments. It was popular in the early 18th century and could be combined with engraving.

FLAT POINT

A type of needle-made lace in which no part of the design is raised.

FLEMISH SCROLL

A double-curving scroll found on William and Mary chairs and also earlier with Flemish cabinetmaking.

FLINT GLASS

It is today usually termed lead crystal; other names include: lead glass, crystal glass and English glass. It was produced by George Ravenscroft (1618–81) in about 1675. The discovery gave the English almost a world monopoly for about 150 years.

FLINT-LOCK

A lock for a gun or pistol that had a flint fixed in the cock, or hammer, which, on striking the battery or cover of the pan, ignited the priming which communicated its fire to the charge through the touch-hole.

FLOCK PAPER

A type of wallpaper in which the design is painted or stencilled on with an adhesive and then immediately a coloured flock is sprinkled all over the surface. When the adhesive has dried, the surplus flock is brushed off. A method that was developed in France early in the 17th century.

FLÖRSHEIM

A faïence manufactory near Frankfurt-on-Main which was started by Ludwig Müller in 1765; eight years later the Carthusians from Mayence took it over, but they disposed of it in 1797. The wares included: openwork table centres and cream earthenware. The mark in the early period was the monogram FH and later an impressed bunch of grapes and MIW.

FLUTE

A tall, slender, deep, conical drinking glass.

FLUTING

Grooves cut parallel in a surface, wood or stone, that usually have a half-round or rectangular section. It is the opposite to reeding.

FOIBLE

With a sword this is the part of the blade between the middle and the point.

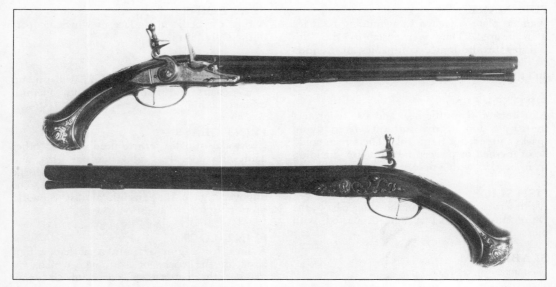

Pair of French silver-mounted flint-lock holster pistols, by Mazelier, Paris, 1708. Courtesy of Christie's

FONTAINEBLEAU TAPESTRIES
The Royal Manufactory was founded by François I (16th century), and a leading weaver was Pierre Lebries.

FORE-EDGE PAINTING
An odd vagary of the craftsman. It means the painting of a picture on the page edges of a book. To do this the painter fanned out the pages, painted his picture and then the book was squared up once more and its edges gilded in the usual manner with expensive editions. The trick was that the picture was invisible in the normal way until the pages were once more fanned out.

FORGERY
The unpermitted imitation of an original work made with intent to deceive, or the production of articles in the exact style of a master with the intention of passing them as works by him. Examples of forgery go back almost as long as there have been patrons of the arts. The deceitful art of the forger is encouraged when the demand for a certain category of art object exceeds the legitimate supply. Examples of the forger's activity appear in practically every field of antiques and the fine arts.

FORKS
They were probably introduced from Italy into England at the beginning of the 17th century. Although they were possibly in use

for serving meat, rather than for eating with, in the 14th century. The first English-made fork is recorded as being dated 1632. At first it was two and then three tines, until in the middle of the 18th century the four tined fork came into use, and is still used by the majority today.

FORM WATCH
A watch made in a manner that is stylistically out of the ordinary for the period in which it was made. Thus odd ones appear as skulls, baskets of flowers and musical instruments.

FOUR POSTER
A large bedstead with tall posts, often carved at the corners to support curtains.

FRANKENTHAL
One of Germany's outstanding porcelain manufactories. It was started in 1755 by Paul Hannong under the patronage of the Elector Palatine, Karl Theodor. It produced until 1799. The wares were hard-paste with a slight creamy-white tone, and included figures and vases. The painting of decorations was exquisite and faultless. Marks include 'PH' with a lion and shield, an incised 'H', and 'JAH' with or without a lion.

FRANKFURT-ON-MAIN
Among the oldest faïence manufactories in Germany, being started in 1666 by Johann

Simonet. It had a number of owners before shutting down in 1772. Some wares have been mistaken for Dutch delft, others took their inspiration from the Chinese late Ming. The mark most used was 'F'.

FRANKLIN CLOCK
A shelf clock with a wooden movement made by Silas Hoadley about 1825. Silas with another clockmaker, Seth Thomas, had bought out Eli Terry the celebrated maker who more or less started factory production for clocks in America. Terry had made a small fortune for himself when, owing to the shortage of metal because of Napoleon's blockade, he received an order for 4000 clock movements to be made from wood.

FREE BLOWN GLASS
Material that is worked entirely by hand and lungs, and has not been moulded or mechanically treated.

FREIBERG
Grey stoneware jugs with geometric decoration were made there during the 17th century.

FRIT
A compound of alkalies, boric acid, and lime, with silica and sometimes lead oxide, partly or wholly fused and used as a basis for certain glazes. It is also a semi-fused stony mass containing silica, alumina and alkalies, used to impart density to soft-paste porcelain.

FUKIEN
See Blanc-de-Chine

FULDA
A promising faïence manufactory in Hesse, Germany that was helped by the Prince Bishop of Fulda and was founded in 1741. To Fulda came two of the talented Meissen painters, Adam von Lowenfinck and his brother Karl Heinrich from Bayreuth. The production lasted only to 1758, but during this short time many pieces of exceptional quality were made. Much of the ware was of a dark red material to which an application of white enamel was given. The following painting and gilding was quite brilliant. Marks included 'FD' and 'Fuld'.

In 1765, the Prince Bishop also gave his patronage to a porcelain factory that was to remain working until 1790. Distinctive features of this porcelain were its perfection with both paste and glaze and the high quality of painting and finishing. The modelled figures are held with the best from any manufactory in Germany, they include rustic country romantic figures and characters from Italian Comedy. Marking was often with a cross.

FULHAM CARPETS
A carpet-knotting workshop opened in about 1750 under the patronage of the Duke of Cumberland. It was under the direction of Père Parisot, an ex-Capuchin from Lorraine, who enticed craftsmen from the Savonnerie; but still failed to remain solvent.

FULHAM STONEWARE
The pottery was established by John Dwight (*c* 1637–1703) who took out a patent in 1671 to produce stoneware. The works remained in his family until 1864, when it was taken over by a Mr Bailey. A fine series of busts and statues of royalty and mythical people were produced there, and also Bellarmines, small mugs and pear-shaped bottles with applied reliefs.

FUMED OAK
Oak that has been given a weathered look by exposure to ammonia fumes.

FÜRSTENBERG
An important porcelain manufactory started in 1747 by the Duke Carl I of Brunswick. The most flourishing period was from 1770 to 1814. Wares included: figures, candlesticks, clockcases and vases, mostly in a lavish exhuberant rococo manner. Painting was sometimes in monochrome working from engravings. A series of well-modelled medallions and busts of scholars and writers are included in the latter period. The mark was normally an 'F'.

FUSAIN WOOD
The timber from this tree, *Euonymus europaeus* the spindle tree, is hard with a pale yellow tint and is sought after by French *ébénistes*. The wood also makes excellent charcoal.

G

GADROONING
A set of rounded or lobed mouldings with notching, carving, fluting or reeding, stamped or cast curves. These were set vertically or slanting either to the right or left. A very popular ornament in the late 17th century and into and through the 18th. It was used not only on silver, but also with embroidery and sometimes with glass.

GAGLIARDI, GIUSEPPE (1687–1749)
An Italian silversmith who had his patent granted in 1742. He excelled in flamboyant large works, including a Madonna, in silver, gilt, nearly six feet high for the King of Portugal.

GALLÉ, EMILE (1846–1904)
The great French artist glassmaker from Nancy. He brought to the decoration of glass a feeling of the painter working 'alla-prima'. He sought out ethereal effects with soft gentle cloudings, and for his decorative ideas he used etching, flashing, wheel engraving and now and then enamel. He showed great skill with the handling of cameo glass. Since his time the copyists have been at work and also have not forgotten to sign their works 'Gallé', all of which has given many a headache to the collector.

GALLERY
A small decorative railing that can run round the edge of a shelf, a table or tray. It may be of plain wood strip, or fretted, or of brass, or other metals.

GALLIPOT
A small vessel used by apothecaries.

GALVANOGRAPHY
A means for copying objects such as coins, plaster-casts, stone, wood and also engraved copper plates. This can be done in copper and bronzed or gilt.

GANOSIS
A process developed by the Greeks for toning down the shine on polished marble. It involved warming the marble and applying a little wax and then buffing to a soft sheen.

GARDEN RUG
A Persian rug of the 16th and 17th centuries with a complicated design of a garden with paths, plants and the rest.

GARDNER PORCELAIN
A manufactory for porcelain was started by an Englishman, Francis Gardner, in about 1765 at Verbilki, near Moscow, and it produced under him and his family until 1891 when it was taken over by the Kuznetsov Works. Gardner made a number of figures inspired by the peasants and simple folk. In painted biscuit porcelain they expressed a sense of vigour and strength showing an influence from Meissen. Other ware made was of a quality to compete with the Imperial factory for orders from Catherine II.

GARNIER, PIERRE (c 1720–c 1789)
A leading French *ébéniste* who became a master in 1742. He had a particular skill in handling lacquer for decorating furniture and designing such as secrétaires with large panel space to show off the lacquer work.

GATE-LEG TABLE
A style of table with drop leaves supported by gate-like legs which are folded back against the frame when the leaves are dropped. It came into vogue at the end of the 17th century. The early examples generally had just one drop leaf with a single gate-leg. It arrived in America at about the same period and retained its popularity there and in England until the advent of the swing-leg table. It is also called forty-legged, hundred-legged or thousand-legged table.

GATES, WILLIAM
English cabinetmaker active around 1780 who was a specialist with inlay work and received the patronage of George III. His workshop was in Longacre, London and he was in partnership with the young Benjamin Parran.

GAUDREAU, ANTOINE ROBERT
(c 1680–c 1751)
One of the greatest *ébénistes* of the Louis XV period, he was under the patronage of the king

from about 1726. He seldom signed his work, although there are a number of pieces extant that are unquestionably from his hand; these include a medal cabinet for the king which is now in the Bibliothèque Nationale and a commode made for the king's personal apartment at Versailles.

GAUDY DUTCH
A certain type of brashly painted Staffordshire earthenware produced in the early part of the 19th century for the American trade and, in particular, the Germans of Pennsylvania.

GAUDY WELSH
A similarly treated ironstone to the foregoing, made in England for the American trade for the approximate period 1830 to 1860.

GEMINI, THOMAS
Instrument-maker who was active during the reign of Elizabeth I. He made a number of instruments for the Queen, including two astrolabes, and was a particularly skilled metal engraver, with not only his instruments but also printing plates.

GENOA LACE
A gold and silver plaited lace made from the 15th century which evolved into pillow lace. The points of Genoa were much sought after in the 17th century.

GENOA VELVET
A cut silk velvet of the late 14th century.

GENOUILLIÈRE
In armour it is a covering for the knee, introduced in medieval times.

GENOVINO
A gold coin of the Genoese Republic used between the 13th and 16th centuries; it showed a cross and gateway.

GEORGIAN STYLE
The fashion of design and decoration which had its vogue during the reign of the four Georges in England from the beginning of the 18th century until about 1830. The craftsmen of this period, particularly with furniture, were among the finest in the world.

GERMAN SILVER
An alloy introduced during the 19th century to imitate silver for jewellery settings, and tableware. It consisted of copper, zinc and nickel, the general proportions were copper 50 per cent, and equal portions of the other two. It is also called nickel silver, and white silver. The Chinese have a similar alloy, but of different proportions, which they call paktong.

GESSO
In the broad sense it is a mixture of a plaster-like substance and a glue. Gesso was and is used to cover the parts of furniture that are to be gilded. When it has hardened, a bole, generally Armenian earth, is applied to provide an enrichment for the gold-leaf.

GHIORDES KNOT
A very fine knot used with a certain type of Anatolian rug, and also termed the Turkish knot.

GIBBONS, GRINLING (1648–c 1721)
The outstanding carver, he was born in Rotterdam and came to England when he was fifteen, and by the time he was twenty-five had established himself. It was John Evelyn who was so impressed by Gibbons' carving of a 'Crucifixion' that he introduced him to Sir Christopher Wren. For Wren he worked the choir stalls in St Pauls. Other examples of his genius can be noted at Blenheim Palace, Chatsworth, Petworth and Belton House. He could carve foliage, fruit and floral designs with a fine sense of delicacy. Statues by him include Charles II, Chelsea Hospital and James II, Whitehall.

GILDING
The art of overlaying or covering with gold. It is a practice that goes far back into history. Gilded gesso decoration was used, at least, as early as the ancient Egyptians of the Fifth Dynasty. Since then gilding has been employed by craftsmen with ceramics, furniture, glass, leather, papier mâché and silver.

GILLOW, ROBERT (1703–73)
English furniture maker who set up his workshops in Lancaster about 1730 and opened a shop in London around 1761. His work was broadened and developed by his sons, Richard, Robert and Thomas. The telescopic table was an invention by Richard. The firm prospered to become the leading 18th and early 19th century furniture makers. Designs used by them came from such as Adam, Hepplewhite and Sheraton.

GIMP
A narrow ornamental fabric of cotton, silk or wool, sometimes with a metallic wire or coarse cord running through it, used as a trimming for upholstery or dresses.

GIRANDOLE
An ornamental branched candelabrum or candlestick which was generally made from metal, in particular silver or gilt-bronze. It came into fashion in the latter part of the 17th century.

GIRANDOLE MIRROR
An ornate wall mirror carrying candle branches.

GIRDLE-BOOK
One dating from before the Reformation that had an attachment allowing it to be fastened to a belt.

GIRDLE-PLATE
An iron sheet used in Scotland for cooking oatcakes on.

GISARME
A medieval weapon mounted on a long staff and carried by foot-soldiers. It generally had a broad cutting blade with a hook on the end.

GLAIVE
A somewhat similar weapon to the gisarme, but generally with a longer blade with the hook set about half way down the back. It was mainly for use by foot-soldiers when attacked by or attacking cavalry.

GLASS
A usually transparent substance, hard and brittle, made by fusing together sand and potash, or soda or both, and other ingredients. The first production of glass was probably by the early Egyptians working in the 15th century BC. It is possible that the first glass-blowing was done by the Romans in the 1st century BC. Since then there have been a number of outstanding centres of production: the enamelled Islamic glass of the 13th and 14th centuries, much of it produced in Syria; the glasshouses of Murano and Venice active from the late 13th century; the German manufactories of the 17th century with the Bohemian glass; the English flint glass developed by George Ravenscroft; the Irish Waterford; and across the Atlantic the Wistarberg glass.

Party frock with glass bead decoration, *c* 1927. Courtesy Christie's, South Kensington

GLASS CANE
Rods of glass between $\frac{1}{8}$ and $\frac{1}{4}$ of an inch (3–6 mm) in diameter used in the making of patterns in certain kinds of paperweight.

GLASTONBURY CHAIR
A type of chair with X-supports, panelled back and arm-rests, generally made of oak. A colloquial name derived from the chair at Wells which reputedly has some link with the last Abbot of Wells.

A pair of George IV Cary's globes. Celestial on the left and Terrestrial on the right. Courtesy Christie's

GLAZE

The vitreous coating of pottery or porcelain; especially one that is transparent as opposed to enamel. Among the most important glazes are lead, tin, salt and feldspathic.

GLOBES

Spherical representations of the heavens or the earth; known as celestial or terrestrial globes. Originally these were made for philosophers and astronomers in the Middle Ages. The maps were either drawn by hand and then fixed to the globes, or the details were engraved in a metal-surfaced globe. Cabinetmakers produced many elaborate and well designed stands both for table models and the larger globes that would be stood on the floor.

GLYPTOGRAPHY

The art of engraving upon precious stones.

GOBELINS

One of the world's leading tapestry manufactories. It was founded at the start as a dye-house by the Gobelin family in the 16th century at Faubourg Saint Marceau, Paris. Tapestry weaving started there about 1601. In 1662 it was bought by Colbert for Louis XIV and placed under the direction of Charles Lebrun the painter. From 1826, handmade carpets were also produced.

GOBLET

A drinking vessel with stem and foot which usually holds about one gill. It may be of glass, ceramics or metal, and may have a cover with a finial.

GODDARD, JOHN (1723–85)

The American cabinetmaker who was associated with the development of the block-front furniture made in the latter half of the 18th century.

GOFFER
To make wavy, crimped or fluted by the use of a hot iron. It is the name of the iron used. In bookbinding it means embossed or indented as with cover edges.

GOMBRON
A small port in the Persian Gulf, later called Bandar Abbas, where the English East Indian Company started a manufactory for ceramics in the first part of the 17th century. The productions included the so-called Persian ware and a kind of white porcelain, known as Gombron ware.

GOODISON, BENJAMIN
English cabinetmaker active between 1727 and 1767 in London, where he had his workshop at the Golden Spread Eagle, Longacre. An outstanding craftsman he numbered royalty among his clients.

GÖPPINGEN
A faïence manufactory set up in 1741 by Andreas Pliederhäuser at Göppingen, Württemberg. The wares were mostly low grade with a grey tin glaze. The mark when used was a stag.

GOREVAN
A type of Persian rug from the Herez district, it has a shortish wool pile set in a cotton base.

GORGET
A protective collar in armour, and a small ornamental plate on a chain worn at one time by officers with some armies. It is also a decorated neck ornament of antiquity.

GOTCH
A large stoneware jug or pitcher with a bulbous shape.

GOTHIC
In architecture the period is dated at around 1160 until 1530. The domestic furniture of the time is distinctive for the massive strength of the pieces, mostly made in rectangular forms, principally from oak. One of the exceptions was the curule chair with some curved legs. The decoration that was used was largely borrowed from their buildings – pointed arches

Gilt-metal Tabernacle clock by Caspar Hoffman of Augsburg, c 1640. Courtesy of Sotheby Parke Bernet

and graceful tracery. Foliage, especially leaves such as those from the vine, gave inspiration.

In the 18th and 19th centuries there was a Gothic revival, particularly in England.

GOTHIC CLOCKS
A rather wide and loose term for German, Italian and Swiss clocks made during the 16th and 17th centuries which had a Gothic feel about the design of their cases.

GOUTHIÈRE, PIERRE (1740–c 1813)
One of the leading workers in metal during the time of Louis XVI. His talent was various ranging from exquisite ormolu mounts to candelabra, andirons, mounts for vases, and many other decorative items for the embellishment of living. He had a long list of titled patrons, but the more they ordered items from him the longer they seemed to be in paying, so much so that the unfortunate man went bankrupt in 1788 and lingered on to die in poverty. He is best recalled for his decorations to Madame du Barry's château at Luciennes.

GRAHAM, GEORGE

English clockmaker and scientific instrument-maker, active during the first half of the 18th century. He was an assistant to Thomas Tompion.

GRAINING

Imitating the colour and grain of a fine wood on the surface of a lesser one. This can be done by means of combs, cut-corks and brushes with a variety of stains often one on top of another. The practice dates from the 17th century in England, and was at its height of popularity in the 19th century.

It is also a ring of little grains in relief near the edge of the face of a coin.

GRANDFATHER CLOCK

A term for a long-case clock, in all probability derived from the popular song 'My Grand-father's Clock', that ran through the halls of Britain and America in the 1880s.

GRAND FEU

The high-temperature kiln that will reach 1400°C for firing the body and glaze of porcelain.

GRAND GUARD

A piece of armour to give extra protection to the left shoulder and breast during a tilting tournament.

GRANDMOTHER CLOCK

A small long-case clock not overall more than about six feet tall. They are rarer than the grandfather clock, and if found should be carefully inspected for signs of alteration or marriage.

GREATBATCH, DANIEL AND WILLIAM

Skilled ceramic modellers active around 1750 to 1770, who were also producers of cream-ware from Lane Delph, Staffordshire. Much of their work had considerable originality.

GREAVE

Armour to protect the lower leg; variations were in use from the 11th to the 17th century.

GREEN, JOHN

A Sheffield cutler, active at the end of the 18th century. To gain some idea of the great variety of items being made, there is a catalogue issued by Green in which he quotes for such diverse items as: cruet frames, chamber candle-sticks, sand boxes, tumbler stands, tureens, mustards and the rest; he was also offering a substantial discount.

GREEN GLASS

Glass in its original colour, it will generally have a green cast or sometimes a tawny cast, these being the result of trace metallic substances. Such glass is generally used for bottles and some window glass, and earlier for domestic items.

GREENWICH

The site of the only royal armoury founded there by Henry VIII in 1515. The craftsmen were largely imported from Germany.

GREGORIAN CALENDAR

It was introduced by Pope Gregory XIII in 1582 and was adopted in Britain and the colonies in America in 1752.

GRIDIRON

An iron utensil in the form of a kind of grating that could be used for cooking over a fire. It was also an iron grating used for torture by fire.

GRIFFIN

A fabulous animal that appears with the body of a lion and the head and wings of an eagle. It has been used as a decorative device in several ways.

GRISAILLE

A painting in monochrome which can give a very realistic appearance of bas-relief. It was a device that Adam used on medallions, depicting classical figures.

GROAT

An English silver coin to the value of fourpence. It was issued from the time of Edward III to that of Charles II, since then it has been included with maundy money. It is also the old Scottish fourpenny piece.

GROLIER

Finely-tooled gold bindings for books were executed by Jean Grolier about 1535 when he was working in Paris. Since his time, the term Grolier has been used to describe work carried out in his manner or influenced by him. His work progressed from simple geometrical interlacings to the use of shaded or azured leaves and interlaced strapwork, often with colour being introduced into the leaves.

18th-century bottles bearing name and date seals. Courtesy Christie's

GROS

A minor coin issued by a number of European countries from the 12th century.

GROS POINT

One of the two most popular stitches in canvas embroidery, the other being Petit Point. The stitches with Gros Point are made over four cross threads and the yarn worked in quite thick.

GROTESQUE

A term applied to decorative ornament which might be painted or carved. The ornament consisted of imaginative fantastic human beings, animals and mystical objects, foliage and flowers interlaced in a fantasy of shape and colour. It was often found in the Greek and Roman palaces, and the fashion was revived in the 15th century in Italy and from there it spread.

GUARD

A protective edge for a piece of material; it might be a strip of embroidery.

GUBBIO

A place celebrated for the majolica made there. It is in the Duchy of Urbino and the potters evolved a beautiful ruby and gold lustre decoration. One of the most famous lustre painters there was Giorgo Andreoli who signed himself as Master Giorgo, and he was active in Gubbio around 1500.

GUENDJE

A Caucasian rug with a fairly fine pile and one which has geometric patterns akin to the Kazak rugs.

GUÉRIDON

A small table intended to take a light source, such as a candelabrum or large candlestick. Some early ones were made in the representation of a young negro holding a small tray. The name is probably derived from that of a young Moor who had been a galley-slave and was brought from Africa to be a page; a fashion that was popular in the late 17th century.

GUILDER

A 17th and 18th century silver coin of the Netherlands.

GUILLOCHE

A continuous repetitive decoration of two or more ribbons or bands that interlace each other and leave circular spaces for another ornament.

GUINEA

An English gold coin issued in 1663, it had initially a variable value, but settled finally at 21 shillings. It was discontinued in 1813.

GUIPURE

A loose term applied to several types of lace. It is itself a heavy lace that could be made by needle or bobbin. Guipure made of gold or silver was one of the most expensive laces, and was worn with some pride by the noblemen of the medieval courts and the ruling ones of the Renaissance. The best was made either in Italy or Flanders.

GUISARME

A long-handled axe, a foot-soldier's weapon of the Middle Ages.

GUMLEY, JOHN

English cabinetmaker and glassmaker active around 1694 to 1729 at Salisbury Exchange in the Strand, London. Chatsworth has a mirror carrying his signature.

GURI

A type of Japanese lacquer work in which a number of different coloured lacquers are layered one on the other and then are exposed as a carver works into them.

HABANER WARE

A peasant majolica produced in Moravia, the start appears to be about the end of the 16th century. Apparently the earliest potters were Germans who had emigrated. The painting was free and had a naïve brightness; characteristic wares included large dishes with wide rims and little jugs with round bodies and rather short necks.

HABERMEL, ERASMUS

A leading instrument-maker of the 16th century. From his workshop in Prague came fine instruments so exquisitely finished that they are works of art. He was particularly skilled in the handling of fire-gilding.

HADLEY CHEST

A rectangular chest with a hinged top; the front had three sunken panels and underneath there were generally two or three long drawers. It stood on short legs which were a continuation of the stiles. The whole of the front would be covered with incised carving featuring tulips, vines and leaves. The chest took its name from Hadley, Massachussetts and was a typical dower chest at the turn of the 17th and 18th centuries.

HAEMATINON

A kind of glassy substance of a beautiful red that would take a fine polish. It was used to make small cubes for mosaic or small works of art and was employed in enamels.

HAFNER

The name given to the potters during the Renaissance who were especially concerned with the production of tile-work stones. The early tiles had a green glaze but later this gave way to a white and the decorations were lively representations of allegorical and historical subjects. In the 16th century, Nuremberg was one of the main centres.

HAGUENAU

An offshoot of the Hannong manufactory at Strasbourg, it was in production in Alsace from 1724 till about 1781. The faïence made there was of exceptional quality, a tribute to the work of Adam von Löwenfinck, the talented Meissen painter.

HAIG, THOMAS

English cabinetmaker active in the latter half of the 18th century. He was the partner of Thomas Chippendale and of Chippendale's son when the father died.

HAIR
During the 19th century there was a vogue for souvenirs, memorial objects and adornments made from hair. In lockets, in the backs of watches, in pendants appeared miniature scenes and decorative patterns woven, 'embroidered' with human hair. Early in the century came bracelets, rings and necklets made from horsehair, sometimes dyed.

HALBERD
A long-handled weapon with a pikehead, which had an axe-like blade on one side and a sharp spike on the other; it was in use during the 15th and 16th centuries. For a time the halberd was the distinctive weapon for a sergeant. It was essentially for use by foot-soldiers against cavalry.

HALLMARK
In the strict sense it is the mark of authenticity and shows that the piece so marked is of the required standard and where and when it was assayed; it would also signify that duty was paid between 1740 and 1890. Included in the English hallmark would be the symbol or mark of the assay office, the maker's mark and date-letter. The marks have unfortunately drawn the attention of the fiddler who has used a number of ploys including: cutting out the marks from a genuine small piece and transposing them to a larger less quality object, and taking casts from a good set of marks and from this preparing his own dies.

Hallmark has been used in a loose way to describe the maker's mark which must be on all gold and silver objects.

HAMADAM
A Persian rug with a long pile of camels' and goats' hair, as well as wool, on a cotton base with bright strong colours and lively patterns sometimes using animals. Hamadam has recently become a trading centre for rugs.

HANAP
A medieval name for a goblet or wine cup, it usually had a stout stem and a moulded foot and sometimes a cover.

HANAU
A faïence manufactory set up in 1611 by two Dutchmen, Jacobus van de Walle and Daniel Behagel, near Frankfurt-on-Main. The early wares had a similarity with Delft, motifs showed not only a Dutch influence but also a Chinese; productions included: inkstands, radially ribbed dishes, narrow-necked jugs called Enghalskrug and vases in the Chinese design. Marks used were 'HV', and a monogram of crossed 'A's with the word 'Hanau'.

HANDKERCHIEF TABLE
One that has a single drop leaf, and the top and leaf are both triangular so that folded it will fit into a corner, but opened out it is a square. The name was probably derived from the fact that when closed it looks like a triangular folded handkerchief.

HAN DYNASTY (206 BC to AD 220)
A period of great advance in the arts in China. Ceramics are represented by collections of mortuary ware of great variety, models including animals, cooking utensils, images of deceased, and servants. The potters of the Han dynasty had learned well the techniques of their trade, notably glazing. A red-toned earthenware carried a brown or green glaze which after being buried emerged with a misty soft, almost metallic looking, patina. Some glazed Han ware has relief decoration and a shallow incised marking.

HANNONG FAMILY
Charles-François and his two sons, Paul and Joseph, who were associated with the faïence manufactories at Strasbourg and Haguenau; from which came some of the finest faïence ever produced in France.

HARDANGER
A beautiful type of openwork embroidery done in the mountainous district of Norway that lies to the north-west of Oslo. It consists of a system of patterns built up with squares or diamonds.

HARD-PASTE
This implies porcelain made from kaolin and Cornish stone, petuntse, this latter substance being fusible imparts translucency.

HARE'S FUR GLAZE
Found with some examples of Sung pottery, it exhibits attractive radiating rust-tinted streaks evocative of the fur of the animal.

HAREWOOD
The wood of the sycamore maple, *Acer pseudoplatanus,* it is generally stained and used in cabinetmaking.

HARLAND, THOMAS (1735–1807)

A clockmaker working around 1773 to 1806 in Norwich, Connecticut. He ranks high in the list of American horologists.

HARLEIAN

A bookbinding style of the late 17th and early 18th centuries. It was named after Robert Harley, 1st Earl of Oxford, and was distinguished by broad tooled borders and centre panels with pineapple figures.

HARLEQUIN CHINA

In particular, sets of cups and saucers that have different colours and designs applied to them. It had a certain vogue in the late-Victorian period.

HARPSICHORD

A keyboard instrument that came just before the piano, it has two keyboards and the strings are plucked by a quill or leather point, rather than struck. In appearance it looks like a small grand piano.

HARRIS, PHILIP

A London locksmith active around 1700. He was skilled in working latten by engraving and using a variety of decorative punches.

HAUBERK

A coat of chain-mail that resembled a long tunic. It was worn by the Normans at the time of the conquest. It had a slit in the skirt at the back and the front to enable the wearer to sit in a saddle, and the sleeves only came to just below the elbow.

HÄUFEBECHER

A small German silver cup. It was generally found in sets, the cups being made to nest one inside the other. It was introduced in about 1550.

HAWKSBEAK

A Greek compounded moulding based on a *cavetto*. When ornamented it carries leaf patterns found with the Doric order.

HEADING SWORD

A long, broad, double-edged sword with either a round or squared point. It had a hilt long enough to accommodate two hands and was the weapon for execution on the continent, notably Germany, where it was employed from the 16th century until the first years of the 19th century.

HEAUME

A 13th-century great helmet of strong construction. At first it had a flat top and covered practically the whole head and neck, nearly to the shoulders. Later the top was made conical with a rounded point, the idea being that with this shape blows were more likely to glance off it. Underneath the knight generally wore a close fitting steel cap or a hood of mail.

HELMET CREAMER

One in the form of an inverted helmet, popular from the first quarter of the 18th century; although usually made from silver there have been examples in earthenware and porcelain.

HELMETS

These head protective devices have progressed through the ages and have included: the Greek, which sometimes had a nosepiece and generally a crest; the Roman, normally with some form of crest and at times cheek or jaw pieces; the 11th-century Norman casque with rigid nosepiece; the 14th-century basinet; the 15th-century sallet; the 15th-century tilting helmet; the 16th-century armet; and the late 16th-century morion.

HEMSTITCH

A type of drawn-thread work in which a few parallel threads at the head of the hem are pulled out, and then the cross threads are fastened in small clusters.

HENRI DEUX WARE

A beautiful ivory-coloured pottery which was at first thought to have been made at Poitou, then at Orion, and later most experts ascribe its origin to Saint-Porchaire; basing their thoughts on records from the Château de Thouars and also an inventory of the property of the Lord of Saint-Porchaire.

HEPPLEWHITE, GEORGE

Although he was one of Britain's leading cabinetmakers, very little is definitely known about his life. He certainly started off as an apprentice to Gillow at Lancaster and later carried on his business in the Parish of St Giles, Cripplegate, London, and when he died in 1786 the administration of his estate was granted to his widow Alice. She nobly carried on calling the firm A. Hepplewhite & Co. The principal sources for identifying his work are *The Cabinet Maker and Upholsterer's Guide*, which was first published in 1788, and *The*

Cromwell lobster tail helmet and Japanese helmet. Courtesy Phillips

Cabinet Makers' London Book of Prices in which there were ten of his designs.

Distinctive characteristics of his work include lightness, delicacy and elegance. As with Chippendale, much of his creative force went into designs for chairs; the backs of many of his examples being enriched with festoons of wheat-ears, fern leaves and the Prince of Wales feathers. He was skilled with the use of exotic woods for inlay work. He was also noted for his bedsteads.

HERAT
A fine rug or carpet woven at Herat in Afghanistan. The pile was of medium length on a cotton foundation. The pattern was generally an overall one featuring fish or leaf motifs. The Herat is generally thought of as the finest of the Persian rugs.

HERCULANEUM POTTERY
A manufactory founded on the right bank of the Mersey in about 1793 by Richard Abbey. When it was taken over by Worthington, Humble and Holland, they named it Herculaneum. The main wares were creamware which were often printed in black and blue, and in addition there were some objects in the Staffordshire manner. The mark was as its name.

Liverpool was a loose term in America for creamware made at the end of the 18th and beginning of the 19th century, not only from Liverpool (Herculaneum) but also certain Staffordshire workers' production.

HEREK
Rugs made from about 1850 in Turkey, many of which were for the Imperial Court.

HEREND
A porcelain manufactory set up in the Bakony Forest, Hungary, in about 1839, under the supporting eye of Count Charles Esterhazy. Most of the production was centred on copies and imitations of such as: Meissen, Sèvres, Capodimonte and Chinese and Japanese.

HEREZ
A rug in the Persian group; it has a cotton base with a short woollen pile.

HERRING BONE BANDING
See Feather Banding

HERRING BONE STITCH
A decorative embroidery stitch in which the threads are worked in a cross-stitch manner. It is also used to secure the edge of material too thick to be hemmed.

HERROBØE

A Norwegian faïence manufactory established there in 1757 by Peter Hoffnagel who had found a suitable clay on his estate. In all, production lasted until 1778; wares included: 'Bishop' bowls, table trays and tableware. They had a rococo flamboyance and were painted with a blue or manganese purple.

HESS, SEBASTIAN AND PAUL JOHANN

The brothers were born in Bamberg, Germany, and were active in the last half of the 18th century. They were highly-skilled ivory carvers, working in miniature they left some exquisite detailed tiny landscapes.

HICKORY

An American hardwood, *Carya alba,* useful in cabinetmaking. Akin to it is the Australian featherwood.

HIGHBOY

An American piece, it usually consists of a tall chest of drawers mounted on a lowboy; the whole is often surmounted by a broken-arch pediment and often has finials. It came in about 1690 and the peak of the vogue lasted until about 1780. In decorative appearance it varied from the richly-carved versions from around Philadelphia to the austere plain finish from New England. In England it is known as the tallboy.

HIGHDADDY

A similar piece to a highboy, but one where the chest of drawers is mounted on a lowboy or frame without drawers.

HIGH-TEMPERATURE COLOURS

Those that can stand the fierce heat of the high-temperature kiln; also termed Grand Feu Colours.

HIGH-WARP TAPESTRY

One made on a loom, in which the warp is arranged on a vertical plane, as the Gobelins; low-warp tapestry is made on a flat loom, as at Aubusson and Beauvais.

HILLIARD, NICHOLAS (*c* 1547–1619)

The leading miniature painter of his time, he was born in Exeter and then moved to London where he set up his studio. He also produced some medals including that to celebrate the defeat of the Armada in 1588; in heavy relief this shows a powerful likeness

Queen Anne Fan-carved Mahogany Highboy. New England 18th century. Courtesy Sotheby Parke Bernet

of Elizabeth I on one side and a tranquil sea swept clear save for a few distant vessels and some sea beasts on the other.

HIRADO WARE

Fine-quality Japanese blue-and-white porcelain produced at Mikawachi in the Hizen province; the best came from the time between about 1750 and 1830.

HISPANO-MORESQUE

A Spanish lustre ware made by the Moorish potters for the period about 1450 to 1520. The painting was bold with an attractive pure naïve quality. Motifs included: leaves, writhing stem forms, and sometimes animals such as gazelles.

The term can also apply to oriental rugs found in Spain.

HITCHCOCK CHAIR

One that is named after Lambert Hitchcock; he was a 19th-century Connecticut cabinet-maker. The seat started off as rush but later was often cane or solid wood. The front legs were generally splayed and tapered to ball feet. The back had a turned crest rail and was slightly bent. The finish was generally black paint with some gilding and bright floral motifs.

HIZEN WARE

The production of the province of Hizen, including such celebrated wares as: Hirado, Imari and Nabeshima, noted for rich decoration.

HO CHOU

The pottery in the Shansi province in China that is credited with producing some of the finest ware during the T'ang dynasty.

HÖCHST

A manufactory in this German town that produced quality faïence and porcelain from about 1750 to the end of that century. Influences came from Meissen and Strasbourg and wares included: figures, reliefs, dishes and tableware. Marks used were a wheel with six spokes, and later the Electoral Hat over the wheel.

HOCK GLASS

One that has a round bowl curved in slightly at the top and is mounted on a tall slender stem.

HOCK LEG

A cabriole leg having a broken curve on the inside of the knee.

HOGARTH CHAIR

A loose term for a splat-back chair with distinctive curving lines and cabriole legs. It was a type that turns up in William Hogarth's (1697–1764) paintings. The basic double curve being related to Hogarth's declared 'line of beauty'.

HOLITSCH

A Hungarian faïence manufactory started in 1743 and in production until about 1827. Wares included a number in imitated styles such as: Castelli, Wedgwood's Queen's Ware and black basalt.

HOLLIE POINT LACE

A needle-point lace of various types, made in Britain for ecclesiastical purposes; the name being a corruption of holy. The practice started in the middle of the 16th century. Two hundred years later it was also used for caps and babies' gowns. It uses a kind of twisted buttonhole stitch with skipped stitches which gives it an attractive look of lightness.

HOLLINS, SAMUEL

A potter of Shelton, Staffordshire, active in the latter part of the 18th century, who produced colour stoneware in the manner of Wedgwood. He marked it 'S. Hollins', and the small pottery was continued by his sons.

HOLLY

Fine-grained, hard, pale wood, *Ilex aquifolium*, useful with marquetry and inlay.

HONAN

Wares from the time of the Sung dynasty, and probably produced in the Honan province. It is distinctive by the black and brown glazes. Objects included: bottles, bowls, vases and jars.

HONEY

At one time gold was ground in honey to produce a powder; when the grinding was finished the honey was dissolved away in water.

HONITON LACE OR GUIPURE

A famous type made at the town in Devonshire, from at first a coarse thread and then from about 1600 a fine thread. This latter was said to have been introduced by the Flemings who had escaped from the persecutions of the Duke of Alba. Honiton lace owes its great reputation to the sprigs made separately with bobbins on a pillow; afterwards these were either worked in with a delicate pillow net or sewn on to it. This net was made of the finest thread from Antwerp.

Heathcoat's invention, however, dealt a fatal blow to the trade of the net-makers, and since then Honiton lace is usually made by uniting the sprigs on a pillow, or joining them with a needle by various stitches.

HON-ZŌGAN

Japanese inlay technique which is used to decorate iron vessels by hammering gold or silver wire into previously engraved lines.

HOPFER, DANIEL

German armourer active in Augsberg around 1510, and one who was concerned with the development of etching for decorating armour.

HORN

The types most often used came from buffaloes, cattle and rams. It was either used in the natural shape or split and flattened. Objects made included: drinking vessels, handles for tableware, combs, snuff-boxes and fans.

HORN BOOK

A type of childs' primer, it was generally a piece of parchment or paper on which would be the alphabet, or simple religious texts or prayers that would be mounted on a board. It would be protected by a piece of flattened and transparent horn. It was in use from about the late 16th century to the early 18th century.

HORSE BRASSES

Their origin is possibly two thousand years ago when like objects were used to adorn the mounts of the important and noble. Opinions have been expressed that some designs were evolved as a protection against the evil eye but these cannot truly be proved. It is more probable that they were just for decoration. Although fairly frequent examples started to turn up in the 18th century, it was not until about 1850 that their popularity grew. It is possible to gain some idea of their date by the colour and quality of the brass.

Today, they are much sought after by collectors, preferably on the original leather harness. But it is an area heavily infiltrated by the faker and it is wise to give particularly the backs of specimens a thorough examination with a magnifying glass.

HORSEHAIR

An upholstery cloth which was made partly with horsehair and used from around the last quarter of the 18th century onwards. It was particularly popular for chairs as it was hard-wearing.

HUGUENOT WORK

In the 16th and 17th centuries many French Protestants were so savagely persecuted in their own country that they fled to America, Britain, Germany, the Netherlands and Switzerland, bringing their skills with them they greatly enriched the decorative arts in these countries.

A large group of Huguenot silk-weavers set themselves up in workshops around Spitalfields, London. The largest evacuation of these people came in 1685 after the Revocation of the Edict of Nantes by Louis XV. Highly talented silversmiths of Huguenot extraction who came to work in Britain included Pierre Harache, Augustin Courtauld, and Paul de Lamerie.

HULL

A pottery started in 1802 in Yorkshire; it produced earthenware in the Staffordshire manner. From about 1825, William Bell was in charge and from this time the wares may carry a date and 'Bellevue Pottery Hull' circling a single bell or two bells.

HUMPEN

A large German cylindrical drinking vessel of glass that was normally well decorated with enamel; in vogue during the latter part of the 16th century and through the 17th century.

HUNGARIAN POINT

A type of embroidery worked on a coarse foundation using parallel zigzag patterns which give it a sawtooth look.

HUNTING CHAIR

A somewhat nebulous term. Sheraton mentions such a chair being 'stuffed all over except the legs, which are of mahogany'; he also has an illustration in his *Cabinet Dictionary*, published in 1803, which shows a chair that has a leg rest which would pull out. The younger Chippendale has mention of his version that had a caned seat.

HUNTING RUG

A Persian rug of the 17th century which used intricate designs with forests, huntsmen, hounds and their prey.

HUNTING SWORD

One with a single-edged blade and a gentle curve that was intended for the chase; but was also worn for show by some commanding officers in the 18th century. It would have been of little use in combat as it had no protective guard for the striking hand.

HUSK FESTOON

One that uses a decorative garland of husks, the outer pods and covers; a motif that was popular in the latter part of the 18th century.

HUTCH

An early primitive and massively constructed type of chest often raised on legs and of more than one tier. It was in use in the late medieval time. The name is derived from the French *huche,* meaning in a broad sense 'a kneading trough'. It might also be used for grain storage and even as a clothes receptacle.

HUTCH TABLE

A stout simple early table that would have a cubby or box-like container below a hinged top.

HYALINE

A substance resembling glass, transparent as glass, crystalline.

HYALITE

A colourless variety of opal; it is sometimes as clear as glass, at other times translucent with a whitish haze.

HYDRIA

An ancient water jar that can be distinguished by its horizontal side handles and a single vertical back handle.

HYDROSTATIC BALANCE

One for weighing substances in water to find their specific gravities.

HYLOGRAPH

An instrument for tracing designs on to glass. Hylography is the art of engraving on glass.

ICE GLASS

It is also termed crackle glass. The effect of an overall crazing of tiny cracks is caused by immersing the still warm, recently worked glass into cold water. The surface and object is consolidated once more by reheating.

ICE PAIL

For cooling a single bottle of wine; it may be made from silver, plate or china and will consist of an outer container for the ice, or inner for the bottle, and generally a lid. Simpler versions may be just the outer container and no lid.

ICONOGRAPHY

The science that deals with statues and images, bas-reliefs, busts, medals and other similar representations.

IGEL

A German squat glass dating from the 16th century. It will usually be found made of green glass, and if decorated will have a series of small prunts fused to the main body.

ILMENAU

A porcelain manufactory started in 1777 in Thuringia. The ware was partly influenced by Meissen, and at times used the crossed swords mark, also made were medallion reliefs imitating Wedgwood's jasper.

IMARI

A Japanese porcelain that was initially treated with an attractive underglaze of blue and then a brownish-red was added, and latterly gold. It took its name from the port of Imari. The porcelain became a sought-after export in the middle of the 17th century. As orders came in from Europe so did the decoration show European influence.

IMPASTO

With ceramics it is a technique for putting on the colour so thickly that it remains standing up in relief.

IMPERIAL FACTORY

The leading pottery in Russian that, after several abortive starts, began successful operation in the reign of Catherine II from about 1763. With usual affluence of style she ordered painters and modellers to be brought in from France and Germany. Early production, not unexpectedly, favoured the Meissen style. In 1779, Jean Rachette came from Copenhagen to direct the figure modelling. Parallel to this was the production of beautiful vases with medallions bearing not only the likeness of Catherine but depictions of allegorical beauties, and magnificent tableware.

The love of ceramics flowed strongly in the Russian Imperial family, for after Catherine came her son Paul, who, although he lived in a demented state of self-exaltation, possessed to the full this passion. He founded an extension of the potteries near his private palace at Gatchina. He had the craftsmen producing large wares that bore medallions showing important buildings and landscapes. Murder struck this one down, but his successor, Alexander I, kept the factory fully occupied in spite of Napoleon's ill-judged invasion. It was Alexander who brought in a high import tariff for foreign ceramics, an action which gave considerable impetus to private businesses in this line in Russia. The Imperial patronage continued through Nicolas I, Alexander II, Alexander III, until Nicolas II under whom standards started to fall.

The marks from the Imperial Factory began with a black double-headed eagle, and went on from the reign of Catherine II with the sovereign's initials – often surmounted by the Imperial crown.

IMPERIAL RUSSIAN SERVICE
Surely the largest service ever ordered or made, it consisted of 952 pieces and was of cream earthenware decorated with 1244 scenes from England, and each piece also carried on its border a shield in which was painted a green frog. From this came the secondary name of the 'Frog' service. It was ordered in 1773 by Catherine II from Josiah Wedgwood.

IMPRESSED MARKS
In ceramics they are those which are stamped or pressed into the clay before firing or glazing. They make matters a little more difficult for the faker than the painted marks, but with a quartz stick these too can be ground off.

IMPRINT
The publisher's and printer's names on the title page or pages at the front or at the end of a book. Books printed before 1465 did not bear an imprint. After this date until the last part of the 16th century the imprint was put at the end of a book, then it appeared at the front and the publisher's name and the printer's are often combined. Finally the publisher appeared at the bottom of the title page and the printer on the reverse.

INCE, WILLIAM and MAYHEW, JOHN
English cabinetmakers active from about 1758 to 1810 at Broad Street, Golden Square, Soho and at Marshall Street, Carnaby Market, London. They are best recalled for their designs that were published in *The Universal System of Household Furniture* which had some 300 plates which showed influence from the Gothic and rococo styles.

INCISED DECORATION
Ornamentation applied to objects of silver or some other metals, woods, ceramics and glass by engraving or fine chiselling. It can sometimes be termed sgraffito.

INCUNABULA
In the broad sense it implies books printed before 1500. The singular form is incunabulum.

INCUSE
In numismatics it is a mark struck or impressed into a coin by a punch.

INDIAN EMBROIDERY
Work that exhibits great richness in choice of colours and is worked with a variety of stitches. The beginning of the art probably goes back to the 4th century BC. One of the most sought after items is a cashmere worked shawl; the ground may be either silk or fine wool and very elaborate border patterns are built one on the other until the whole shawl is nearly covered with embroidery.

INDIENNE
A painted or printed cotton which was first produced in India, and which has been imitated in a number of other places.

INGLE
A medieval Scottish word for a fire upon a hearth against a wall, and also for a fireplace.

INKSTANDS
These have been made according to records since the Tudor times, although the earliest existing silver example dates from about 1630.

English Art Nouveau bronze inkstand, *c* 1900. Courtesy of Sotheby's, Belgravia

They were first called standishes and the most usual type consists of a rectangular tray which carries an inkwell, a bell, a taper stick and a sand or pounce box (to hold the blotting material); there would also be depressions or small racks for the quills or pens. By the time of the late 18th century, cut glass silver mounted bottles were used for the ink to prevent the staining of the silver holder.

Inkstands could also have a small knife to sharpen the quills and a little pot for holding shot into which the pen could be thrust to clear congealed ink.

INLAY
The decorating of a wood surface by cutting out the design and letting in thin pieces of other woods with a variety in their colours and grain, and other materials. For instance: ivory and bone, semi-precious stones such as amethyst, lapis lazuli and agate; mother-of-pearl, marble, glass, tortoiseshell, brass, bronze and other metals. The final surface presented is absolutely flat. The method is in contrast to marquetry which is a veneer technique.

INRŌ
A small case or set of cases for holding medicines and perfumes used by the Japanese and carried from the girdle. They were generally exquisitely decorated with lacquer.

INTAGLIO
Forms or designs that are sunk into a surface as opposed to those that are raised in relief. The term applies particularly in the context of antiques, to jewellery with incised gems.

INTARSIA OR TARSIA
A type of inlay decoration of a wooden surface which was in fashion during the Renaissance. It relied only on the inlaying of different kinds of woods to build up elaborate landscapes, figures, flowers, fruit, architectural scenes, scrolls and arabesques.

IRIDESCENCE
With ceramics and particularly glass it is the quality of exhibiting changes of colour. With Roman glass it can often be seen very clearly and in this case it is caused by a long burial

in damp conditions that brings on a surface decay.

IRISH POINT LACE
Largely this started with work carried on in a Convent school at Youghal which began about 1852. The designs were to a degree adaptions from earlier Flemish or Italian points. Other notable centres include a convent of the Poor Clares at Kenmare, Co. Kerry, and the Carmelite Convent at New Ross, Co. Wexford. In many places quite exquisite and delicate crochet work was carried out and exists through to today.

IRISH STITCH
A long upright stitch used on fine canvas for grounding, its distinctive characteristic is that the stitches start alternately from the last row of the canvas and the third. This lets the stitches of one line reach to the centre of those in the next line and this can produce an even gradation or change with the colours used.

IRONSTONE
A hard white pottery first made in England in the 18th century. It was patented in 1813 by C. J. Mason as 'Ironstone China'. The decoration was generally blue-printed or painted using elaborate and flowing floral patterns. Plates had scrolling and wavy edges, and larger vessels such as tureens had a rococo appearance and often had some red painting and gilding. American potters of the latter half of the 19th century produced a large amount of similar ware describing it as flint china and white granite.

ISOCEPHALIC
A type of relief in which all the heads of the principal figures, standing, sitting or mounted, are arranged in a horizontal line, or very near to; as might be noted in a bas-relief or carved decoration, particularly that worked with a Classic inspiration.

ISPAHAN
A Persian rug from the 16th century in which imaginative designs and patterns were built up, using beautifully blended colours. The foundations were of linen or sometimes silk with a fine wool pile.

ISTORIATO
A type of painted decoration, associated with Italian ware and Urbino in particular. It

£10 note showing a Ploughman, issued in 1929 by the Currency Commission and the Bank of Ireland. Courtesy Stanley Gibbons

implies an overall painted ornamentation, that seldom leaves any border, using landscapes with figures and architectural features. The manner was said to have been brought to its highest peak by Nicola Pellipario, working after 1528, one of the leading majolica painters.

IVORY

A material which comes from a variety of mammal sources, including elephant, narwhal and walrus, that has been used for carving since prehistoric times. Egyptian and Assyrian specimens of the art are of a date at least as early as that of Moses. The early Greeks and Romans worked small statuettes, and the carvings from the 4th to the 7th century had considerable quality and are also useful visual records for the study of Early Christian Art.

Some hundreds of years later comes the time when, for many, ivory carving was at its height, a period from around 1250 to about 1450. All manner of objects drew the craftsman's skill; small diptychs and triptychs, crozier heads, covers for books, holders for relics, combs, jewel caskets and crucifixes. Centres for workshops included Germany, Italy, France and England.

IVORY PORCELAIN

A ware developed by Worcester; a glazed Parian, which has a surface like ivory.

JACARANDA

The wood of the south American tree genus *jacaranda,* which is extremely hard with a pleasant black and near-white blotched look which has been used in cabinetwork.

JACK

A coarse, short, medieval protective jacket worn by foot-soldiers. It was made of thick cheap leather and sometimes was lined with metal plates.

A large leather jug, *see* Black Jack.

JACK BOOT

A large, heavy, thick leather boot which reached to above the knee, with reinforcement over the instep to take stirrup wear, a flared top and spur; worn by cavalry during the 17th and 18th centuries.

JACKFIELD

A Shropshire pottery and one of the oldest in the country; parish registers of Stoke-on-Trent record in 1560 potters 'from Jackfield'. The ware from around 1760 was a red earth covered with a very black glaze, sometimes having scrolls and flowers in relief.

JACOBEAN

A collective name for the Arts during the reign of James I (1603–25), by a rather free extension the name can take in the whole of the Stuart period (1603–88).

JACOBEAN EMBROIDERY

See Crewel Work

JACOBITE GLASSES

Drinking vessels carrying cryptic decorations connected with the Jacobite cause and associations that were propaganda for the Pretenders. Motifs included: the rose for the House of Stuart, the star, the oakleaf, and the word *Fiat* which means 'let it be done' and was a common toast and also password with the Jacobite sympathisers. They were used in the first half of the 18th century.

JACOBS, LAZARUS AND ISAAC

Father and son who were in business in the latter half of the 18th century and early part of the 19th in Bristol as glass-makers and cutters. Isaac produced a number of quality blue glass decanters, some with gilt ornamentation.

JACQUARD

An attachment for a loom which facilitates the weaving of figured fabrics, it consists of a chain of differently perforated cards which activate devices to lift the warp threads in the correct succession to produce the pattern. It was named after Joseph Marie Jacquard of Lyons who died in 1834.

JADE
A mineral, a semi-precious stone used in jewellery. It is generally green, but may range from a blackish to a milky translucent white colour. It will take deep and open carving. The clear white and green specimens are the most prized. The Chinese term the dark green, Pi Yü and the beautiful emerald Fei-ts'ui.

JALOUSIE
A blind or shutter with horizontal slats intended by adjustment to admit air and light but to keep out sun and rain. It was probably introduced around the end of the 16th century. In Europe, early in the 18th century, it was referred to as a Venetian jalousie. From this it was named a Venetian blind, and at least one workshop in Philadelphia was advertising them at the end of the 18th century.

JAMBEAU
See Greave

JAMBIYA
A vicious, double-edged and curved dagger with a strengthening rib down the middle of the blade. It is particularly a weapon of the Arabs.

JANUS
An ancient Roman deity, probably the god of the household door, he appears on the old Roman coin, the As, with two opposite faces which could be symbolism for the two faces of a door. The As was a bronze coin which originally weighed about twelve ounces, but by 89 BC it had been reduced to half an ounce.

JAPANNING
Giving a high finish to woodwork. There are many different approaches to this; one of the basic methods is to apply a number of layers of pigmented shellac varnish to a white or coloured glue-whiting priming. Copal oil varnish may also be used. The recipe for the famous 'Vernis Martin' has been lost, but it is believed to have been something like: copal 3 parts, linseed oil $1\frac{1}{2}$ parts, turpentine $4\frac{1}{2}$ parts.

The fashion for lacquered furniture and other objects started about 1660 and reached its height in the second quarter of the 18th century. When japanning was applied to metals, after each coat of the rich toned varnish, the object would be baked to harden and consolidate the layer. Decoration was by painting and gilding,

the gold sometimes being reduced to a powder (*see* Honey) and then mixed with a medium.

JARDINIÈRE
An ornamental stand or small table to display or hold flowers or plants in pots. In ceramics it is often in two pieces; the upper part being the receptacle and the lower the stand, and these can range from about three feet to upwards of five feet. The table type was brought in during the reign of Louis XVI and sometimes included Sèvres plaques set in the veneer on the top and a surrounding metal frieze.

JASPER WARE
A fine stoneware produced by Wedgwood that could be coloured right through by the addition of various metallic oxides; the process was mastered in 1775. The principal body colours are the famous blue and green, a warm lilac, and black. On to these coloured bodies were applied the white reliefs. From 1780, the colouring of the bodies was done by dipping (Jasper Dip as it was known.) For a period Wedgwood made a good profit with the Jasper; apparently none of his workmen had any idea what the material they were working with was made from. But at last the secret came out when a dishonest employee found a letter giving details of the ingredients, and this he sold. Soon there were imitations of Jasper not only coming from Staffordshire but also in Europe where even the celebrated house of Sèvres joined in the copying.

Böttger, the genius of Meissen, produced in about 1707 a ruddy-red stoneware which he named 'Jasper' after the semi-precious stone. The experimenting was carried out in conjunction with Tschirnhaus, and the finished red Jasper ware was so hard that it could be cut and polished by a lapidary and gilded by a goldsmith, it was made from a red-brown clay found at Meissen.

JELLY GLASS
An early 18th-century one for holding the sweet was a simple little round glass with a folded lip. Later came a trumpet bowl on a straight stem and sometimes with handles. Another type had a bell-shaped bowl on a round foot.

JELLY MOULD
A bygone from the kitchen of yesterday that is now sought after, often to act as an ornament. They have been made from glass,

china and metal and appear to have been used from around 1700. Wedgwood made them in creamware. Some examples were in two parts, the outer case holding the jelly, whilst into the middle of the setting jelly a slender cone or pyramid would be put, and left in place when the jelly was turned out in order to support it.

JENNENS AND BETTRIDGE
A Birmingham firm active from about 1816 to 1864; they were probably the largest manufacturers of papier mâché, from which material came a wide selection of objects including: boxes, trays, screens and bed-heads and ends.

JENSEN, GERREIT
English cabinetmaker active from around 1680 until his death in 1715. He supplied furniture to the Royal Households of Charles II and Queen Anne. One of his specialities was the making of fine mirrors. Crown records show that he also worked with lacquer and inlaying metal and it is possible he was the only craftsman of his time using the Boulle style.

A dish by Thomas Toft. It is nearly 18 ins (45 cms) in diameter. Courtesy Christie's

JERSEY GLASS COMPANY

American firm active from about 1824 for around forty years, they did considerable work on the development of machine pressing. They were situated over the Hudson from New York.

JERSEY PORCELAIN AND EARTHENWARE COMPANY

American firm, set up in 1825 in Jersey city, New Jersey; it was later sold to David Henderson and became known as D. & J. Henderson Co. The first porcelain made in America came from here, and the quality was high; in 1826 the company received a silver medal for excellence. Decoration was mainly carried out in gold. Later they also produced creamware and a form of Rockingham. Mark generally used was the firm's name plus 'Jersey City' impressed in a circular manner.

JESUIT WARE

Porcelain produced in China which used decoration inspired by the Jesuit Fathers. Early pieces carried crucifixions painted in blue on a white ground. Later came the use of other Biblical motifs. The French Jesuits were active in China from about 1600 and in the end established quite a thriving export line.

JET

A very dense velvet-black mineral similar to coal, which on being worked will take a very high glass-like polish. Particularly in the Victorian period it was much in demand for mourning jewellery. It was also used to make such as: buttons, paper-knives and toy ornaments. It was copied in a cheap black glass, and today has been largely superseded by an artificially-blackened chalcedony that is termed Black Onyx.

JEWELLED PORCELAIN

A distinctive decoration adopted by Sèvres in 1787, it consisted of dropping small spots of coloured enamel on to previously laid gold and the whole was fused by firing. Probably the first work in this manner was done earlier in the 18th century at the St Cloud works. In Britain the method was taken up by Copeland, Goss, Wedgwood and Worcester.

JEWELLERS' CEMENT

An adhesive used by jewellers which is made up from mastic resin, isinglass and sal ammoniac dissolved to saturation point in alcohol.

JEWELLER'S ROUGE

A reddish powder, ferric oxide, it is used for polishing gems, glass and metals.

JOEY

Slang term for the fourpenny piece. It was also a small glass taking its name from the coin which at one time would have been the price for a measure or tot.

JOGGLING

A primitive method of decorating a soft alloy or metal like pewter. It is done using a very small sharp chisel which is held at a slight angle from the metal and then pushed with a rocking motion. The marks left have a fuzzy appearance and the lines are laboured.

JOHNSON, THOMAS

English furniture designer and carver active in 1755 in Soho, London. He is best recalled for two books; *Twelve Girandoles* and *The Book of the Carver*, and also a part work on new designs.

JOHNSON AND REAT

Skilled armourers active in Philadelphia during the first half of the 19th century; makers of fine quality swords and sabres often with chased and modelled silver hilts.

JOHNSTON, THOMAS

A leading American exponent of japanning, he was at work around the middle of the 18th century in Boston, Massachusetts, which town was a centre for the craft.

JOINED FURNITURE

That made by a joiner employing such as mortise and tenon joints held by pegs as opposed to the use of glue.

JOINT STOOL

One made by a joiner with the parts held by mortise and tenon joints. Often made from oak, early examples still around date back to the 15th century.

JONES, INIGO (1573–1652)

English architect, born in London, who also spent some time designing furniture.

JUNGFRAUENBECHER

A double celebration drinking cup associated with Germany, introduced about 1565. It was made in silver in the form of a girl. Her full skirt was the larger container, whilst in her uplifted arms she holds a smaller swivelling cup. The main purpose for the jungfrauen-becker was as a toast cup for the bridegroom and bride. He would empty the skirt container and then turn it over without spilling the wine from the smaller cup and hand it to his espoused.

JU WARE

A blue or white porcelain of the Sung dynasty (960–1278), it was originally made at Ju-Chou, Honan province, hence the name. Largely it was made for the Imperial Court. The body was a rather pale reddish-brown with a crackled glaze.

KABA-KARAMAN

A rug of Turkish classification, with a fairly long, coarse wool pile.

KABISTAN

A Caucasian rug that is considered one of the finest; a fine wool pile with mosaic patterns sometimes with small flower details. It was woven in the Baku area.

KAENDLER, J. J. (1706–75)

The most talented of the modellers at Meissen and the inspiration for so many modellers to come. He had with him a number of skilled men, including Johann Eberlein and Peter Reinicke. He worked under the patronage of the eccentric and colourful Count Brühl of whom, *Chambers Journal* in 1857 reported 'The Dresden porcelain reached its highest development under the administration of the famous Count Brühl, the same in whose wardrobe Frederick the Great, when he took Dresden, found 1500 wigs, with suits of clothes and snuff-boxes to match. His taste for magnificence made itself felt at Meissen, and we owe to him the most beautiful specimens it produced.'

Kaendler modelled men and animals of natural size as well as the delightful and exquisite small figures that have a life and vitality of their very own. Their influence is evidenced in the modelling which was to come from Bow, Chelsea and Derby.

KAIRAKU-EN WARE

A Japanese porcelain, commissioned from Eiraku by the chief of the Kishū province.

KAISERTELLER

A pewter plate from 17th-century Germany, which was ornately worked and usually had an emperor's head included in the design.

KAKIEMON

A Japanese potter of Nangawara in Arita, active around 1650, who was probably the first to enamel Japanese porcelain.

It is also a Japanese ware, a development of Imari, which had a blue underglaze and delightful refined decoration in enamel, with sea-green, violet and rust-red among the predominant colours. The results were to influence a number of the European establishments, including Chelsea, Chantilly and Meissen.

KAMASHIMO ZASHI

The first sword that a young Japanese boy will wear when in full ceremonial dress. It has a short blade and a decorated lacquer scabbard.

KAOLIN

This is from the Chinese word for china clay and has been adopted into English usage and describes all porcelain clays that endure firing without discolouration.

KARATSU WARE

It was produced by a pottery in the Hizen province from around the 13th century. Productions included a stoneware made largely by imported Korean craftsmen.

KAS

A type of Dutch cupboard or wardrobe, generally panelled and often decorated with floral designs, and only very seldom carved. It had two doors and normally just one drawer at the bottom. There were also double versions with two sets of double doors. Both types had a broad overhanging cornice.

KASHAN

A city famous for its fine carpets and rugs, the foundations of which can be cotton, linen or even silks, and the pile short and of fine wool or silk, with rich colours and the use of ivory as a base tone. Unfortunately, beautiful rugs such as these and others from the area have become a target for the fiddler. A few years ago, he would leave his imitations beside a road to 'age' in the sun and dust. Today the more up-to-date operators give the rugs what they call an 'antique wash' in a bath of chemicals, which at times will do more than just age, they have been known to change some of the colours.

KASHI

Enamelled tilework of the 16th and 17th centuries in Persia.

KASTRUP

A Danish faïence manufactory founded about 1755 by Jacob Fortling. The wares included: large decorative rococo vases, figures and tableware marked with 'F'.

KATANA

The national weapon of Japan; it is a single edged sword with a long, slightly curved blade. They were made of very high-quality steel and the finest would bear the mark of the armourer who had made them. The guards to these weapons were the often exquisitely decorated tsubas, which are fitted between two seppas, or washers.

KATÁR

A short, broad-bladed Hindu sword or dagger used mainly for thrusting. It has a handle of two parallel bars joined by a cross-piece which the hand grips.

KAUFFMANN, ANGELICA (1741–1807)

A Swiss portrait and decorative painter who apart from studio commissions executed work for interior decoration for Robert Adam. Her style was, and has been, much aped by lesser furniture decorators.

KAZAK

A Caucasian rug woven by nomad Cossacks, it has a long, rather heavy pile.

KEITH, JAMES

A crystal glass craftsman from Newcastle-upon-Tyne who emigrated to Norway and worked at Nöstetangen. He was active around 1753.

KELLINGHUSEN

A faïence manufactory founded in Holstein, Germany in about 1760 by Carsten Behrens. The wares were of simple but brave design, tulips and carnations predominated in the floral decoration.

KELSTERBACH

A German faïence manufactory set up in 1758 in Hesse-Darmstadt. In 1761 the Landgrave of Hesse-Darmstadt took over and ordered the making of porcelain. The mark was a monogram of HD surmounted by a crown.

KEN

An early two-edged sword from Japan.

KENT, WILLIAM (1685–1748)

English painter, architect, and the father of modern gardening as Horace Walpole in his *Anecdotes of Painting* describes him; to this could also be added interior decorator and furniture designer. He started out as an apprentice to a coach-builder. His designs for interiors and furniture showed a strong baroque influence. He enjoyed using flamboyant carving and gilding. Tables had a massive richness about them, chairs echoed the then current French vogues. In his handling of large pieces, such as bookcases, he used a strong architectural treatment.

KENTUCKY RIFLE

A long-barrelled weapon that evolved from the juncture of several ideas from immigrants from Holland, Germany and Switzerland to Pennsylvania. The final result had a smaller calibre than current European weapons and a longer barrel. It was also called the Pennsylvania rifle. The first recorded use of the term 'Kentucky Rifle' was in a song written in 1815.

KENZAN, OGATA (1664–1743)

The Japanese potter, painter and poet who worked in Kyoto. At the start he was influenced in pottery by Ninsei but then turned away

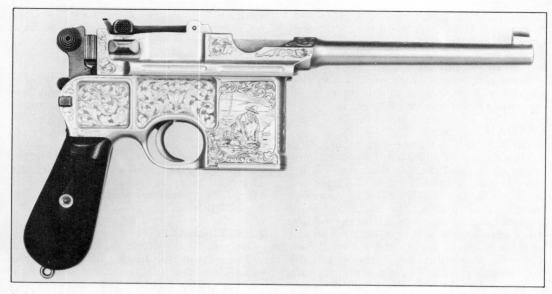

A Mauser No. 11867 made in 1896. With gilt engraved decoration on one side showing a prospector panning gold and on the other bear shooting. Weapon is signed Von Lengerke and Detmold, New York. Further inscribed 'James Beatty. The gift of his friend Pat Salvin. Dawson City. 1899.' Courtesy Christie's

from the flamboyant manner and sought his expression in the soft, subtle tones of a limited palette with the use of talented brush-work and caligraphic inscriptions in line with Zen Buddhist ideas. His brother Korin was one of the most skilled and accomplished lacquer artists of any period.

KERR & BINNS

A manufactory at Worcester run by these two gentlemen brought out what they termed 'Worcester Limoges', or enamel painting on a dark-blue ground. The finest of these pieces were executed by Thomas Bott, a student from the School of Art, who joined them in 1853. These were usually enamelled in light-blue *camaieu*, heightened with white in a very close imitation of the beautiful Limoges enamel on copper. Mr George Wallis, in his account of Worcester Porcelain at the International Exhibition in 1862 said: 'The examples amply prove what can be done by an intelligent and correct continuity of action; and whilst the specimens themselves are of a very varied character, some of them are the most perfect things of the kind ever produced. The dark-blue ground contrasts admirably with the gold enrichments, whilst the white enamel in its various delicate gradations, from the extremely relieved high light downward gives

a delicacy and purity to the general effect of each piece which renders them covetable objects to all persons of taste.'

KETTLE-HAT
A helmet that served, generally for foot-soldiers, from the 13th to the 16th century. It was of open design with a kind of brim. Eventually it was superseded by the morion.

KETTLE-SHAPE
A loose term to describe a chest of drawers, a bureau, or similar piece that has swollen convex curves at the front and the two sides. It is somewhat in the manner of *bombé,* except that with this manner the swelling curves are rather lower down in the piece.

KETTLE-STAND
An early 18th-century introduction to hold a kettle. It varied in shape, but was generally founded on a tripod or tripods as a base, and the whole made of slender rods. They were made in silver and later also in plate.

KEY FRET
A geometrical border pattern coming down from the ancient Greeks. It is also termed Greek Fret.

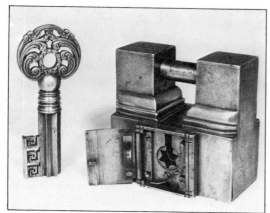

18th century steel and brass mounted double-sided padlock, the keyholes with spring covers engraved with the initials J.M. Courtesy of Phillips

KEYHOLE

A type of openwork, pierced, decoration for the handle of a silver porringer.

KEYS

Today a collectable item in their own right. Some of the older and larger ones having elaborate heads and decorative curved handles.

The possession of the keys of a town or building generally signified a position of authority.

KHANDA

A double-edged sword from India. One of the oldest national weapons. The pommel has a long spike with a knob at the end.

KHORASSAN

A Persian rug with generally a cotton foundation, sometimes a wool, and a rather short pile with fine knotting. The colours are clear and strong in patterns that can include flowers, figures, animals and birds.

KIDDERMINSTER

A centre of the textile trade since around 1334, and probably the oldest carpet-making district in the country. Two-ply carpets were made there from 1735. At first only these 'Kidderminster' carpets were made but in 1749 a Brussels loom was set up in the town and soon 'Brussels' carpets were being made in large quantities.

KIEL

A German faïence manufactory founded in Holstein in 1763 and worked till only 1788.

One of the principal painters was Abraham Leihamer, and the master-potter was Jean Buchwald. The ware was similar to that from Strasbourg with coloured scroll borders and well-handled flowers. The mark was a 'T' over a 'P', both being surmounted by the word 'Kiel'.

KILIJ

The Turkish sabre, a long, curving, single-sided blade, with an off-set curve to the hand-grip.

KILIM

A kind of carpet or rug without a pile, it is tapestry woven. Kilims have been made in the Caucasus, Kurdistan, Persia and Turkey.

KILN

From the Latin *culina,* a kitchen, cooking stove. A place for burning, baking or drying. Kilns may be divided into two classes. Those in which the materials come into actual contact with the flames, and those in which the furnace is beneath or surrounding the oven. Lime kilns are of the first order, and pottery kilns of the second.

KINDJAL

A Cossack weapon with a broad, double-edged blade.

KINGWOOD

A beautiful Brazilian wood, also called violet wood after the colour of its markings; it was much in favour with cabinetmakers.

KLOSTER-VEILSDORF

A porcelain manufactory founded in 1760 in Thuringia which in the succeeding years produced some of the finest porcelain ever made there. Excellent figures were modelled and the painting of tableware was in the manner of Watteau. Marks included 'CV', 'C' and a 'V' each side of a shield, and the same surmounting an 'R'.

KNEEHOLE WRITING TABLE

Introduced in about 1700, it generally consisted of a flat top over a long shallow drawer with a set of drawers each side of a central kneehole, at the back of which could be a small cupboard.

KNIBB, JOSEPH (c 1650–1711)

One of the leading English clockmakers who made many types of timekeepers including:

bracket, lantern and long case clocks. He evolved the Roman strike to conserve spring-power; with this, one bell struck up to three and another with a different tone struck once for five and twice for ten.

KNIFE CASE OR BOX
A container for not only knives but also forks and spoons. They were introduced in the late 17th century and the early versions had a sloping top and inside a fitted inner top with shaped holes cut through to take the cutlery.

KNOP
A swelling, a protuberance used as an ornament in the stem of a drinking glass, a chalice, or candlestick. They were made in great variety and were known by names that are vaguely descriptive; acorn, bell, bullet, bladed, cushion, cylinder, drop, mushroom, etc.

KNOTTED PINE
Earlier, the plank exhibiting knots was looked on by furniture-makers as second-rate so that it was normally only used when the piece being made was destined to be painted. Today a considerable fashion has developed for 'stripped pine' furniture. The old farm dressers, corner cupboards and the rest are being sought out and subjected to caustic soda washes and other such. Then a little minor surgery, refitting, varnishing or waxing and they are collectors' pieces.

KOBAN
A thin, flat, oval Japanese gold coin in use between 1609 and 1870.

KÖNIGSBERG
A small pottery started in East Prussia in 1772 and worked until 1811. The ware was modelled in the rococo manner and much of the decoration was of flowers. The mark was 'HE' and generally a date.

A second pottery in the town was active around 1780 making tableware in the manner of Wedgwood.

KOPEK
A minor Russian coin. In the 16th century it was of silver showing the Tsar mounted.

KOVSH
A Russian vessel roughly in the shape of a boat with a single handle used for ladling out drinks such as kväss. They have been made in silver, gold, wood and sometimes in other suitable materials.

KRIS
A Malay knife that dates from about the 14th century, the blade may be straight or wavy and both edges are honed to considerable sharpness. The Kris may be short, about six inches, or up to three feet long. Versions appear in Java and Bali and other islands around the top of the Malay peninsula.

KUAN WARE
A type of Chinese pottery of the Sung Period, the 12th century. The name is now used for porcelain made at Ching-tê-chên.

KUBA
A fine eastern Caucasian carpet.

KUKRI
The short curved sword with a very heavy blade which is the weapon of the Gurkhas of Nepal. One of the most deadly instruments in its class.

KÜNERSBERG
A faïence manufactory established in Bavaria in 1745 which made a wide variety of wares including: jugs, cylindrical tankards, vases, dishes and some figures. Gold was much used in decoration, and marks were 'Künersberg' and 'KB'.

KURDISTAN
A Persian-type rug of medium pile, which is strong and long wearing.

KWAART
A type of clear lead-glaze sometimes used over tin-glaze to produce a sparkling brilliant surface.

LABELLED FURNITURE

Pieces which still carry small paper labels giving the name of the maker and which may also advertise 'his' business and specialities. It was a custom of many cabinetmakers, both American and British, of the last half of the 18th century to affix these tokens, usually underneath, in a drawer or at the back of furniture. Such items need a very careful inspection as the faker is well aware of this custom and it is not too difficult to produce a convincing fraudulent label.

LABURNHUM

The wood of the *Cytisus laburnhum,* much sought for veneer work, especially when the veneer slicer cuts across a branch to produce a layer suitable to be laid as an 'oyster shell'.

LACE

(Corresponding to the Italian *merletto;* Genoese *pizzo;* German *spitzen;* French *dentelle;* Dutch *kanten;* Spanish *encaje;* the English word owes something to the French *lacis,* but both are connected with the Latin laqueum.)

A delicate open-work fabric that is made from threads of linen, cotton, silk, metal or wool. The hand-made varieties come under two principal headings: first, needlepoint or point lace; second, bobbin or pillow lace made with bobbins and pins on a pillow. The hand-made lace has patterns that are influenced by, and traditional from, the places in which it is made; it is always distinguishable from the machine-made product.

LACE GLASS

A Venetian glass having a patterned effect resembling lace, it was developed during the 16th century.

LACIS

A square-meshed net used as a ground with some types of lace-making.

LACQUER

A yellow varnish of varying tones and tints prepared by dissolving shellac from different sources in alcohol. It may have additional colouring added to it by the use of gamboge, saffron or other pigments or dyes. It sets with a high gloss and a very hard brittle film; therefore it should only be applied to a firm and stable base. The oriental lacquer derives also from the lacquer tree, *rhus vernicifera.*

A clear and weaker solution of shellac has been used as a protective coat for brass, copper and other metals.

LACQUER WARE

A broad term for articles of furniture, or ornaments that have been treated with lacquer in one form or another.

LACROISE, ROGER VANDERCRUSE
(1728–99)

French *ébéniste* active during the 18th century who made a number of fine pieces of furniture for the Tuileries and Versailles. He had a particular flair for marquetry.

LACY GLASS

American pressed glass that was a vogue during the second quarter of the 19th century. It was distinctive by the use of overall patterns of lace-like appearance.

LADDER-BACK

An embracing term for chairs with backs of two upright posts connected with horizontal plain or decorated slats.

LADIES ECCLESIASTICAL EMBROIDERY SOCIETY

Founded by the architect G. E. Street (1824–81) with the aim of producing needlework for church use of a high standard.

LADIK

A fine-textured rug from central Anatolia.

LADLES

Cup-like spoons with long handles. They have been made from silver, Sheffield plate, Britannia metal, pewter, iron, ceramics and wood, and are for serving.

LALIQUE

A French glass developed by the jeweller and inventor Réné Lalique (1860–1945). It was

Nightdress of fine lawn, formerly the property of Queen Victoria. Courtesy of Bonhams

ornamented in a unique manner with flowers, figures, animals and birds. His technique involved pressing and engraving. Productions included: scent bottles, bowls, vases and a number of sinuous figures evoking a mystical captured movement.

LAMBETH WARE
It implies delftware and faïence produced by a group of London potteries active at Aldgate, Southwark, Vauxhall and principally Lambeth itself. In the *History of Lambeth* it states that some Dutch potters established themselves about 1650. One Dutchman was probably John Ariens van Hamme who obtained a patent in 1676.

The decoration was naturally influenced by the Dutch, although later some English manners came in and also imitations of the Italian majolica work. Wares included considerable variety: barrel-shaped mugs, large pear and globular jugs, wine bottles, candlesticks, octagonal plates, tiles, apothecaries' slabs, architectural ornaments and puzzle cups and jugs. In the early 19th century the Doulton

Manufactory was active – they used glazed stoneware which was almost identical to the German *Steingut* or the so-called *Grès de Flandres*. Doulton later made items such as: chemical vessels, sanitary ware and the famous Toby-fillpot jugs.

LAMBREQUIN
An ornamental drape to hang from a shelf or to hide the curtain fittings in the manner of a pelmet.

A scallop or lace-like decoration used with Rouen faïence in the 17th century.

A small drape attached to a helmet as a protection from the sun.

LAMÉ
A heavy fabric that is interwoven with metal threads or has a brocade pattern in metal, silk or rayon threads.

LAMELLÉ
A method of decorating leather by cutting parallel slits and threading slips of coloured leather or metal through and so building up simple geometrical patterns.

LAMERIE, PAUL DE (1688–1751)
The son of a French Huguenot, he was born in Holland, the family coming to London in 1691. Paul began his apprenticeship with the silversmith Pierre Platel who was also a Huguenot. After this Paul entered his mark in 1712 and from then on produced some of the finest worked silver of any time. His decoration verged towards a rich rococo with the use of engraving, gadrooning, strapwork scrolls and much original invention.

LAMETTA
A foil or wire of gold, silver or brass.

LANCE
A cavalry weapon, a shaft with a sharp steel head. The medieval lances were so long and heavy that they had to be supported on a rest.

LANCET CLOCK
A bracket clock popular around 1800. Its name came from its pointed top which was in the form of the early Gothic lancet arch.

LANGE DE BOEUF
A short broadsword or dagger popular with the Venetians. It was also a pike with a wide blade that tapered quickly to a point which was used in the 15th and 16th centuries.

A Webb's cameo vase in deep rose-pink glass overlaid in white. Courtesy of Phillips

Spinach green jade boulder carved in high relief, 18th century or earlier. Courtesy of Phillips

Road map by John Ogilby. Courtesy of the Regent Gallery, Cheltenham

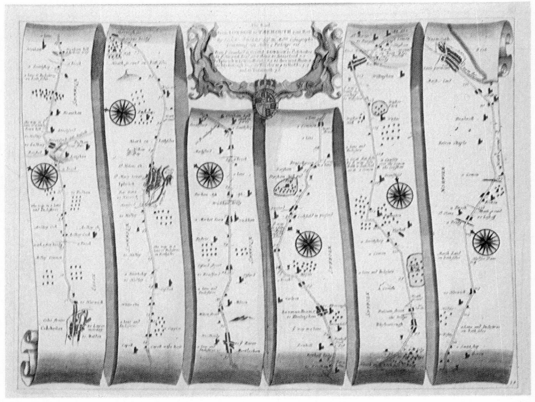

Working model of a 2-inch scale Burrell Compound road engine, the front inscribed 'The Burrell Road Locomotive', length 1·04m. Courtesy of Phillips

Cire Perdue Glass Vase by René Lalique, *c* 1906. Courtesy of Christie's

'Tenture des Chancelleries', a rare Louis XIV Royal Armorial Tapestry by the Gobelins works, late 17th century. Courtesy of Christie's

Fine inlaid Mahogany Vitrine by Emil Gallé (1846–1904). Courtesy of Christie's

Detail of a 16th-century
French 'Animal Kingdom'
tent stitch bed hanging.
Courtesy of Bonhams

Pot lid entitled 'Bear
Hunting'. Courtesy of
Bonhams

Magnificent inkstand made in 1639 with repoussée
decoration and cast figures. Courtesy of Christie's

'Improved Phantasmagoria and Dissolving Lantern' made by T. & H. Doublets, 1880. Courtesy Christie's, South Kensington.

LANTERN CLOCK

A native English development brought in during the first half of the 17th century. A bracket or wall clock that was weight driven, with metal frame and a rounded bell-dome. It was also called a birdcage clock and at times, wrongly, a Cromwellian clock.

LANTERNS

They came into common use in the Middle Ages. They were designed for outside and inside use. Their frames were generally made from iron or brass and with the earlier models thin sheets of horn were used to protect the flame from draughts.

LA ROCHELLE

A faïence manufactory started in 1749, most of the potters coming from Marans. The productions showed influences from Nevers, Rouen and Strasbourg.

LATTEN

A thin sheet hammered out from brass or a brasslike alloy; it was at one time much used for church utensils and also by some locksmiths.

A Japanese Lantern Clock. The pendulum is at the rear. Courtesy Sotheby Park Bernet

LATTICINIO
A type of glass containing milk-white canes or threads made in Murano near Venice.

LAVY FAMILY
Living in Turin they controlled the mint from the middle of the 18th century and produced some well engraved medals which showed a strong French influence.

LAWRENCE FRAME
A richly carved gilt frame with spandrel corners, it would often contain an oval, thin wooden mount that was popular with some clients and their painters. It took its name from Sir Thomas Lawrence (1769–1830).

LEAD GLASS
One fused with lead oxide, a development from the flint glass of Ravenscroft, made in 1675.

LEATHER
A wide variety of animal skins that have been treated to remain flexible and stable; processes can include boiling, tanning and sun-drying.

Leather has been used amongst other purposes for: book-bindings, wall-hangings, screens, armour and coverings for chair seats, upholstery of a chair or sofa, chests and table and desk tops. It has been decorated by dyeing, painting, gilding, stamping and blind-tooling. Final treatment may be by varnishing, wax polishing or leaving a natural surface.

LEAVES
Ornaments in furniture, ceramics, glass or metal that have been taken from or inspired by such as: laurel, palm, olive and acanthus. Totally imaginary leaf shapes are also found.

LEEDS
Pottery was probably first made in Leeds in 1760 at Hunslet by two brothers named Green. The early ware was black but was soon superseded by cream. By 1783 the business had grown to encompass many partners. It was under the direction of William Hartley, Joshua Green, John Green, Henry Ackroyd, John Barwick, Samuel Wainwright, Thomas Wainwright, George Hanson and Saville Green and in 1800 also with Ebenezer Green and E. Parsons. Not surprisingly this crowd disagreed and the firm ended in Chancery and was bought by Samuel Wainwright. Ware produced included: wicker pattern plates and baskets with perforated borders, cream tableware, bell-shaped tygs, vases and modelled animals.

LEEK EMBROIDERY SOCIETY
Founded by Thomas Wardle in 1879. Inspiration came from the work of William Morris, who was a friend of Wardle's.

LEROI, DESIRÉ
A French boy prodigy who was working at Sèvres when only eleven years old. He joined Minton in 1874, and then in 1890 went to Crown Derby. He had a particular talent with the handling of flowers and birds.

LEROUX FAMILY
Celebrated Huguenot silversmiths active in New York during the first half of the 18th century.

LE ROY, PIERRE (1717–85)
The leading French clockmaker of his time. He was awarded the Academy of Science prize for his work on timepieces to be used at sea.

LESUM
German faïence manufactory started near Bremen in 1755. The ware included: bird and animal tureens, openwork baskets and tankards. The mark was rather complicated, a 'V1' plus the date and a scrolling leaf.

LEVANT
A type of morocco leather with a large and irregular grain. It is much used for quality bookbindings.

LEY
A poor quality pewter which can have as much as 40 per cent lead in the alloy. It was used for wine measures, etc (which must have been a lethal practice), and such as candlesticks.

LIGHTHOUSE CLOCK
A shelf-clock made by Simon Willard and patented in 1822, it had the approximate shape of a lighthouse with a dome-shaped glass hood, hence the name. Later the term was applied to novelty clocks with the case produced from not only metal and glass but also wood and serpentine.

LIGNUM VITAE
A tropical American tree, *Guaiacum officinale*, found particularly in the West Indies. It is an exceptionally hard, dense, dark-coloured wood.

It has been used for veneers, but more in turning bowls and some drinking vessels.

For a long time it had considerable medicinal value.

LILLE LACE
A bobbin lace made since the 16th century and noted for its delicacy and beauty. The designs and parts of the patterns are outlined with a heavy thread. The ground has an hexagonal mesh.

LILLE WARE
A faïence manufactory started there in 1696 by Jacques Feburier of Tournai and Jean Bossu of Ghent who set out to make ware à la façon d'Hollande. A second faïence works was started in Lille in 1711 by Barthélémy Dorez which went on for nearly a century. In 1740 a third establishment was set up by Jean-Baptiste Wamps a maker of Dutch tiles. A fourth workshop came in 1774 with M. Chanou who made 'ouvrages de terre brunes appelés terres de St Esprit à la façon d'Angleterre et du Languedoc'. A fifth was started by a M. Heringle in 1758 and a sixth by an Englishman William Clarke in 1773 making earthenware.

LIMBACH
A porcelain manufactory founded in 1772 in Thuringia. It mainly produced tableware and some figures.

LIME GLASS
Produced first by William Leighton in 1864, it is clear, but has not the strength of lead glass.

LIMERICK LACE
A method that started in about 1829, a variety of tambour lace, worked in a similar manner to tambour embroidery. The pattern was embroidered on net with stitches run with a pointed needle or hooked with a tambour needle.

LIMOGES ENAMEL
A type of enamel which has a dark-blue ground colour fused to the surface of the metal. Decoration was achieved on the blue by applying different thicknesses of white enamel. This difficult art was perfected at Limoges in the 16th century.

LIMOGES WARE
A hard-paste porcelain manufactory established by a decree of the 8th of October 1737 by Le Sieur Massié subsequent on the discovery of kaolin at St Yrieix. Massié was joined by Monsieur Fourneira and the Grellet Brothers and later also produced faïence.

LINENFOLD
A carved ornament simulating simply-arranged folded drapery in vertical lines. Popular in the 16th century, it is likely to be of Flemish origin.

LINEN PRESS
Intended for flattening slightly damp linen after washing. It consisted of two large thick boards, in between which the linen could be put and then pressure would be applied by a large wooden screw and handle. Sometimes the bottom board served as the top of a table. The first examples date from the middle of the 16th century.

LING LUNG
Delicate pierced work or openwork used to decorate some Chinese ware of the 17th and 18th centuries.

LINNELL, JOHN
English cabinetmaker active around 1765. He was an imaginative designer with ideas spanning: beds, chairs, commodes, desks, mirrors, sconces and tables.

LINWOOD, MATTHEW
A silversmith from Birmingham who was working around 1800. After an apprenticeship with Joseph Hunt he produced a number of fine works in silver, mostly of small size: nutmeg graters, snuff-boxes and such as wine-labels.

LION-AND-RING HANDLE
It was employed in the latter part of the 18th century, particularly with Sheraton-style furniture.

LION MASK
A motif used with furniture in the Louis XIV period, Empire and Regency.

LISEUSE
A small stand for a book or books. It may also be a revolving table fitted with open shelves. Developed in France in the 18th century.

LITHOPHANE
A decorative technique with which porcelain is impressed with figures which are made

distinct by transmitted light. A patent for the method was held by Grainger, Lee & Co., of Worcester, early in the 19th century. Later, other establishments produced a like product, especially Meissen.

LIVERPOOL

It is likely that faïence punch bowls were made there in the first half of the 17th century, decorated in blue camaieu, with ships and inscriptions. A number of vessels during the period of production carried advisory or warning verses, such as this from a large jug which had a scene in a court-room on the other side:

> One female companion to soften my cares,
> Two thousand a year to support my affairs,
> Three dogs and a gun when to sport
> I incline,
> Four horses and chaise to indulge me and
> mine,
> Five jolly companions with whom to
> make merry,
> Six dishes each day, with six glasses of
> sherry.

The faïence made was similar to that from Bristol, and delftware was also made, with great ship bowls and cream-coloured earthenware. In 1765 Richard Chaffers produced a soapstone porcelain. This came about only after the good man had travelled far in his search for a vein of the elusive material. Apparently he set off in some style on horseback with a pair of saddle-bags, a supply of linen, a thousand guineas to pay the wages of the miners, and a brace of pistols.

LIVERY CUPBOARD

A large cupboard standing on its own legs, or a smaller version that might be hung from the wall; both these were evolved during the 16th century. They were intended to display food to be taken to the bedroom for the night, and candlesticks. The store cupboards generally had some kind of ventilation provided by perforation.

LOBSTER TAIL HELMET

One with a flexible neck-guard, a Burgonet, worn in the 17th century.

LOCK, MATTHIAS

English woodcarver and designer working around 1740 to 1769 at Castle Street, near Longacre, London. He played a considerable part in the introduction of the rococo style

William III marquetry longcase clock, signed Jno. Gavell, London. Courtesy Christie's

with furniture. He published amongst other works: *A New Drawing Book of Ornaments, Shields, Compartments, Masks* and *A New Book of Foliage.*

LONG-CASE CLOCK
Grandfather or, in America, Tall-case clock.

LONGTON HALL
A porcelain manufactory near Newcastle-under-Lyme, Staffordshire active from about 1752 to 1760. Early on it was under William Littler and his brother-in-law Aaron Wedgwood (the third). Products included: sauce-boats, tureens, butter-dishes and some figures.

LOTUS
A water-lily much used as the model for decorations with the ancient Egyptians, versions subsequently appear in the 18th century.

LOVE SPOON
A carved spoon often of quite large size given in Wales as a sign of betrothal from the early 18th century.

LOWBOY
A dressing table with drawers standing on its own legs, the lower part of a Highboy or Tallboy. In England it appeared in Queen Anne and Chippendale styles; generally with cabriole legs.

LOWENFINCK, ADAM FRIEDRICH VON (1714–54)
Porcelain painter who started with Meissen, from there he went to Chantilly, Fulda, Höchst and Haguenau. A highly-talented hand with flowers and imitations of the Chinese manner.

LOWESTOFT
A pottery established for soft paste in 1756 and for hard paste in about 1775. The former contained bone ash and resembled the soft paste from Bow. The wares had a simple naïve charm, unpretentious, with enamel colours and sometimes transfer decoration. Items were inscribed with such as: 'A Trifle from Lowestoft'. Marks from other establishments, such as the crescent from Worcester and the Meissen cross swords, were often imitated. This was not a practice of Lowestoft alone by any means. Many of the big potteries were also involved, copying each other's manners; all of which creates possible confusion for the collector.

LUCERNE HAMMER
A long-handled mace or war hammer used generally by medieval foot-soldiers.

LUDWIGSBURG
Important hard-paste porcelain manufactory established in 1758 by Ringler under the patronage of the Duke Charles Eugène of Württemburg. It became famous for the fine painting of the vases and table-services. The mark was a double 'C' under a Ducal Coronet, and sometimes stag's horns were used.

LUNAR DIAL
One for showing the hour of the night by the shadow of a gnomon in moonlight.

LUNG-CHÜAN
The highly important centre for celadon in the Chekiang province. It was at its peak during the Sung dynasty (*see* Celadon).

LUSTRE
An iridescent sheen given to ceramics. Lustre ware was achieved by firing on metallic oxides from such as copper and silver.

LYRE
An ornament that was popular with Robert Adam. It also appeared as a chair-back and as the basic idea for the ends of some sofas, particularly those from the hand of Duncan Phyffe the New York cabinetmaker.

McABE, JAMES
London clockmaker active between 1781 and 1811, he was a specialist in the making of bracket and carriage clocks.

MACE
A heavy club, often spiked and used during the Middle Ages for breaking armour.

A ceremonial staff carrying some symbol of authority.

MACRAMÉ
A coarse lace, usually with a fringe, made by tying threads into knots and forming geometrical patterns, originally made at Genoa, Italy in the 19th century. It was used for decorating linen or in conjunction with furniture upholstery.

MADEIRA
White embroidery on cambric or linen made by the nuns of Madeira. With its use of eyelets it has an appearance of Broderie Anglaise.

MADELEY
Thomas Martin Randall set up a small pottery at this place in Shropshire in 1826, after some years of changing jobs. He went from Caughley to Derby and then to Pinxton. After this to Islington where he decorated Nantgarw white china in the manner of Sèvres. At Madeley he had with him Thomas Wheeler, William Roberts and F. Brewer and they used a fine body in the manner of Nantgarw and Sèvres, and decorated as in the way of Sèvres very successfully. Some figures were also modelled. The pottery lasted until about 1840.

MAGDEBURG
In 1754 Johan Guischard opened a faïence manufactory here and produced creamware and faïence ware with open basketwork borders.

Johann Wagener started a tile stove workshop in 1791.

In 1799 a third pottery came into being under Elias Rousset and making creamware.

MAGGIOLINI, GIUSEPPE (1738–1814)
He was from Parabiago, Italy, and studied with a monastic workshop and then set up on his own. His specialities were commodes and tables of excellent and simple design, decoration being limited to marquetry.

MAHOGANY
The most popular wood for fine furniture, the genus *Swietenia mahagoni*; its use on a large scale dates from about 1720 although it had been known in England from Elizabeth I's time. Originally it was imported from the island of San Domingo; today it comes from the Cuban and Jamaican forests. Mahogany is a very hard compact grained wood which will rarely shrink or warp and is not greatly affected by changes in humidity or temperature. Today, most mahogany furniture is veneer over a firm base because of cost. The wood will take a very high polish or it may be left in a natural smooth state.

MAIL
Body armour made of interlinked rings, its beginnings are probably somewhere in the second century BC.

MAINFERRÉ
A piece of armour, a gauntlet, to protect the bridle hand of the knight, used from the 14th century onwards.

MAIN GAUCHE
A short, straight, double-edged dagger held in duelling whilst the rapier was in the right hand. It was principally for parrying rapier strokes from one's opponent. It was a 17th-century introduction.

MAJOLICA
The name derived from *maiolica,* given to earthenware with a tin-glaze and painted, made in Italy. Sometimes it was applied to tin-glazed earthenware of an early kind made in France, Germany and the Low Countries in the Italian style. The word is an Italian version of the place-name Majorca and was originally used for lustre-decorated, tin-glazed

Louis XVI Mahogany Secrétaire à Abbatant.
Courtesy of Christie's

pottery thought to have been made there. Anyway this pottery was shipped by Majorcan merchants from Spain. In the 16th century the word came into use for all kinds of tin-glazed enamelled earthenware. The majolica industry seems to have spread from Tuscany, and in the 17th and 18th centuries it continued north-westwards to Genoa and Savoy, and southwards to Sicily. Some of the painters and craftsmen of this industry wandered further afield, so that it began to spread to France, Spain, Switzerland, Poland and England. Strangely, under competition from this last-named, the Italian majolica industry began to decline to the level of a peasant craft, but revived once more in the 19th century.

MAKER'S MARK
The personal mark of the gold or silversmith implying responsibility for the standard of the metal in a particular piece. The earliest example is around 1479. Prior to 1697 the mark was generally a symbol, after that year at first it was the leading two letters of the craftsman's name and then the initials of the first Christian name and surname.

MALTESE LACE
A heavy bobbin lace of either black or white silk probably made in Malta from around 1833.

MANSELL, SIR ROBERT (1573–1656)
English Admiral of the Fleet who turned to glassmaking in about 1608 and who by 1618 had gained control of the English glass industry. At the height of his direction he had some four thousand men working for him and was paying an annual monopoly fee of £1500 to Charles I. Although he achieved much in the way of organisation, his bluff quarterdeck manner was not appreciated by many of the craftsmen, who subsequently left.

MANWARING, ROBERT
English cabinetmaker and chair-maker active around 1760 to 1770 in the Haymarket, London. His published works include: *The Cabinet and Chairmaker's Real Friend and Companion* and *The Chairmakers' Guide*.

MAPLE
A tree of the genus *Acer,* a hard, light-coloured, close-grained wood, often producing interesting curly and bird's-eye effects for veneer.

MARBLED PAPER
A treatment given to paper to produce the look of marble. Sheets are lowered onto the surface of liquid size which has manipulated colours floating on it. Marbled papers have been used for bookbindings and also at times for wall coverings.

MARBLED WARE
A practice of intermingling the surface colours in ceramics to simulate some marbles, it is distinctive from agate ware which was through the body. From around the 16th century it was achieved by the use of slip, from the 18th century with glazes.

MARIEBERG
A Swedish faïence manufactory founded in 1758 by Jean Eberhard Louis Ehrenreich, the

Victorian marquetry side cabinet by Holland and Sons of Mount Street, London, one of the most prominent in the 19th century. Amongst other commissions of note were those for furnishing Balmoral, Osborne and Sandringham. The top of the side cabinet is veneered with three panels of sycamore, cross-banded with kingwood, tulip-wood and pale stringing lines. The frieze is richly mounted with ormolu, above three panelled cupboard doors with raised satinwood borders and ormolu inner frames. It is profusely inlaid in contrasting woods and ivory on a sycamore ground with neo-classical scrolling foliage. Courtesy Christie's.

dentist to King Adolphe Frederick. In that year the persuasive dentist begged for the privilege of being allowed to produce 'differentes espèces de porcelaines fines et ordinaires, vraies et fausses, ainsi que des grès cérames' at the same time asking for 10 000 silver dollars. He made his point and the pottery went on to produce cream-coloured earthenware and porcelain figures based on the French comedies and some fine faïence. They had a particularly attractive marbled glaze using deep violet and grey. Marks included 'MBE' surmounted by three crowns and date.

MARKS
Indications of date, craftsman, country or district, that have been put on items of at least: ceramics, furniture, glass, gold, silver and other metals and alloys and also textiles such as tapestries and carpets. They can be a

dangerous guide if they are always believed at first sight; for with the possible exception of glass, the faker has fiddled with them in many cases, either by erasing and re-marking, or by altering and making additions.

MARLI
A decorative raised border for a dish or platter in ceramics.

MAROT, DANIEL (c 1661–1720)
Born in France he escaped to Holland after the Revocation of the Edict of Nantes in 1685. He entered the service of William of Orange. His talents were varied and he worked on designs for not only furniture, but also ceramics and gardens. It is possible on a stay in England of four years that he worked on the interior decoration of Hampton Court Palace.

MARQUETRY
Laid work, used in the decoration of furniture of many periods and countries. A wide variety of materials have been used in this way: wood of the same type or different varieties, ivory, bone, mother-of-pearl, tortoiseshell and metals. It was used by the early Italian craftsmen in their cabinetwork and often elaborate pictures of figures and landscapes were created. Its introduction in Britain dates from about 1670. Patterns may include abstract forms, flowers, foliage and grotesques.

MARROW SCOOP
A form of double-ended spoon for extracting the marrow from bones. Of silver and also Sheffield plate, it dates from the late 17th century.

MARSEILLES
An early French faïence manufactory set up in about 1697. The first quality objects seem to have come from Saint-Jean-du-Désert, a suburb of the town. A porcelain manufactory was set up there in 1766 by Joseph Gaspard Robert, and from about 1777 he produced such items as fine vases and table services in the manner of Sèvres. The pottery closed about the time of the Revolution in 1793.

MARTHA WASHINGTON CHAIR
A style of mahogany chair, with or without arms, but with a high flat back, with seat and back upholstered. It is supposed to have taken its name from an original design used by Martha Washington, the wife of George Washington, the first President of the United States, at Mount Vernon.

MARTHA WASHINGTON TABLE
A style of work table that could be oval or octagonal with four slender reeded legs. A small set of drawers and receptacles for sewing materials were included under each end. The name was derived as with the Martha Washington chair.

MARTIN BROTHERS
The producers of some of the most original stoneware, the four brothers worked first at Fulham and then at Southall in the latter part of the 19th century. Their subjects covered all manner of weird and strange animals, birds and fish. It was the boast of Charles Martin that 'We make it a matter of pride never to repeat a single specimen of our work.' The mark was usually a signature incised into the paste. In particular, their colouring is unique and they even took on architectural pieces for the Earl of Carlisle, Lord Egmont and Sir Edward Clarke.

MASK
A decorative ornament in the shape of a human, an animal or a birds' head, often grotesque, that has been used in many crafts; ceramics, furniture, metals and even as part of designs with textiles.

MASON, MILES
An English potter active in the last quarter of the 18th century and early years of the 19th century. He worked from Lane Delph, Staffordshire and made some good porcelain, usually printed in red and blue with Chinese designs. His son patented 'Ironstone' china in 1813.

MATCHLOCK
The earliest form of mechanical firing, a part called a serpentine held the match and swung it down to the flashpan; this could be controlled by a trigger. It was introduced early in the 15th century.

MATTING
A technique for slightly roughening a metal surface, such as silver, by the use of a punch making marks very close together.

MAUNDY MONEY
Alms distributed on Maundy Thursday; originally in connection with the ceremony of washing the feet of the poor on that day.

MAYER, ELIJAH
The English potter active at Hanley at the end of the 18th century and early 19th century. His speciality was black basalt.

MAYHEW, JOHN
See Ince, William

MAZARINE
A silver or Sheffield plate dish with a straining plate used for serving fish in the late Georgian period. It was named after Cardinal Mazarin.

MAZARINE BLUE
A blue of deep tone, somewhat strangely named also after the Cardinal Mazarin.

MAZER
A large drinking bowl, often of a wood like maple and with gold and silver mounts.

Sometimes it had a cover. The earliest use was probably in the 13th century, but by the time of the 15th and 16th centuries it had become popular.

MECHANICAL BANK
An innovation of the last half of the 19th century. The designs were exceedingly various and although not long ago they were looked on as not much more than toys, well preserved examples are now sought after and they have featured in major sales.

MECHLIN LACE
A delicate attractive lace made at Malines in Belgium, it is worked on a hexagonal mesh ground.

MEDALLION
A square, rectangular, circular or oval tablet on which are carved or painted busts and figures. They have been used for ornament in interior decoration, and with furniture, ceramics, glass and metal. They are also struck for commemorative purposes.

MEDALS
Circular, star or cross-shaped metal objects that have been struck in memory of victories or campaigns and famous men. The earliest use dates from Greek times.

MEDICI PORCELAIN
A private manufactory for soft paste established in Florence in 1580 under the patronage of Francesco I (de' Medici), Grand Duke of Tuscany. A laboratory was set up in the Boboli gardens. Records claim that the first artificial porcelain in Europe was made here. Vasari, chronicler of the artists, speaks of the translucid pottery. Fine vases as of a high quality equal to the most ancient came from here. M. Jacquemart gives a recipe for making this porcelain which is taken from a manuscript discovered in the Bibliotheca Magliabechiana, compiled by some person in the Duke's employ. The mark was the dome of the duomo in Florence with an 'F' underneath.

MEDICI TAPESTRY
A workshop started in 1546 by the Duke Cosimo I in Florence. Among artists who contributed designs was Bronzino.

MEISSEN
The famous manufactory founded at Meissen on the Elbe, about twelve miles from Dresden, by Augustus II, King of Poland and Elector of

Pair of Louis XV ormolu and Meissen porcelain figures of begging pugdogs. Courtesy of Christie's

Saxony for the manufacture of hard paste or true porcelain. The experiments of Tschirnaus and Böttger started in about 1706 (see Böttger).

The manufactory had almost total supremacy from 1710 to 1756, during this time some of the finest examples of the ceramic art were made and set the seal on the great influence Meissen would have over the other houses in Europe. With the Seven Years War Sèvres took the lead. But later when Count Marcolini took over the direction success came back. Joseph Kaendler (see p. 138) did much for the manufactory, using his brilliant skill for more than forty years. The famous crossed swords mark was first used in about 1724 and is probably the best known ceramic mark of all.

MELES
A type of Turkish rug with a short pile and patterns showing Caucasian influence.

MELON FLUTING
An ornamental device to give strength to a silver or other metal vessel and so help prevent denting or buckling.

MENDLESHAM CHAIR
A Suffolk chair related to the Windsor. It has a lower back with a straight top rail and a saddle seat.

MENNECY
A French faïence and soft-paste porcelain pottery started in 1735 under the patronage of the Duc de Villeroy and the direction of

François Barbin. Early wares were similar to those of St Cloud and Chantilly. In 1766 the ownership changed to Joseph Jullien and S. Jacques. Later productions were mostly faïence. Marks used were 'DV' and 'BR'.

MENSULA
A device that allows for the drawing of a plan directly on a plane table whilst surveying. This is done by using the sight rules for drawing alignments. Johann Praetonius describes one in about 1600.

MENTONNIÈRE
A piece of armour to protect the chin.

MERCATOR, GERHARD (1512–94)
One of the great early cartographers he also made a number of large terrestrial globes. Born in Flanders he studied at Louvain and was a friend of Gemma Frisius. He made a set of instruments for the campaigns of Charles V; and during his life did much to develop the art of map-making.

MESAIL
The adjustable visor on medieval helmets.

MIGNONETTE
A beautiful delicate lace, a blonde, it was made near Paris and was much used in the 17th century.

MILAN LACE
A type of bobbin lace also termed Milan Point. Milan has been a lace-making centre from the 15th century.

MILK GLASS
An opaque white glass intended to be an imitation of Chinese porcelain. It was made in Venice as long ago as the 16th century.

MILLEFIORI
Highly regarded paperweights made by a difficult process which included the fusing together of slender rods or tubes of coloured glass, cutting the result across and joining the sections or embedding them in clear glass. The paperweights were first made in Venice; then centres such as St Louis, Baccarat and Clichy followed suit.

MILLE FLEURS
Literally a thousand flowers; with tapestry, fabrics and carpets it implies an overall design

Pair of Chinese polychrome covered vases. Ming Period. Ormolu mounts and frame-work. French Regency Period. Courtesy of Ader, Picard, Tajan

using small flowers, leaves and plant stems. This type of decoration originated in China and was imported into Europe.

MING DYNASTY

During this period, covered by the reign of the Ming Emperors from 1368 to 1644, there was an attempt to revive past glories, but despite the achievements of many fine works, the heights of the T'ang and Sung periods were not again reached. There were, however, notable technical advances. New porcelain techniques were evolved, such as blue under-glaze painting and the use of enamel colours over the glazing. To some degree, Chinese methods and designs of this period were copied by European porcelain factories. Technical perfection was also attained in jade and ivory carving, and in *cloisonné* enamel.

MINIATURE SILVER

Contemporary small and sometimes tiny reproductions or copies of full-size pieces of silver, such as candlesticks, coffee-pots, cream jugs, goblets, porringers and tankards, were made by skilled craftsmen. The reason may have been for specialist collectors, or as toys to go with the magnificent dolls of the late 17th century onwards. For a time there was the suggestion that these small creations were intended as trade samples, but this is unlikely.

MINT MARK

A distinctive letter or mark placed on a coin at the time of striking to identify the mint.

MINTON

The pottery was founded at Stoke-on-Trent, Staffordshire by Thomas Minton (1765–1836) who had previously served his apprenticeship at Caughley and who had also had a period with Spode. Minton started a production in 1796 which has continued right through to the present day. Early wares were often blue-printed, and creamware was also produced. Porcelain appeared from 1798 to 1811 and then again from 1821. In the mid-19th century Leon Arnoux joined the firm and remained as art director until 1902. Early marks included an 'M' between two inter-linked 'Ss' on impressed 'Minton' and 'HM & Co.'

MIRRORS

The ancient mirrors of the Etruscans, Greeks and Romans were disks of metal which was usually the alloy bronze; they were often

George III Irish gilt-wood mirror. Courtesy of Christie's

slightly convex and polished on one side. Pliny mentions a manufactory for mirrors of glass at Sidon.

Small metal mirrors with a highly-polished surface were still being used during the medieval times. There was a fashion for small metal, pocket mirrors carried in richly-orna-mented cases, often made of ivory and carved with hunting scenes, love interludes and sometimes illustrations from poetry. Gold, silver and enamels were also used on the cases.

The method of backing glass with thin metal sheets was known; Vincent of Beauvais mentions one backed with lead in 1250. The first guild of glass mirror-makers seems to have been in Nuremberg in 1373.

Sir Robert Mansell (*see* p 159) was making glass mirrors in England with the help of Italian workmen. In 1670 the Duke of Buckingham had an interest in a glass-works at Lambeth that was making flint glass mirrors. These old English mirrors with bevelled edges in the Venetian manner are still well known. The Venetians tried very hard to protect their secrets, and threatened to imprison the family of any glass craftsman who went abroad, and if he did not return, assassins were dispatched to kill him.

Despite the punishment some twenty Venetian glass workers did go to France in 1665 and set up a glasshouse at Faubourg St Antoine.

The term 'silvering' was a misnomer up to 1840 as till then no silver was used, a tin amalgam was employed. The 'silver on glass' mirror was a development by J. von Liebig who in 1835 found that by heating aldehyde with an ammoniacal solution of silver nitrate in a glass vessel a deposit of metallic silver was formed on the surface of the glass. Manufacture of the method started in 1840.

MISERICORD
(From the Latin *misericordia* meaning compassion or pity.) A kind of shelf projection found on the underside of the hinged seats in the choir stalls. Its purpose was for a chorister to support himself during the lengthy services. The seats were often carved underneath with richly-imaginative skill.

A thin-bladed medieval dagger, similar to a stiletto; it is so-termed as it would have been used to give the 'mercy' stroke to a fallen enemy.

MITRE
A term used in joinery for the angled joint where two mouldings or bands of veneer come together at right angles. A diagonal cut made across two pieces so that they may be joined together at right angles.

MOCHA
A fine soft leather made from the skin of an Arabian goat.

MOCHA WARE
A ceramic decoration in which the pot was ornamented with coloured bands of irregular form, that gave vague suggestions of plant forms, trees, moss. It was named after the Mocha stone, moss agate and was made during the period 1780 to 1914.

MOHAIR
A fine material woven from the hair of the Angora goat. Close imitations are made from wool and cotton.

MOHUR
A gold coin of India and Persia now obsolete. The last issue was made by the East India Company in 1835, it contained about $7.10 of fine gold and was worth 15 rupees – there has been a recent striking of a mohur in India, this is also worth 15 rupees.

MONSTRANCE
A receptacle in which Holy relics can be exposed to view. Later, a vessel in which the Host is exposed to receive the veneration. The name is derived from the Latin *monstrare*, to show. It is generally of gold or silver.

MONTEITH
A punch bowl, with a scalloped rim which was sometimes made removable. It was introduced late in the 17th century and took its name from a strange eccentric Scot who was at Oxford in the 1680s, and who liked to wear a great cloak with a scalloped edge. Monteiths were also made in glass.

MOORFIELDS CARPETS
Hand-knotted carpets in the Turkish style made in London from about 1760. Robert Adam was among the leading designers who used the works.

MOQUETTE
A kind of upholstery fabric or fine carpet with a velvet-like pile.

MORION
A foot-soldier's helmet without a visor that had the edge turned up, worn in the late 16th century. It was of Spanish origin and was often decorated with engraving or etching.

MORNING STAR
A medieval weapon which consisted of a heavy and viciously spiked ball on the end of a short staff or sometimes attached to the shaft by a short length of chain. It was also called a Holy-Water Sprinkler.

An important musical timepiece by Charles Clay of London, active early part of the 18th century. This has an organ mechanism. It is 93 ins (236 cms) high and 32 ins (81 cms) wide. Courtesy Christie's

MOROCCO
A fine leather from France, Switzerland and Turkey made from goatskin which has been tanned with sumac and dyed on the grain side. Imitation morocco is made from sheepskin. It is possible it was first processed by the Moors. It is strong and firm but retains flexibility and is useful for bookbindings.

MORRIS, WILLIAM (1834–96)
English artist, designer, architect and poet. He was the leader of a group of intellectuals, artists and craftsmen, who sought to stem the mass of machine-made objects that they felt were set to destroy the true purpose of the craftsman. As with John Ruskin, and later with Walter Gropius, Morris sensed the deep-running social problems that could develop from a lack of satisfaction and a lack of feeling of accomplishment for a large number of artisans. He and those around him brought back an inspiration to work with printed and woven textiles, wall-papers, carpets, furniture, stained glass, metal work, book-printing and binding; in fact almost every aspect of domestic design was explored. Ornaments included a rich and strong use of plant and flower forms. Morris was a friend of the Pre-Raphaelites and he started a firm 'Morris, Marshall, Faulkner & Co.', in 1861, whose credo was 'fine art workmen in painting, carving, furniture and the metals'.

MORRIS CHAIR
A large easy chair, with an adjustable back, of the late 19th century; it had big loose cushions and it is reputed to have been developed by William Morris.

MORTAR
A mixing vessel, with its pestle that has been in use in Europe certainly from the Middle Ages; in the Orient much longer. They have been made from bronze, marble, pewter, wood and other suitable materials and are an adjunct to the work of an apothecary and a cook.

MORTLAKE TAPESTRY
Weaving mills near London established by James I. Francis Cleyn was art director and one of the chief weavers was Philip de Maecht.

MORTLAKE WARE
An English pottery manufactory started in 1800 by Joseph Kishere where brown stoneware was made. Decoration was in the manner of

Fulham with reliefs. Productions included: jugs, mugs and flasks.

MOSAIC BINDINGS
A full-leather binding with inlaid or onlaid small fragments of thinned coloured or different leathers. The term may also be used for a decoration to imitate the foregoing with paint.

MOSBACH
A faïence manufactory at Baden that was established by Pierre Berthevin in 1770. Much of the ware showed the influence of Strasbourg. One speciality was a type of jug with inscriptions in black intended as a presentation pot.

MOSQUE LAMPS
They were designed to hang from the ceilings by chains and had an oil lamp. The quality of the enamel decorated glass was of the finest; the craftsmen being mostly in Syria or trained there. The best of these lamps were probably made during the 13th and 14th centuries.

MOTHER-OF-PEARL
The hard, pearly internal layer of several kinds of shell, including: oysters, mussels and abalones. The iridescent quality was exploited with inlay, and was also used for costume jewellery, buttons and cutlery handles.

MOUNTMELLICK
A type of raised embroidery worked in Ireland which was started in about 1830. It was carried out on a closely woven linen or drill with a thick cotton; natural plant forms were treated with great detail.

MOUSTIERS
An important French faïence manufactory that was active from 1686 to 1800, although there is evidence that ware was made there considerably earlier. In the late 17th century Pierre Clérissy was the driving force. Productions include the blue and white Berain style, decorated with motifs from artists' engravings.

In 1738 a second pottery was opened by Joseph Olerys and here the Spanish influence was evident with the treatment of the ware by a kind of polychrome fired to a high temperature.

There was also a third establishment worked by Jean Ferrat between 1718 and 1791 that copied the Marseilles and Strasbourg manners.

MUDEJAR
A style in ornament which shows the coming together of Christian and Moorish Art in Spain during the period of 1250–1500.

MUDGE, THOMAS (1717–94)
English clockmaker born in Bideford, the son of a local schoolmaster. After an apprenticeship with George Graham he set himself up in Fleet Street, London. He developed the 'lever' escapement which made a reduction in the size of clock and watch movements possible. This advance was incorporated in a watch George III gave to Queen Charlotte. Later Mudge moved back to Devon, to Plymouth, and worked on marine chronometers.

MUFFINEER
A small caster for salt or spices intended for muffins; those tea-time delicacies which are either a thick yeast risen spongy cake or a batter bread with egg that is baked in a small shallow batter-pan. It was introduced in the late 17th century.

It may also be a special muffin dish with a cover made of silver or porcelain.

MUG
One of the most used drinking vessels, it was generally cylindrical with a handle. They have been made in silver, Sheffield plate, pewter, tin, copper and nearly every kind of ceramics: earthenware, stoneware and porcelain. Decoration has varied from elegant designs to comic inscriptions. Other shapes did include the barrel and baluster.

James II mug made by George Garthorne, dating from 1686, and only 3¾ ins (9·5 cms) high. Courtesy Spink

MULE CHEST
An early 18th-century chest with two single drawers underneath and mounted on short legs. It is also called a blanket chest.

MULL
The name for a snuff-box in Scotland. In this context they could be large community boxes for passing around a gathering of friends. Some were made from horn with fine silver decorations.

MURANO
See Venetian Glass

MURRHINE
Glass that is transparent and can thus show pieces of coloured glass that are embedded in it.

MUSICAL AUTOMATA
Developed parallel with the music box from the 18th century. They had considerable variety: dancing dolls, monkeys, groups of figures, birds, marching soldiers, and acrobats.

MUSICAL BOXES
Developed during the latter part of the 18th century, the early models had little quality of sound; but during the 19th century they improved quickly as new ideas were incorporated. Devices were brought in that could produce the sounds of mandolines, bells, drums and flutes. Mechanically they became long playing with multi-tune cylinders.

MUSIC STAND
A small table with an adjustable sloping top for holding music in front of a player. It was developed in the 18th century.

MUSKET
A hand firearm evolved in the latter part of the 16th century; owing to the weight of its construction it normally had to be fired from a rest. At first it was fired by a match-lock then a wheel-lock and later a flint-lock and lastly a percussion cap.

MUSKETOON
A short musket with a large bore.

MUSTARD POT
The small cylindrical pots came in at the beginning of the 18th century with a lid normally with a thumb-plate for lifting and a handle at the side. Later the shape might be octagonal, or oval. The custom in the early days was that the pot would contain dry mustard and it would be mixed on the plate.

MUZZLE LOADER
One that receives the charge and projectiles or bullets into the muzzle.

NAILSEA
English glasshouse which was started by John Robert Lucas in 1788 a few miles to the west of Bristol, and which was in production until about 1873. The glass made there ranged from a brown to dark green with a speckling of white to clear glass with coloured strips. An extraordinary variety of items were produced: inscribed rolling-pins, walking sticks, ornamental flasks, mugs, jugs, bowls, witch-balls, tobacco pipes, ale-yards, bells and cream jugs.

NAMAZLIK
From the chief prayer of the Mohammedans, it is a small rug that can be identified by the point at one end which represents the niche of the mosque. One is normally owned by every follower of Mahomet.

NANCY TAPESTRIES
A weaving house set up by the Duke Leopold in the early part of the 18th century near his palace at Nancy, France. Gobelins craftsmen did most of the weaving.

NANKING WARE

Chinese blue-and-white porcelain shipped from Nanking during the 18th and 19th centuries.

NANTGARW

This south Wales porcelain manufactory was established in 1813 by William Billingsley, the famous flower painter from Derby, and Samuel Walker. A certain amount of excellent porcelain was produced, although some of it was likely to react to the high temperature of firing and there are pieces about that show distortion and cracking of the glaze. In 1814 the pottery was moved to Swansea. After three years Billingsley and Walker returned to Nantgarw and for a time carried on until their funds ran low and they packed up and went to Coalport. Marks included: 'Nantgarw' impressed and Nantgarw above 'CW', and also 'Swansea' impressed or written.

NAPIER'S BONES

Numbered rods which can be used for calculating. Napier's set consisted of ten oblong pieces of wood. Each of the four faces of each rod is numbered. The bones can be used for multiplying and dividing. John Napier, the Scottish mathematician, was born in 1550 and lived until 1617.

NARGHILE

The Middle-East hookah or hubble-bubble pipe. It consists of an enclosed container of water surmounted with the bowl for the tobacco and a long tube with a mouth-piece which when drawn on sucks the smoke through the water.

NAUTILUS SHELL CUP

One made from the pearly nautilus and mounted, often with very elaborate silverwork. It was a vogue that started about 1550.

NÉCESSAIRE

A French word that implies a small casket or box which was fitted for and contained the things required for needlework, or writing, or toilet accessories, or personal cutlery and possibly a glass or metal cup. The boxes and contents were often exquisitely made; bottles would be fine cut glass with gold or silver mountings, and the boxes themselves would be highly finished with chased precious metals and semi-precious stones. These are mentioned in French records as early as the 14th century.

NECK OR NECKING

A part of a column considered as interposed between the spreading (ornamental) part of the capital and the shaft. Sometimes this is between two neck mouldings and may have a separate decoration. In a general sense, any ornamental member at the lower part of a capital. It is also known as Gorgerin.

NEEDLEPOINT

A lace made with a needle as opposed to that made with bobbins. It is made on a parchment or paper pattern.

NEF

A table vessel to hold napkins, cutlery, and salt. They were very often in the shape of a ship and made of gold or silver and exquisitely wrought. A show-piece for the owner, the quality reflecting his standing and riches.

A clock in the form of a ship of the 16th century, with mechanical devices that could demonstrate astronomical movements.

NEO-CLASSIC

A movement in design, architecture, painting and sculpture of the last part of the 18th century

A gold-mounted nécessaire 4½ ins (11·4 cm) high. Courtesy Christie's

and the first part of the 19th. It was partly sparked off by The French Revolution which brought a reaction against the luxury and elegant excesses of Louis XV. A second reason was that the excavations at Pompeii and Herculaneum turned men's minds back to Antiquity, and there was an attempted revival of the more Spartan manners of the Greeks and Romans. In architecture and interior decoration, furniture and other domestic items there was a simplification in design. In 1764, Winckelmann wrote his *History of Ancient Art,* in which he referred to the 'noble simplicity and calm grandeur' of Ancient Greece. Neo-Classical architects in Germany included Langhans and Schinkel; in England there were Sir John Soane, Hamilton and Smirke. The period in France has been termed the Neo-Grecque and in America the Neo-Greek.

NEO-GOTHIC
The Gothic revival of 1840 in England and similar movements in Germany, France and the United States.

NEST OF DRAWERS
Generally implying a small chest of drawers or a small box of drawers.

NETSUKE
A very small carving, often only about one and a half inches long, in wood, or ivory. It is a form of button to attach the inrō (a small box for medicines) to its silken cord and belt. Examples from the 18th and 19th centuries often display brilliant and imaginative carving, even if a little grotesque and macabre at times. Earliest examples date from around the 16th century. Main centres for the production of these sculptures in miniature have been Asaka, Kyoto and Edo or Tokyo.

NETTING
The making of fine material for use as a basis for embroidery or lace; it could also include larger scale nets for the garden. This was quite a popular hobby with some men in the Victorian period.

NEVERS
In the year 1590 the alchemist Gaston de Cleves dedicated a book to Louis of Gonzaga, Duke of Nevers. He praised this prince for having brought into his states expert artists and workmen in the arts of glass making, pottery and enamel. About this time the name of Scipio Gambyn is found on a parish register and he is described as 'pothier'. A relation Julien Gambyn of Faenza had established a faïence manufactory at Lyons. But the earliest evidence of one at Nevers is that founded by Domenique Conrade in about 1602. During the 17th century much good faïence was made there; it was distinctive by the fine drawing and painting. Motifs included birds and foliage, flowers, and later Chinese influence was evident.

The glasshouses flourished in Nevers from the last part of the 16th century, and one speciality was the production of small glass figures of lay and religious subjects.

NEW HALL
The pottery was at Shelton, Staffordshire, and had been built by Mr Whitehead who made white salt glazed stoneware. In 1782 the premises were taken over by a company of potters who had bought Champion's unexpired patent for the making of porcelain which had been renewed in 1775 in spite of opposition from Wedgwood and others. The party consisted of: Samuel Hollins of Shelton, Anthony Keeling of Tunstall, John Turner of Lane End, Jacob Warburton of Hotlane, William Clowes of Port Hill, Charles Bagnall and Mr Heath of Shelton. The wares consisted of hard-paste porcelain with simple but charming decorations using mainly floral motifs. Latterly a change was made to a rather glassy bone porcelain. Marks included: 'New Hall'.

NICKEL SILVER
A silver white alloy, which contains no silver, it is made principally from copper, zinc, and nickel. The resulting alloy is hard and tough and is used extensively for tableware; from 1840 as a basis for electro-plating with the EPNS mark.

NIDERVILLER
French faïence manufactory established about 1760 by Jean Louis, Baron de Beyerlé. Principally German potters were employed and the wares were rich in decoration using flowers in garlands and bouquets; figures were also made which were modelled by the sculptor Charles Sauvade called Lemire who was in charge of this department for more than twenty years. The marks were 'JLB', crossed 'C's' under a crown and monograms of B and N and also C and N.

Natural stereoscope by J. Wood, Birkby, Huddersfield, c 1862. Courtesy of Christie's, South Kensington

NIEDERMAYER, JOHANN JOSEPH

He was the master modeller, figure maker at the Vienna porcelain manufactory for nearly forty years from 1747, and his work was noted for his light decorative touch with a rococo flourish.

NIELLO

From the Italian, it is the art of chasing or engraving out lines or forms, and inlaying a black composition called *nigellum* or niello; it was probably also known to the Greeks. It has been used in Russia, and earlier by the Byzantines, who compounded for this purpose silver, lead, sulphur and copper, and laid it on the silver in a powder, after which it was passed through a furnace, so melting and incorporating with the solid metal. It was practised during the Middle Ages; and although rare, specimens can be found in museums. In the 15th century these designs were engraved with great delicacy. The origin of taking paper impressions from metal plates is ascribed to the practice of Maso Finiguerro, a Florentine

goldsmith, who in the middle of the 15th century used to take impressions of his incised work on cups and plaques in a viscid water-ink on paper, so as to test the state of his work. Such impressions of the early fathers of copperplate printing still exist, and are known as niellos.

NIGHT TABLE

A bedside table, an early 18th century introduction; one type was a small oblong table rather like a small washing stand.

NOCTURNAL

An instrument for finding the time at night by the position of the stars, and also for determining the latitude.

NOGGIN

A small mug or cup holding about a gill.

NONSUCH CHESTS

Late 16th-century chests possibly made by Flemish or German craftsmen. The name comes from the usual decoration which was a building supposedly resembling Henry VIII's palace at Cheam, called Nonsuch. The picture was built up with great detail of towers, cupolas and windows by inlay.

NORMAN, SAMUEL

The English cabinetmaker active around 1760. He was in partnership with John Mayhew and James Whittle near Covent Garden, London. They offered a complete service of furniture-making, gilding, carving and upholstery. They would have supplied items to Windsor Castle.

NORMANDY LACE

Bobbin laces were made from the early part of the 16th century. Important centres included: Dieppe, Fécamp and Honfleur. The styles of Mechlin and Flanders, black and white, were imitated cleverly.

NORTON, EARDLEY

The English clockmaker of St John Street, London who was working during the third quarter of the 18th century. His specialities included: delicate cases of tortoiseshell and complicated and ingenious constructions of automata.

NORTON, CAPTAIN JOHN

He set up the Norton Pottery in 1793 at Bennington, Vermont, which continued in production until 1894, being passed down through his family. The main production was stoneware and much of the clay was brought from Troy, a heavy haul across some steep hills.

NOTCHING
A very simple form of decoration found in primitive woodwork. It would consist of just small hollows cut out.

NOTTINGHAM
The pottery produced was principally salt-glazed stoneware between 1690 and 1800. Decoration was by piercing, incising and impressing. The grey body was covered with a light-brown glaze and a light metallic lustre. Commonest forms were two-handled loving cups, cylindrical mugs, tea-pots and jugs.

Lace made in Nottingham was largely an imitation of bobbin, and woven by machinery.

NULLING
A square sectional, carved or cast ornament somewhat similar to gadrooning.

NUTMEG GRATER
A small cylindrical grater made in silver with a cover and dating from the late 17th century. They were in demand when making hot toddies.

NYMPHENBURG
A porcelain manufactory opened in 1747 which was to come under the protection of Maximilian Joseph, Elector of Bavaria. In its early days it employed the talented sculptor Franz Anton Bustelli. His principal work was the group of sixteen Italian Comedy figures. He also created services and decorations for banqueting tables. Later, in the time of Crown Prince Ludwig, who was to become Ludwig I, and who was the builder of Munich in the Classical style, one of his architects, Friedrich von Gärtner, became artistic director of Nymphenburg in 1820. Porcelain of this period was decorated with landscapes, copies of famous paintings from the Pinakothek, portraits and town scenes.

NYON
The Swiss hard-paste porcelain manufactory at this place near Geneva was established about 1780 by Ferdinand Müller of Frankenthal. Much of the painting was done by Genevese artists and they generally marked it with a 'G' or 'Geneve' in full and sometimes with a fish. This can be misleading as there never was a pottery in Geneva. The best of the decorators were: Delarive, Gide, Hubert and Mulhouser.

OAK
The wood of the genus *quercus,* it is hard and compact, with a pleasant colour. It was the most important wood for furniture in the Medieval, Renaissance, Tudor and Jacobean periods in England, Flanders and Germany. Its popularity lasted until about 1660 when it began to be superseded by walnut.

OBAN
A large, oval gold coin of Japan from the 16th to the 19th centuries; now obsolete.

OBERKAMPF, CHRISTOPHE PHILIP (1738–1815)
A leading cloth printer and dyer, born in Germany. When he was nineteen he went to Paris and became a French citizen. He set up his workshop at Jouy near to Versailles and soon gained the appreciation of Louis XVI who gave him the Royal appointment. His speciality was the so-called Toiles de Jouy, printed work on fine cotton, with designs using classical themes, landscapes, flowers and often in a warm-toned monochrome. Many of his patterns have been freely borrowed from since his time.

OBOL
An ancient Greek coin which was at first a weight and weighed one sixth of a drachma. The Attic obol was silver and weighed eleven and a quarter grains.

An oak press (cupboard) dating from the early 17th century. The decoration includes inlays with holly and fruitwood. Courtesy Christie's

OCTANT
An instrument for measuring angles, similar to a sextant.

OEBEN, JEAN-FRANÇOIS (c 1720–63)
German born he moved to France when he was twenty and became the finest *ébéniste* of his time. He was appointed to Louis XV after the death of Boulle. His particular talent was with marquetry.

OEIL-DE-PERDRIX
A type of decoration with porcelain which involves a repeating pattern made of tiny spots of colour each of which is surrounded by a ring of smaller dots. Sèvres used the idea from about 1760.

OGDEN, THOMAS (1692–1769)
English clockmaker who specialised in long-case clocks that had a rotating device that gave the

phases of the moon. An idea which a number of makers after him were to imitate, with various versions such as that with a disc that showed the rising and setting sun and the hours of darkness.

OGEE
A moulding with a double curvature as with an S. It has been used with furniture, glass, silver and ceramics.

OGEE BRACKET FOOT
A cabinet foot that came in during the late 18th century.

OGEE CLOCK
An American design incorporating the above moulding in the front; early 18th century.

OGILBY, JOHN (1600–76)
The Scottish cartographer particularly associated with the mapping of the coaching roads, using a strip or ribbon method.

OLD HALL
A pottery at Hanley run by Job Meigh from about 1780 and then by his sons Job and Charles. Good pieces were produced early in the 18th century using the designs of the sculptor Giarinelli. Job, the son, was awarded the Society of Arts gold medal in 1823 for giving the public a glaze for common pottery that was free from the dangerous qualities of the usual lead glaze with cooking pots. Before this it was known that coarse, cheap, red pottery made for cooking food was covered with a very dubious glaze which was compounded with litharge; the result being that when this kind of vessel was used for baking or boiling, the heat tended to make the glaze soluble and it mixed with animal fat or acids from fruits and became a fairly lethal condiment.

OLIVE WOOD
A hard close-grained wood, *Olea europaea,* it has a good working quality and exciting grains. It has been used from far back in history. Records point to early Egyptians, Greeks and Romans and other Mediterranean peoples being conscious of its worth.

OMBRE TABLE
A triangular table for use when playing the Spanish card game of ombre, which was played by three people and became a vogue in the 17th and 18th centuries.

O'NEALE, JEFFRYES HAMETT
(c 1734–1801)
The Irish painter who worked in London, he was a freelance decorator with Chelsea during the red and gold anchor periods and also possibly with Worcester.

ONION FOOT
A flattened ball foot.

OPAL GLASS
A translucent opalescent glass used for stained glass and ornamental ware, it often had surface decoration applied of enamel and gilding. Other names have included cornelian and topaz glass.

OPAQUE CHINA
An early 19th-century term for improved earthenwares.

OPUS ANGLICANUM
A form of early English embroidery which used long and short stitches in a free manner so that the result appeared to imitate painting.

OPUS ARANEUM
Embroidery in which long straight lines form a pattern reminiscent of a spider's web.

OPUS CONSUTUM
Appliqué or cutwork of medieval times.

OPUS PECTINEUM
A woven work carried out with a tool, such as a comb, to imitate embroidery.

OPUS PHRYGICUM
Embroidery of great richness, often with gold thread.

OPUS PLUMARIUM
Work done mainly using featherstitch.

OPUS PULVINARIUM
The use of cross stitch and tent stitch on canvas.

OPUS SARACENICUM
A medieval name for carpets and rugs not made in Europe.

OPUS TIRATUM
Early name for drawn thread work.

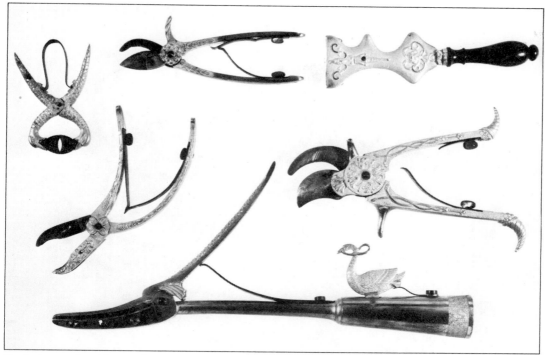

Gardening tools with ormolu mounts. A. Durant, 19th century. Courtesy Christie's

ORDERS

In architecture this refers to the Doric, Ionic and Corinthian, and later to the Tuscan and Composite. Features of all these have been used in furniture, particularly with long-case clocks, and also with silver in candlesticks.

ORIBE WARE

Pottery made by the talented Japanese Furuta Oribe (c 1544–1615), the celebrated tea master. His work appeared as seemingly rough forms decorated with great simplicity, and is divided by the Japanese into green, red and black.

ORLEANS

A faïence and porcelain manufactory started in 1753 by Sieur Jacques Etienne Dessaux de Romilly and it was called the *Manufacture Royale*. Wares included glazed statuettes in the Italian manner; and stoneware and marbleware during the early part of the 19th century.

ORMOLU

Gold that has been ground (*see* p 128, Honey) for use as a pigment on bronzes and brasses, ornaments that can be intended for furniture or such as candlesticks.

ORMOLU VARNISH

One used to imitate true gold on metal mounts.

ORNAMENT

Something that is added from an aesthetic standpoint to a structural or functional form of an object. It may be applied by painting, texture, relief, engraving, carving or moulded.

ORPHREY

Rich embroidery, usually with gold, a band of such work affixed to ecclesiastical vestments and formerly the robes of knights.

ORRERY

An astronomical instrument which consists of an apparatus which shows the principal movements of the solar system; the members are represented by spheres of different sizes and their movements in circular orbits are controlled by arms and uprights moved by geared wheels. The original instrument to bear the name orrery was made by John Rowley, London, in 1713. In itself it was not a new invention but a near copy of one that had been made at an earlier date by a leading horologist and instrument maker, George Graham (1673–

Original and historically important Orrery made by John Rowley. Courtesy of Sotheby Parke Bernet

1751), who had been assisted in his task by his renowned uncle, Thomas Tompion. It was Prince Eugene of Savoy who had commissioned the orrery from Graham. Rowley had managed to make his copy from it whilst it was waiting transport to Europe. The name orrery arose when the Rowley copy came into the possession of Charles Boyle, 4th Earl of Orrery.

In truth it cannot be said that the orrery was suddenly invented, it was really a development from planetariums and similar devices to show the movements of the heavenly bodies. Although there are no examples of the very early machines of this nature, there are records that point to experiments in the field. It is possible that the Chinese in the third millenium BC were operating water-driven instruments. Cicero makes a mention of a complicated

globe made by Archimedes in about the year 225 BC. Ptolemy in his *Almagest* mentions a globe which he had made which would show the movements of the sun and the moon.

ORVIETO
One of the oldest Italian ceramic centres, pottery was made there from the 13th century. Majolica made its appearance there about 1400. The forms were somewhat crude and lacking in elegance, but the painting had strength with a use of flowers, masks and animals treated in a Gothic manner.

OSTRICH CUP
One in which the body or bowl of the cup was made from an ostrich egg which was then richly and ornately mounted with and in gold and silver. First examples date from about 1500.

OTTOMAN

An upholstered settee with or without a back that was originally used in Turkey.

OTTWEILER

German faïence and porcelain manufactory established in about 1784 by Etienne-Dominique Pellevé. Wares included English-style lead-glazed earthenware, and tableware charmingly decorated with scenes from mythology and Italian comedy.

OUSHAK

A rug in the Turkish category with a deep wool pile.

OYSTERING

Veneering using specially selected veneers from cross-sections of branches and roots. The vogue started with Charles II and continued until about 1700.

PAD FOOT

A simple plain end to a cabriole leg, a club foot.

PADOUK

A Burmese tree, *Pterocarpus macrocarpus,* a heavy brilliant-coloured wood, it has the texture and tone of rosewood and was popular with the French *ébénistes*. It is also termed Vermilion or Andaman redwood.

PAESI

The term for majolica paintings of landscapes with buildings.

PALISSY, BERNARD (*c* 1510–*c* 1589)

The celebrated and inventive genius was born at La Chapelle Biron in Perigord. This alchemist and master potter started as a painter on glass. He spent many years with trial and error to discover his secret glazes, often in his creative impatience heating the kiln with his broken-up furniture. As he was a Protestant, after the Edict he was taken under the protective arm of Catherine de' Medici and settled in Paris, thus escaping the blood-letting massacre of St Bartholomew. But, sadly, he was taken in the end and in 1588 was immured in a Bastille dungeon where he died.

The modelling of his dishes and ornaments of fish, reptiles and animals remain unique, despite a host of desperate imitators and would-be forgers.

PAMPHLETS

Printed booklets, leaflets, sale catalogues, travel brochures, timetables, programmes of theatrical productions and sporting events are all rising in importance as collectors' items. If being displayed, they should be put under ultra-violet ray inhibiting glass to slow down or prevent fading and yellowing of the paper.

PANCHETTO

A small three-legged stool with a single plank back which was generally chip-carved; it originated in Italy during the Renaissance.

PAP BOAT

A small boat-shaped silver vessel with a lip at one end for feeding infants.

PAPER MOSAIC

A late 18th-century hobby of building up small pictures and likenesses of flowers and plants from tiny fragments and slivers from different coloured papers.

PAPERWEIGHTS

The finest examples of glass weights have come from France from the three principal centres – Bacarat, Clichy and St Louis. English producers include Bristol, Nailsea and Stourbridge. American weights have come from Sandwich, New England Glass Company and several others. First examples were probably made at St Louis in about 1820.

Parasol dating from around 1860. Courtesy Christie's, South Kensington

PAPIER MÂCHÉ
(From the French meaning literally chewed paper.) A modelling material that is made from pulped paper with size. It has been used for ornaments and objects including trays, small boxes, bed ends, snuff-boxes and tabletops. Its use dates from about 1750.

PAPPENHEIMER
A rapier with a distinctive perforated hilt used in the middle of the 17th century which took its name from Marshal Pappenheim.

PARCEL GILT
Silver or other metal that has been partially gilded.

PARCHMENT
Animal skins that have been treated by scraping, by the use of lime, to remove hair and by rubbing. Skins of sheep, pigs and goats have been used. For top-quality vellum those of young calves or still-born lambs are favoured. It remained the finest support for writing until nearly modern times, but from the 13th century onwards paper began to replace it.

PARDOE, THOMAS (1770–1823)
English freelance pottery decorator, he was born in Derby and went to Bristol in 1809

where he had an enamelling shop in Bath Street. From there he went to Nantgarw and probably assisted Billingsley with the painting of the famous service made for Prince Albert.

PARGET (or Pargeting)
A type of decorative plasterwork in which the designs are either in relief or cut or pushed in. Italian craftsmen brought the art to England in about 1520.

PARIAN WARE
A fine-grained porcelain with a surface finish like Parian marble that was developed by Copeland at Stoke-on-Trent in about 1846. Chief use was for modelling figures which would be left unglazed.

PARQUETRY
A mosaic of woods laid in geometric patterns; it is more applicable to floors than furniture.

PARTISAN
A kind of halberd or pike; also a staff or truncheon. It was first used in the 15th century.

PASTILLE BURNERS
Ceramic holders for fumigant or perfuming pastilles. These would be basically a paste of gum, benzoin, charcoal and cinnamon. They came in about 1700.

PATCH BOX
A small box to hold face-patches that came into use in about 1675. They were made of gold, silver and other metals decorated with enamel.

PATCHWORK
A type of fancywork in which fragments of cloth of differing colours, textures and shape are sewn together generally in some form of design. The results have been made into quilts, pillow covers and aprons. The craft started in Europe during the Middle Ages.

PÂTE-SUR-PÂTE
A technique for decorating ceramics in which the effect is gained by building up low relief with successive layers of slip laid with a brush. It was developed by Sèvres about 1850, and a Mr Solon who worked there brought it to Mintons when he changed his employer.

PATINA

The colour, texture and feel of a surface which is the result of age and wear, of polishing and affectionate care.

It is a film or encrustation by oxidation or other processes on bronze or other metals; for example, the darkening of silver when exposed for a period to the atmosphere. Often a patina is artificially applied to a piece of sculpture or metal work to achieve a desired effect; this may be done by applying chemicals such as weak acids, exposure to weathering, or by burial in places such as a peat bog which will attack the metal.

PATRON

A small box with a hinged lid and fixed divisions inside to hold pistol cartridges.

PAULDRON

A piece of armour that covers the joining of the arm-piece to the cuirass.

PEAR-DROP HANDLE

Small brass pendant handle for a drawer, it came in during the latter part of the 17th century.

A butterfly-leaf Pembroke table veneered in hardwood, cross-banded with satinwood with two opening frieze drawers. It stands on square, tapering legs, terminating in brass casters. Courtesy Spink

PEARL WARE

A pure white earthenware developed by Wedgwood around 1779. It was not iridescent.

PEDESTAL

The base for a column, statue, vase, candelabra, etc.

PEDESTAL TABLE

One which has one central support or pillar that is carried on spreading feet.

PEDIMENT

In classical architecture the triangular top over a gable or portico. In furniture it can be found at the head of cabinets and similar pieces. It was a feature of the Georgian period and also in France in the 18th century.

PEDOMETER

A meter for the rough measurement of distances, it responded to the movement of the wearer and counted the paces taken. Early examples from the beginning of the 18th century were sometimes operated by a cord attached to one of the feet of the wearer and then passed up to the pedometer which would be hanging from his belt.

PEGG, WILLIAM

A painter attached to the Derby porcelain manufactory and working there from about 1795. He was skilled with flowers and plants. But as a member of the Society of Friends he felt that it could be sinful to make the likeness of anything, so he retired and took a small shop. Apart from other stock he apparently sold red herrings and at this point seems to have modified his former scruples as he painted a water-colour group of his herrings to advertise their sale. Known as 'Quaker Pegg' later on he returned to the Derby works.

PEG TANKARD

A late 17th-century communal drinking vessel that had a vertical row of pegs inside that marked off measures for each man to drink down to as the tankard was passed round.

PEMBROKE TABLE

A small table with drop leaves supported by brackets in the frame or swing legs. It was introduced about the middle of the 18th century.

Pewter. The flagon in the centre is by John Heaney, Dublin *c* 1775, the one on the left is English *c* 1770 and that on the right is Scottish by Lachlan Dalls, *c* 1690. Courtesy of Richard Munday

PENDANT
A carved, moulded or modelled ornament that hangs downwards.

PENNY
Originally this was of silver and it was the principal Anglo-Saxon coin with the king's name on the obverse. In about 760 it would have shown Offa and on the reverse a cross motif. At the end of the 18th century it was made of copper and from 1860 bronze, except for a few still made of silver that were given out as Maundy money.

A coin used in Scotland up till 1707, by which time it had become so devalued that it was worth only one twelfth of the English penny.

The tribute penny of Matthew, Chapter XII, verse 19, was a denarius of Tiberius.

PEPPER BOX
A strange kind of revolver that had a set of barrels grouped together round a central axis that were fired by a hammer and trigger, the former could be either on top or underneath. On some models the barrels would turn automatically, with others they had to be turned by hand. Most pepper boxes had about six barrels but there were some savage weapons that had eighteen. The invention of the pepper box has been credited to Ethan Allen at about the time of the American Revolution, certainly he made the largest quantity of the pistol.

PERCUSSION LOCK
One that is fired by a hammer or striking pin striking a fulminating powder. It was reputedly thought up by the Reverend Alexander Forsyth who received a patent for it in 1807.

PETIT POINT
Embroidery which uses a very small satin stitch on a fine canvas.

PETRONEL
A 16th century short gun with a large bore, somewhat similar to an arquebus.

PEWTER
Any of the various alloys having tin as their principal constituent. The oldest-known pewter that has been found in England is Roman and this was made of tin and lead alone. In the Middle Ages, about one thousand years later, lead was still a main ingredient. A synod at Rouen in 1074 allowed the use of pewter as a substitute for gold and silver in church vessels. It is recorded that the cauldrons used to boil the meat at the coronation of Edward I, in 1274, were made of it. At first it provided the vessels for the rich but gradually its use spread until most people used it in one way or another.

Pewter can be enamelled and inlaid, but usually it is worked by itself, being hammered into shape. Its popularity for making drinking vessels dropped off as the people knew of the danger of lead poisoning when the liquors had any acid content.

PHYFFE, DUNCAN (1768–1854)
A very important American cabinetmaker. He was born in Scotland and emigrated with his family and arrived in New York in 1783. He was influenced by Hepplewhite and later by Sheraton, developing an American Directoire manner. He was conscious of the classical in his designs and latterly used a fair amount of carved decoration.

PIE-CRUST TABLE
A small round table generally with a tilt-top on a three-legged base. It took its name from the raised and decoratively carved edge to the top.

PIED-DE-BICHE
An early foot to a cabriole leg in the shape of a cloven hoof of a doe or stag. First appearance was about 1690 with French furniture.

PIERCED WORK
It occurs with metals, lace, furniture and ceramics. With metal the work is done with a fine saw with a rounded back which allows curving cuts to be made and also small chisels have been used. In ceramics the cutting is done before firing whilst the clay is still slightly malleable.

PIER MIRROR
One that has been designed to hang on a wall between two windows, normally over a console table, thus it acts as part of the general design of a room, balancing in with the window arrangement.

PIER TABLE
One designed to stand against a wall between windows. Robert Adam favoured a semi-circular kind, usually in pairs, that would be an integral part of the symmetry of the interior decoration of a room.

PIETRE DURE
A fine mosaic in which the tesserae were cut from semi-precious stones such as lapis lazuli, agates, cornelian, porphyry, onyx, jasper, as well as fine marbles and ivory which was applied in low relief; some examples added gold, silver and diamonds. The sumptuous decoration attracted the rich princes of Florence, Ferrara and Urbino, who competed with those from Rome, Venice and Naples as to who could possess the greatest example of this almost profligate use of gorgeous and valuable materials. It was also known as Florentine Mosaic.

PIGGIN
A wooden or ceramic vessel with a long handle used as a ladle for liquor. Principally made during the 17th and 18th centuries.

PIKE
A foot-soldier's weapon, a long staff with a spear head, sometimes with a hook or pick, it was superseded by the bayonet.

PILASTER
In furniture it is a rectangular or half-round pillar or column 'engaged' into the background. It may be in the manner of one of the orders, complete with capital or may be in the form of a figure or carved with a variety of motifs.

PILGRIM BOTTLE
One that has a flattened circular shape, generally with two rings to hold a shoulder cord. Early examples go back to the T'ang dynasty (618–907). Silver bottles appeared about 1600 and they would have silver chains.

Painted pine cabinet in the style of William Burges, with Zodiac signs, *c* 1865. Courtesy of Sotheby's, Belgravia

PILGRIM INSIGNIA
Small badges or labels, generally made from lead, which were handed out to pilgrims when they reached a particular shrine as evidence that they had completed their journeys. These pilgrims' medals or tokens were forged in large numbers in London during the latter part of the 19th century. William Smith and Charles Eaton set about an almost mass-production effort. In a small house in Rosemary Street near the Tower they concocted a 'cock metal', a cheap alloy of copper and lead, and poured forth thousands of medals and trinkets purporting to be from the Middle Ages. They issued them by burying them at midnight in the mud at the river's edge and then in daylight going through a well-acted pantomime of finding these 'valuable' items. They could have become very rich if they had not made a silly mistake over an inscription on one type. They had used an Arabic phrase, which an expert pointed out as impossible because Arabic was not known in Europe until two centuries after the supposed date of the medal. 'Billies and Charleys', as these rough frauds are known, may still be met with in some job-lot or jumbled in a box with other items.

PILLOW LACE
One made on a pillow with bobbins, pins and threads.

PILLOW SWORD
One with a straight blade and plain hilt, intended as a domestic security weapon in the 17th century it would normally be kept within reach of the man of the house when he retired for the night.

PINCHBECK
An alloy of copper and zinc used to imitate gold in cheap jewellery or with poor attempted forgeries. It was first made by Christopher Pinchbeck in about 1700.

PIN CUSHION
First examples would appear to date from the medieval period when they would have been an important adjunct for the ladies concerned with embroidery and needlework. They have been made from ivory, bone, wood, silver, amongst other materials, with the small stuffed pad for the pins and needles. There have been examples that would clamp to the worktable with a wooden screw. In the 19th century they became souvenir gifts on a wide scale.

PINE
Any tree of the genus *Pinus,* it can vary from quite hard to soft, and in colour from the so-called white pine to yellow. It has been used as the carcass for many veneers and also for items that will be gessoed and gilded as well as those where the pine is left showing and waxed or varnished.

PIQUÉ
A rather stiff cotton fabric in white or colour which has a finely-ribbed or raised woven pattern. It may also be in silk or rayon. It may be pricked or dotted; having inlaid work such as small ornaments in metal.

PISTOL
The smallest firearm, and designed to be fired from one hand, it was first introduced about 1540. Firing was at first by wheel-lock, later flint and percussion lock.

PISTOLE
A former Spanish gold coin, a double escudo of the time of Philip II (1527–1598).

PLACCATE
In armour it is a plate to give extra protection to the breast.

PLANISHING
Smoothing a piece of metal, polishing by lightly hammering.

PLAQUE
A commemorative or decorative tablet of metal, porcelain, ivory or bone; round or oval to be inlaid in cabinetwork or if of larger size to be fixed to a wall.

Card from an English pack of 1840 which was hand-painted. Courtesy Stanley Gibbons

PLATING
A thin coating of one metal laid on another metal.

PLAYING CARDS
Games with these go back to at least Tudor times. From early in the 18th century they carried excise duty. They had square corners until 1862 and court cards were single headed until 1867. English pack is 52 and the Italian 40.

PLYMOUTH
The first British hard-paste porcelain manufactory, it was active between 1768 and 1770 after which it was moved to Bristol. It was William Cookworthy, born at Kingsbridge in Devon, who found the secret of making Chinese Porcelain and then discovered the materials of kaolin and petuntse, or as he termed them Moorstone or growan and growan clay in Cornwall. With Lord Camelford he took out a patent for the method that is dated 17 March 1768.

POINT DE GAZE
A delicate needlepoint lace in which the pattern and ground are worked together with the same thread. It originated in Brussels.

POINT DE NEIGE
A lace worked on a brilliant white ground.

POINT DE PARIS
A bobbin lace made from the 17th century, often in narrow strips. Later a very rich lace was produced with gold and silver threads with pearls attached and this became known as point d'Espagne.

POINT DE VENISE
A fragile lace worked on a square mesh ground.

POINTILLÉ
A decoration on metal which is done by pricking or using a fine pointed punch.

POKER WORK
A method of decoration on wood in which the design or picture is scorched or burnt into the surface with a heated iron. It became a popular hobby in the 19th century.

POLE-AXE
A medieval foot-soldier's weapon, a battle-axe often with a hook at the back of the heavy-headed blade.

Flounce of Point de France. Courtesy of Phillips

POLE HAMMER
A medieval weapon with a blunt heavy head for smashing in your opponent's armour.

A documented Copenhagen porcelain bowl which is decorated with a scene from the Battle of Copenhagen and inscribed with the date '2nd April 1801'. Courtesy Arne Bruun Rasmussen, Copenhagen

Military decorations: Army Gold Cross group awarded to Lieutenant General Sir Colin Campbell, including the Peninsular Gold Cross and six clasps. Courtesy of J. B. Hayward & Son

The Guinness Animals and Keeper (set of six) and Horse and Cart pottery figures. Courtesy of Arthur Guinness Son & Co. Ltd.

George III giltwood console table designed by Robert Adam and made by William France and John Bradburn in 1765 for Sir William Dundas. Courtesy of Christie's

'A house-boy' by Carl Fabergé who constructed the figure with various semi-precious stones. Courtesy of Christie's

Silver plaque by Paul Vianen, dated 1607. Courtesy of Christie's

Charles II silver-gilt porringer and cover, 1669. Courtesy of Christie's

POLE SCREEN
A small fire-screen which could be adjusted to keep the heat off the face and so preserve the valued pale look. It was often decorated, on the side away from the fire, with embroidery. It came into use early in the 18th century.

POMANDER
A decorated box to contain perfume powders, perfumed ambergris or musk that was carried by both ladies and gentlemen during the 15th and 16th centuries as a foil against the evil smells and fevers which were abundant in the streets and public places.

POMMEL
The knob on the hilt of a sword, dagger or the like.

PONIARD
A thrusting dagger with a sharp long triangular blade.

PORCELAIN
Vitrified ware with a translucent body made from china-clay and petuntse fused at a considerable heat (see Plymouth).

PORRINGER
Two-handled silver bowl generally with a cover and a matching salver or serving dish. It had its main vogue in the 17th century.

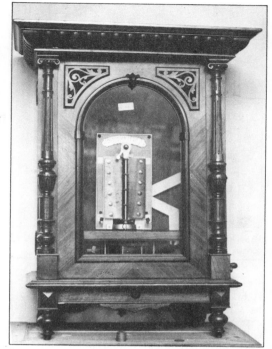

Fortuna Disc Polyphon, penny in the slot operated, c 1887. Courtesy of the Norfolk Polyphon Centre

POSSET POT
A two-handled vessel for holding posset, which was a thick drink made of milk curdled by strong ale or wine and with honey or dark sugar and spices.

POSTCARDS
Examples of art photography, patriotic fervour, early humour, scenes and the rest prior to 1930 are fast becoming sought after.

POSTERS
The field is wide and includes early commercial, theatre, sports meetings and travel which are a few of the categories to be looked for.

POT
A general term for helmets.

POT LID
The decorated lids of white glazed earthenware pots that held fish pastes, pomades, creams, etc.

Brass powder flask with repoussé decoration. 19th century. Photo by the author

POTSDAM
A faïence manufactory established about 1739 by Christian Rewend which produced a delft carrying the mark 'P' over 'R'.

There was also the glasshouse started in 1679 with Johann Kunkel which made fine glass but unfortunately the works were destroyed by fire in 1688.

POTTERY
In the general sense it can include porcelain, stoneware and earthenware. In the specialised sense it implies earthenwares that are only fired to low temperatures.

POUNCE POT
The container for pounce, which was finely-powdered sandarac or cuttlefish bone, that was used to blot the ink or to stop it spreading if writing on vellum. With the latter the pounce would be rubbed into the surface before writing.

POWDER FLASKS
For carrying gunpowder, they could be made of metal or horn and were often decorated.

PRESS
A loose term for a long cupboard with shelves for clothes.

PRESS BED
One that folds into a press or cupboard with doors. Apparently there was a version of this in the late 17th century with which a door was hinged upwards to form the tester and was held up with two removable poles.

PRESSED GLASS
That which is forced into moulds whilst it is still plastic from heating. The first efficient machine for this process was developed in America in the late 1820s.

PRICKET
A spike for securing a candle found in early candlesticks and chandeliers. Later this was replaced by a cylindrical cup. The term can also apply to the candle so impaled, as well as the whole support.

PRIE-DIEU
A chair with a very low seat and high back used for kneeling to say prayers. They were generally present in a bedchamber from the early medieval period onwards. The name was not used until about 1600.

PRINCE'S METAL
An alloy imitative of gold said to have been developed by Prince Rupert, Count Palatine of the Rhine (1619–82). It was three parts copper and one part zinc.

PRINTED EPHEMERA (*see* also
Pamphlets)
Such as bus, train and steamer tickets, price tags, old bills; and also broadsheets, newspapers, periodicals, any once mass-produced printed item now scarce because of age or fragility.

PRISONER OF WAR WORK
During the Napoleonic War some 60 000 captives languished in Britain; and craftsmen amongst them made such as: bone full-rigged ships, straw work, rolled paper filigree and hair jewellery.

PROPORTIONAL COMPASS OR DIVIDERS
These have legs with points at both ends and an adjustable joint. When open the distance between the points at the two ends is proportional to the lengths of the corresponding legs. The dividers can be used for enlarging or reducing drawings. It is likely that they were invented by Joost Burgi towards the end of the 16th century.

PRUNT
A small glass ornament attached to the main glass body by fusing.

PUNCH BOWL
A large vessel of silver, porcelain or glass to hold the liquid which would be based on a

mixture of wine, distilled spirits, lemon juice, sugar, spices and herbs.

Punch pots were often made in the shape of teapots with a top upstanding handle. This would be intended for a tea-based punch.

PURDEY, JAMES SENIOR AND JUNIOR
The father (1784–1863) was also the son of a gunsmith. He opened his business in 1814 just off Leicester Square, London. He did make flint-locks but was primarily concerned with percussion-cap. The son (1828–1909) was apprenticed to his father and continued the work which was to give the firm of James Purdey & Sons one of the leading names in the world, one which is still firmly established.

PURL
Embroidery that is worked with gold or silver threads and twisted wires, sometimes wound with silks.

PUZZLE JUG
A joke pot or drinking vessel, versions of which have been around since medieval times. They can include openwork and numerous spouts and lips which make it difficult to see where the liquid will be poured from.

PYX
The vessel, case, vase, tabernacle in which the Host is reserved. They could be made of silver and often were richly decorated with lapis lazuli, ivory and enamel. It can also be a small watch-shaped vessel in which the Eucharist is carried when the priest visits the sick.

Exeter Puzzle Jug. Courtesy of the Royal Albert Memorial Museum, Exeter

QUADRANT
An instrument formerly used by navigators to determine altitudes. Basically it consists of a brass limb, the quarter of the circumference of a circle, and is graduated to one minute. The zero of measurement or the reading of a vertical line on the limit, was carefully determined in the fixed instruments, whilst with instruments that were movable a plumb-line was used to mark the zero while an observation was being made. There were a number of varieties of quadrant and often these were known by the names of their inventors such as Godfrey's, Gunter's, Hadley's, Sutton's, etc, or they could be called by special names, mural quadrant, gunner's quadrant, surveyor's quadrant.

QUAICH
A drinking cup from Scotland, originally made of wooden staves fixed with metal hoops and having two ears. By the 17th century it was being made from brass, pewter and silver.

QUARE, DANIEL (1649–1724)
Leading British barometer and clockmaker who was in business in London, in his early days at St Martin's Le Grand and afterwards in Exchange Alley. In 1680 he developed a repeating watch and produced fine timepieces that ran for a year on one winding, telling not only the time but also days, months and the difference between mean and solar time. He was Master of the Clockmakers Company in 1708.

QUARRY
A small square or diamond-shaped pane of glass. It may also be applied to a similar shaped piece of stone or tile.

QUARTZ
Semi-precious stones such as amethyst, agate, onyx, rose quartz, sardonyx and cat's-eye; these are all different varieties of quartz. It is basically silica or silicon dioxide; different impurities tint the substance into the wide variety of colours shown in the aforementioned gems.

QUATREFOIL
In French *quatre feuille*. It is a four-cusped figure resembling a symmetrical four-lobed leaf or flower, to be found in windows and panels.

QUEEN'S WARE
A cream-coloured earthenware produced by Wedgwood, it was so named after he had received the patronage of Queen Charlotte in 1765.

QUENCHING
A term employed in metal crafts. It describes the process of plunging a piece of red-hot metal into a container of water or oil with the intention of cooling it quickly and making it brittle and extremely hard.

QUERVILLE, ANTHONY
American cabinetmaker active around 1840 and by repute to have made much of the furniture for the White House during the period of Andrew Jackson.

QUILL CLEANER
A small vessel filled with lead shot into which the quill could be thrust to clean off accumulated residues of ink. Some had covers with holes in which the quills could rest in between use. It was often included with an inkstand set.

QUILL EMBROIDERY
A method used by the Ojibwa Indians in North America in which they use the quills of the porcupine as a type of embroidery. Three kinds of stitches were used: loop, spot or back. Sinew was used for thread. The quill was slipped under the loop and bent over, so that the stitches could not be seen.

QUILLING
A strip of lace or embroidered ribbon fluted or folded and looking like a row of quills.

QUILLONS
The projecting arms of the cross-guard of a sword.

QUIMPER
A small pottery in France, started in 1690, where grey and brown glazed stoneware was made by De la Hubaudière, who also was producing faïence there. An older faïence had been made there imitating that of Rouen.

QUIRK
A sharp-edged hollow or groove between two mouldings.

QUIZZING FAN
One that would have a small spyglass set in the base just above the rivet that would enable the user to observe carefully without necessarily being noticed.

RAEREN

A centre near Aachen in Germany where fine Rhenish salt-glazed stoneware was made from around the 16th century. Outstanding were the large jugs and vases of a bellied cylindrical shape with a central band showing a frieze in low relief of peasants dancing, illustrations from the Old and New Testaments, in particular the story of Susanna, and coats of arms – some with inscriptions. The best-known makers were Baldem Mennicken, Jan Emens and Engel Kran.

RAIL

The horizontal member in framing on panelling, and also the top piece of a chair back.

RAKU WARE

A Japanese earthenware, low-fired and generally with a soft glaze of yellow, red or black. The style was started by Chōjiro (1516–92).

RAMSAY, DAVID

English horologist active around 1600 to 1650. He learnt his skills in France and on returning to London became clockmaker to James I and Charles I.

RANDOLPH, BENJAMIN

American cabinetmaker working around 1760 to 1790 in Philadelphia. He specialised in furniture in the Chippendale manner, and earned the sobriquet the 'Philadelphia Chippendale'. He was a skilled carver.

RAPIER

A straight two-edged sword used for thrusting in the 16th and 17th centuries.

RAPPOIR (also Rasp)

A late 18th-century device for grinding snuff; it was made from iron framed with wood, bone, ivory and sometimes silver. It was generally hinged.

RATTAN

A long climbing vine from Malaya and the East Indies that is used in basketry.

RAVENSCROFT, GEORGE (1618–81)

British glassmaker who, with the backing of the Glass Seller's Company, set up a glasshouse in the Savoy in London, where after some research he came up with 'flint glass' which contained lead oxide and was more brilliant when cut, heavier and stronger and also softer to work with the graver than the Venetian glass. He took out a patent for this revolutionary material in 1673.

READING CHAIR

English chair introduced about 1710. It had a slightly pear-shaped seat, with the narrow part at the rear; the back had a spread horseshoe crest rail and an adjustable back-rest. The reader sat astride and could place his elbows on the padded rests at the ends of the horseshoe. They have been incorrectly called cockfighting chairs.

RÉCAMIER

A luxurious chaise longue with the ends at the head and foot scrolled outward, designed in the Directoire style. It was named after Madame Récamier.

REDWARE

Unpretenious lead-glazed wares with soft porous body of a warm red–burnt sienna tone.

REFECTORY TABLE

A long, narrow table, so called after the type the monks would have used in their refectories from the Middle Ages. Generally of massive timbers with the stretchers low down.

REGENCY PERIOD

Broadly from 1793 to 1820, the time when George, Prince of Wales, later to be George IV, acted as Regent.

RELIEF DECORATION

That in which the ornament is raised or carved above the background.

RELIQUARY

A small box, casket or other small container which can be carried about, and which is used for keeping sacred relics in. Various forms of reliquaries include: pocket versions which were carried by explorers and leaders in the early days of Christianity; shrines or *châsses;* and smaller arm, finger or head reliquaries which were shaped to show the outer contour of those members of the body, or part of the body, which they enshrined.

REMINGTON, ELIPHALET, JUNIOR
(1793–1861)
Early in the 19th century he set up a gunsmith's workshop at Ilion on the Erie Canal. He developed a breech-loading single shot rifled small arm using the rotating block system; and also an efficient revolver.

RENAISSANCE
The magnificent period of creativity of the 14th, 15th and 16th centuries that saw the rebirth of the arts of learning and living. The visual arts burgeoned as never before and were encouraged by widespread enlightened patronage, epitomised by the De' Medici family.

RENDSBURG
German faïence manufactory set up in Holstein by Caspar Lorenzen in 1764. Ware was largely decorated with underglaze blue using motifs such as oriental flowers and forms; items such as snuff-boxes, bishop bowls and pot-pourri containers were in demand. Marks included 'CR', and 'RF'.

RENNES
From the 16th century, potteries were active, and faïence from 1748. This work was started in July of that year by Jean Ferasassi, called Barbarino, a Florentine, in the Quartier des Capucins. A second faïence workshop was started a year later by François-Alexandre Tutrel in the Rue Hue.

RENT TABLE
An English Table, introduced about 1750; round, hexagonal or octagonal, with drawers often marked with relevant figures or dates referring to the properties on an estate.

REPOUSSÉ
The technique for producing a design in relief by hammering from the reverse side. It is employed in metal work with silver, pewter, tin or other similar materials.

REREBRACE
Armour worn in medieval times to protect the upper arm.

RESTORATION
A general term to describe design and decoration in England for the period from 1660 to 1688. It can be also termed Carolean and late Stuart.

REVERE, PAUL (1735–1818)
The great American silversmith who worked in Boston. His father was a French Huguenot, Apollos Rivoire, who had come to Boston in 1718 and then changed his name to Paul Revere. The younger Paul, after learning his trade with his father, set up on his own and produced a number of fine pieces; he marked them with just 'Revere'. Many know of his work in support of the Revolution and his epic ride on 19 April 1775, when he rode out by night from Charleston to Lexington to give warning of the advance of the British troops on Concord. This was the theme for Longfellow's poem; 'Paul Revere's Ride'.

REVOLVER
A hand gun that has a six-chambered cylinder that rotates and is so designed that the chambers can be brought in turn in line with a single barrel. An American came up with what was probably the first model to work with a degree of reliability, this was a flint-lock and Elisha Collier took out a British Patent for it in 1818. Later came Samuel Colt with his various models, and for these he took out patents in Britain in 1835 and in America in 1836; they were made not only in America, but also in London. The first English maker to come up with a satisfactory revolver was Robert Adams who patented a five-shot model in 1851. In 1853 William Tranter patented a double-trigger model. The nearest an English designer came to a Colt was the Daws type patented in 1855. Then came the brothers John and Philip Webley who were, over the years, to arm legions of British officers.

RHYTON
A pottery drinking vessel roughly in the shape of a horn which has on the base a head of a woman, an animal or a mythological beast.

RIBAND-BACK
A feature favoured by Chippendale in which the back splats of a chair carried carvings of simulated ribbons often to be completed with a bow.

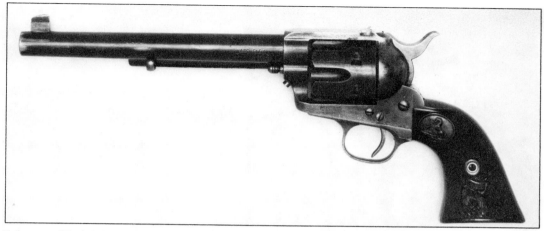

Colt: ·450 (Eley) S.A. Target revolver made about 1890. Courtesy of Christie's

RICHARDSON, FRANCIS (1681–1729)
One of the first American born silversmiths to find success. He worked in Philadelphia and was followed in his work by his son Joseph, and grandsons Joseph Junior and Nathaniel.

RIDGWAY FAMILY
Potters working at Hanley, Staffordshire, and later Cauldon Place, Shelton. They traded as J. & W. Ridgway in the early part of the 19th century, and they made mainly stone-china, domestic wares, and some porcelain.

RIESENER, JEAN HENRI (1734–1806)
Born in Germany he moved to Paris where he worked for Jean-François Oeben and took over his workshops when he died. Louis XVI made him *ébéniste du Roi* and he is considered the greatest of the skilled hands working during this period. He particularly excelled with marquetry and ormolu.

RIFLE
A shoulder-fired firearm that has grooves, rifling, in the bore of the barrel that give a rotary motion to the bullet or projectile to ensure greater accuracy of fire.

RIGAREE
A glass decoration with which there are narrow vertical parallel lines to form small ribs.

RIMBAULT, STEPHEN
English clockmaker active around 1760 to 1780. His speciality was bracket and table clocks that included novel mechanical displays,

such as groups of dancers and musicians performing with sound.

RINCEAU
An ornament composed of leaf scrollwork often developed symmetrically, and inspired by the acanthus.

RITTENHOUSE, DAVID (1732–96)
The American astronomer, clockmaker, mathematician and scientist from Pennsylvania who was the first Master of the American Mint. He was a leading maker of long-case clocks and also other clocks orientated towards astronomy. He made a number of technical instruments as well.

ROCAILLE
A form of decoration developed in the 18th century which was based on shell and rock shapes.

ROAN
A low-grade sheepskin tanned with sumak and dyed to imitate morocco. It has been used for book-binding and some upholstery.

ROCK CRYSTAL
Colourless transparent quartz. Since Roman times it has been worked into ornaments, vases and often elaborate drinking vessels. Craftsmen during the Renaissance left some exquisite examples of carving and beautiful mounting. In the medieval times it was regarded as a protection against poison, the proximity of which was supposed to discolour it.

An example of English Rockingham, typical of a period when it favoured rich baroque decoration. The oval basket has a central gilt entwined branch handle. In the centre can be seen a view of 'Wentworth House', the seat of the Earl of Fitzwilliam in Yorkshire. Courtesy Christie's

ROCKING CHAIR
Mainly an American chair it began to appear about 1725 and went under such names as the Boston Rocker and the Salem Rocker.

ROCKINGHAM
An English pottery established on the estate of the Marquis of Rockingham at Swinton, Yorkshire. The well known mark of the griffin was adopted from the crest of the Marquis. The importance of the workshop started with the Bramfield family's association in 1778. The Rockingham teapot became well known for its distinctive shape, it was taller rather like a coffee-pot, and for the fact that it was able to extract the full flavour of the tea. From 1823, Thomas Bramfield began making very fine porcelain and insisted on the most skilled painters for the decorating. Other wares of this time included cream-coloured and blue-printed earthenware, marbled ware and black basalt.

ROEMER
A popular hock and moselle glass from about the middle of the 17th century. It was generally a glass slightly tinged with green and having a nearly spherical bowl on a stout stem often ornamented with prunts.

RÖENTGEN, DAVID (1743–c 1807)
The son of Abraham Röentgen (1711–93), the skilled worker in marquetry. David inherited his father's workshop near Coblenz. He found most of his patronage in France, particularly Paris, and amongst his clients was Marie Antoinette. He had a skill like his father with marquetry, and he was noted for his mechanical devices which would open drawers, latches and slide panels.

ROLLED GOLD
It was intended as an imitation for massive gold, and was originally copper or a base metal over which a thin plate of gold was rolled.

Now it is more likely to be a kind of filled gold, rolled or drawn out so that the gold is very thin.

ROLLING PINS

A speciality of the Nailsea glasshouse, the fashion lasted from the late 18th century to the end of the 19th century. They appeared in several colours and were decorated with enamel or gilding, often with mottoes. They were used for salt and sometimes sweetmeats.

ROLL TOP DESK

This is somewhat similar to a cylinder top except the top drawers and whole writing area can be covered in by a slatted panel that descends down a slight double curve or wave profile.

RONDACHE

A round shield carried by medieval foot-soldiers.

RONDEL

A 14th to late 15th century sharp pointed dagger with a round guard.

RÖRSTRAND

A Swedish faïence manufactory, working under Jean Wolf from 1725, near to Stockholm. Early wares were in lead-glazed earthenware, much of it sold round the country. By 1743 the pottery was run to waste, buildings in ruins and accounts ill-kept. Elias Magnus Ingman was appointed and he did improve matters. His son took on and for a time made *porcelain de silex,* English stoneware. Later imitations were made of Oriental and Delft ware but very little faïence, and then work in the manner of Marseilles and Strasbourg with flowers and fruit in relief.

ROSE ENGINE

One that controls an engraving point with an eccentric movement that leads to the cutting of a floral pattern resembling a rose. It may be used for decorating or providing a certain textured surface on a metal.

ROSEWOOD

Several trees from Brazil, Honduras and India are styled rosewood, so termed for the fragrance from the freshly sawn timber. It is hard and dense with rich colours and streaking. Much in favour for veneers from about 1760.

ROSSO ANTICO

A name once used for the Wedgwood unglazed red stoneware.

ROTTEN STONE

A soft, friable, siliceous stone that when powdered can be used as a polish with oil for wood, with water it will help to remove scratches on metal.

ROUEN

A centre for fine faïence, where a number of potteries were active from the latter part of the 17th century. Influence from the district affected potters over the rest of France, and also in Germany and Holland. Decoration included imaginative use of lambrequins and scrolls, festoons, flowers and coats of arms. Later the creative approach of the Chinese became evident and the flourishes of the baroque.

ROUNDEL

An ornamental disk containing such as a rose or medallion.

ROXBURGH

A bookbinding of the 18th century, named after the Scottish collector, the 3rd Duke of Roxburgh. It had a leather back with gold titling, paper or cloth sides, the front and bottom edges were uncut and the top edge gilt.

ROYAL COPENHAGEN

A porcelain manufactory was set up in 1772 by an apothecary F. H. Müller and it is still flourishing. Artists employed to carry out the painting were Gylding, Seipius and Ruch. Matters declined during the 19th century until 1885 when the revival began. Marks included three wavy lines.

RUBY GLASS

One of a deep-red colour produced at first by the addition of oxide of copper or gold chloride, now by adding selenium. The German, Johann Kunckel was probably the first to make it successfully in 1679, although he may have been using a recipe found by a Doctor Cassius of Hamburg.

RUMMER

A large-bowled glass on a short stout stem, popular for hot toddies from about 1760 to 1850.

RUSH SEAT

One that dates back to the time of the early Egyptians. In the 18th century they had a certain vogue with such as the ladder-back chair. The rushes have to be harvested at the right time and properly cured or they will rot.

RUSSIAN IMPERIAL TAPESTRY WORKS

They were opened by Peter the Great in St Petersburg in 1716. They flourished most under the enlightened and almost insatiable patronage of Catherine between 1762–96.

RUSTIC WORK

Around the middle of the 18th century there was an odd fashion for rather strange furniture that imitated tree and rock forms, sometimes using actual branches to build up the backs and sides of chairs. These oddities fitted into man-made grottoes, such as the extraordinary echo-filled artificial cave at Pommersfelden near Bamberg, Germany, with its shell-packed hand-made rugged rocks.

SABATON

Foot-armour made from a laminated plate, it is broad and blunt at the toe.

SABRE

A long, cutting blade similar to a sword, it may be straight, slightly curved or with a decided sweep curve to it. The blade has a single sharp edge; some, however, may have a so-called false point with double edges for about six inches.

SABRE LEG

A square-sectioned leg that has a slight forward concave curve.

SACRAMANTHAUS

A shrine for holding the sacrament, in some German churches it is sometimes quite large and decorative.

SACRISTY CUPBOARD

One of the earliest movable cupboards, it was used for keeping sacred vessels. It dates from the Gothic period.

SADDLE SEAT

A seat that has been scooped away to the back and sides in an approximate shape of a flattened saddle. It is often used with Windsor chairs.

SAINT CLEMENT

French faïence manufactory started in 1750 at Meurthe-et-Moselle by Jacques Chambrette in conjunction with Lunéville. Wares produced included gilt faïence, figures, and cream earthenware.

SAINT CLOUD

Porcelain and faïence manufactory near Paris which was founded about 1690 by Pierre Chicanneau. He received letters of patent for his family in 1702. In 1696 the mark of the sun-face and fleur-de-lis was registered, this was followed by 'St C' over a 'T'. The porcelain had a distinctive ivory tinge and some later came close to Blanc-de-Chine.

ST PETERSBURG

The Russian Imperial Porcelain manufactory was founded by the Empress Elizabeth Petrovna in 1744 with craftsmen from Meissen. Catherine II patronised the works and in 1765 she enlarged them. The painter Swebach directed the decoration. In 1825 two potters came from Sèvres. Most of the ware showed influences from German and Austrian centres. The hard paste was often lavishly decorated with gilding. Marks were various and included: three vertical parallel lines, Catherine's cypher Ekaterina of an 'E' with hatching on the middle stroke and Emperor Paul's crown over his cypher.

SALAMANDER

A square or round plate on a long handle that is intended to be thrust into the fire until red hot and then withdrawn and held over pastry, cheese or other foods that call for a quick browning and crisping of the surface.

SALLET

A 15th-century helmet, also termed a salade. It was often worn with a chin-piece, a beaver. The general shape of the helmet tended to be drawn out at the back to give protection for the neck.

SALT GLAZE

One that is produced by throwing common salt into the kiln at the moment of the highest heat.

SALTS

Prior to the middle of the 17th century the standing salt was placed in the middle of the table; and around this arose the social division of 'above' or 'below' the salt. Many of these large salts were superb examples of the goldsmith's and silversmith's art; the finest example being the superb salt by Benvenuto Cellini for Francis I. After the Civil War the salts became smaller and less conspicuous, the bell salt came and then the cylindrical with a steeple cover and later the capstan. At the end of the 17th century small individual salts for each guest made their appearance. Shapes were various, round on feet, boat shaped, shells and pierced work with blue glass liners.

SALVERS

A flat tray, round, square, octagonal and often with gadrooning and lively chasing. They were to present drinks and food, or deliver messages to the head of the house. The name probably comes from the Spanish *salva*.

SAMARKAND

A rug woven in the vicinity of Samarkand with a medium-length pile and showing Chinese influence in the designs.

SAMBIN, HUGHES

The 16th-century French cabinetmaker who published a Book of Designs in 1570. From this can be gleaned the progress of the Italian Renaissance over the Gothic. He was a lively carver, particularly with the handling of figures.

SAMITE

A rich, silk fabric of the Middle Ages, it was

George III silver salver in the Chinese Chippendale Taste. Eben Coker, London, 1763. Courtesy Sotheby Parke Bernet

often interwoven with gold and silver. Mostly used for ecclesiastical vestments and sometimes for large cushion coverings.

SAMOVAR

A metal urn used in Russia for making and keeping tea hot; a metal tube heated by charcoal passes through the urn, and generally has a cup-like top on which the teapot can stand.

SAMPLER

Many were probably done to preserve embroidery stitches and patterns. The earliest surviving date from the first part of the 17th century, although it is possible the custom started much earlier. In the 18th and 19th centuries they were often done by children to illustrate their skill and would bear the name and date.

SAMSON, EDMÉ

The firm, Samson et Cie, was founded by Edmé in 1845 at 7 Rue Béranger in Paris. At the outset a large part of their intent was to make replacements for broken pieces from large services. From this grew a wave of brilliant imitations of the wares from other centres such as Chinese export vases, Derby, Chelsea, Bow, Sèvres, Worcester and many others. All pieces made were supposed to have their mark of an 'S' put on as well as the mark of the imitated ware.

Early 19th-century Sampler. Courtesy of the Royal Albert Memorial Museum, Exeter

SANDALWOOD

The tree, *Santalum freycinetianum*, from the East Indies, it has a pleasant yellow-ochre colour and a fragrant perfume, and is particularly used for clothing drawers and chests.

SAND BLASTING

A process for decorating glass invented by Benjamin Tilghmann in 1870, who came from Pennsylvania. The name was derived from the fact that a controlled blast of hard sand, flint and carborundum is projected against the glass.

SAND GLASS OR HOUR GLASS

A direct descendant of the Clepsydra or Water Clock of the East. The idea of sand sifting through from one container to another certainly goes back to the early Greeks, the tragedian Nato mentions one such device in 280 BC. In 234 BC Athenaeus mentions that sand glasses were carried around then as we carry watches now.

Much later sand glasses not only helped the cooks but were in metal brackets beside the preacher in his pulpit to keep matters within limits. There were ship or marine log sand glasses, often with a particular ship's name cut into them.

SANG DE BOEUF

A fine red, close to the colour of the blood of an ox, found with Chinese porcelain from the K'ang Hsi period (1662–1722).

SARUK

A Persian rug of a fine weave, generally on cotton with a short pile. It has rich, strong colouring.

SATINWOOD

The timber from an East Indian tree, *Chlorxylon swietenia,* it has a good yellow gold colour with veining. It is sought after for veneering.

SATSUMA WARE

A hard-glazed pottery made in the former province of Satsuma in Kyushu. The white dates from about 1640.

SATYR

An ornament in carving, ceramics and metal-work that is in half-human half-bestial form, one of the woodland beings in the train of Bacchus. It was popular during the Renaissance, and the satyr mark appears in the early Georgian period.

SAUCE-BOAT

In silver they appeared about the middle of the 18th century and in two main types. The one had a broad lip at one end with a scrolled handle on the other, the second type had a lip at each end and two side handles. They might stand on three or four feet or a round base. Many examples were lavishly decorated.

A silver sauce-boat, dating from *c* 1765, made by William Townsend, Dublin. Courtesy National Museum of Ireland

SAVONA

During the 17th and 18th centuries a number of faïence factors were active at Savona, Albissola and Genoa. The productions are generally grouped under the collective term Savona. The early work was largely in blue and white. Wares included apothecaries' jars, vases and tableware; decoration motifs were often a lively use of figures on horseback and amorini.

SAVONNERIE

A fine knotted-pile carpet made in the Turkish style at the old soap factory (hence the name) at Chaillot near the Seine, Paris. The works were merged with the Gobelins in the early part of the 19th century.

SAXTON, CHRISTOPHER

The English cartographer who was active at the end of the 16th century, and who is principally recalled as the map-maker for Queen Elizabeth I; he produced an 'Atlas of the Counties'.

SCAGLIOLA

A material which is made of gypsum, isinglass and colouring matter, plus other materials put on its surface whilst still damp; these can be marble dust, spar or granite dust. It imitates marble and will take a high polish and is extremely permanent. Robert Adam used it for decoration with cabinetwork.

SCEAT

A silver coin of the early Anglo-Saxon rulers (about 600), it was small and thick with a head on the obverse and a cross on the reverse.

SCENT BOTTLES

Examples from the 18th and 19th centuries can be found, made from porcelain, stoneware, glass and finely-enamelled metals, and plain metal. Designs can include small flasks, cylinders and miniature figures.

SCHÄPERGLÄSER

A glass decorated mainly with black enamel which took its name from Johann Schäper who was active about 1650. It is really a kind of sgraffito technique, in which the picture or decoration is needled through the enamel.

SCHIAVONA

A two-edged sword with a basket hilt used in Venice and district during the 17th and 18th centuries.

Royal Worcester Jubilee scent bottle with silver cap. Courtesy Corner Antiques, Coltishall

SCHMELZ GLASS

A German term for a glass developed by the Venetians during the Renaissance. It is formed by fusing coloured glasses until they acquire a marbled look.

SCHOFIELD, JOHN

London silversmith working around 1780 and noted for his candelabra, coffee-pots and tea-urns.

SCIMITAR

A sabre-shaped blade with the curve towards the point and the cutting edge on the convex side. A weapon used especially by the Arabs and the Persians.

SCONCE

A backplate holding a candle bracket or brackets that was fixed to the wall. The earliest examples date from the beginning of the 16th century. Many of them were gilt bronze.

SCREENS

The earliest examples seem to have been in China in the 2nd century BC. The first in England probably date from the time of

Edward II (1284–1327) and since then have been used as protection against draughts, surveillance, heat from a fire, and strong sunlight. Built up of framework with a number of hinged panels which can be as many as twelve, they have been covered with leather, textiles and paper.

SCRIBANE
A type of bureau cabinet popular in Holland and France in the middle of the 18th century.

SCRIMSHAW
The art of engraving designs on whale-teeth, whalebone, and making simple souvenirs, corset bones, chessmen, pastry wheels and walking canes. After engraving, the lines were filled with black ink or paint and the surface wiped clean.

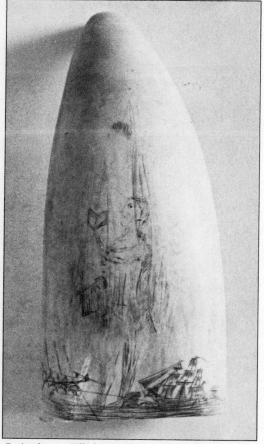

Scrimshaw. Filled sgraffito worked on a sperm whale's tooth. Late 19th century. Photo by the author

SCROLL FOOT
One carved in the form of a scroll, which may be turning either forwards or backwards.

SCROLL TOP
A broken pediment made with two opposed scrolls.

SCUDO
A silver coin used in Italy and Sicily from the 17th to the 19th century. There was also a gold version.

SCYPHUS
A deep cup or bowl with a wide base and no stem, and generally two small handles at the sides.

SEALED BOTTLES
Those dating from the late 17th century that were personalised bottles for wine and carried the owner's crest, coat of arms, a cypher and name of owner or initials and often the date. Generally they are round and rather squat and of dark green or brown glass.

SEALS
A personal item made generally from gold with the crest and or initials cut into semi-precious stones, marble or toughened steel. They were intended to hang from a ribbon or a watch chain.

SECRÉTAIRE
A rather free term that can include: a 17th-century bureau on legs or a stand; a small table in the following century with slender legs, a drawer and surmounted by a small stand of drawers; a fall front desk sometimes with drawers below and a bookcase above; and a desk with drawers and pigeon-holes, sometimes cupboards below.

SECTOR
A mathematical instrument, consisting of two rulers connected at one end by a joint and marked with several scales, as of equal parts, chords, sines, tangents, etc.

SEDDON, GEORGE (1727–1801)
One of the most productive English cabinet-makers of his time; his firm employed at least 200 craftsmen. He took in his two sons, George and Thomas, and his son-in-law, Thomas Shackleton. He had the best display rooms and widest selections for his customers.

Mahogany Military Secrétaire Chest *c* 1850. Courtesy Sotheby's, Belgravia

Louis XV Black Lacquer Secrétaire. Courtesy of Frank Partridge

SERPENTINE
In furniture it implies a wavy or undulating curve. It was used for the fronts of commodes, chests of drawers and also with the tops of desks and card tables.

SETO WARE
That produced from the kilns at Seto in the Owari province in Japan. One of the oldest centres going back to about the 9th century.

SETTEE
A long seat with back and arms generally upholstered; and also a kind of sofa. The name dates from about 1725.

SETTLE
A long wooden bench with arms and a high back; origin dates back to the early medieval period.

SÈVRES
The great French porcelain manufactory that was started at Vincennes in about 1738 with the two brothers Robert and Gilles Dubois, but they were sacked after three years for continued inebriation. In 1756 the works moved to Sèvres from which site it flourished through to today. The early wares were of soft paste, but after the discovery of kaolin by the wife of a poor doctor, Madame Darnet, near her home at St Yrieix, Sèvres started hard paste.

The sculptor Etienne-Maurice Falconet was engaged to supervise the modelling of figures. The painting was exquisite, reflecting the riches and beauty of the pre-Revolution period. The production was large and ranged over a considerable variety of wares. Notably those pieces with the famous turquoise, yellow, green and the pink grounds. There has been much copying and imitating of the best from Sèvres in the past 150 years.

Sextant by Huges with two eyepieces, filters and scale microscope with certificate dated 1882. Courtesy of Christie's, South Kensington

SEXTANT
Invented by John Hadley in 1730 and afterwards improved by him; it enabled the navigator to take the angle between two objects. As the sextant could be held in the hand it was possible to use it on the deck of a ship despite any prevailing motion.

SGRAFFITO
A technique for decorating pottery in which the design is produced by scratching through an overglaze to reveal the coloured ground. It can also apply to a similar approach with paint over metal or wood.

SHAGREEN
The skins of certain sharks and rays that have been treated. It is used for covering microscope barrels, knife cases, tea-caddies, etc.

Originally the term was applied to a kind of untanned leather produced in Russia, Persia and Turkey from the skins of camels, horses and wild asses. The granular surface was achieved by pressing small seeds into the hair side of the skins whilst they were still moist. When dried, the skins were scraped and then given a soaking which brought up the granulation. The skins were finally dyed.

SHAKER FURNITURE
Simple solid furniture produced by members of the religious sect of the Shakers in the late 18th century.

SHARPS, CHRISTIAN
The maker of the celebrated American Sharps rifle, and founder of the Sharps Rifle Manufacturing Company at Hartford, Connecticut in 1851.

SHEFFIELD PLATE
A method of plating a base metal, copper, with silver that was evolved by Thomas Bolsover in 1742. The result was achieved by rolling under pressure and heat a sheet of silver with the copper and a flux. More recently the process has been carried out by electrolysis, depositing silver on to the copper.

SHEKEL
An ancient weight and money unit of Babylonia and also of the Phoenicians, Hebrews and Hittites.

SHERATON, THOMAS (1751–1806)
The English furniture designer and scholar, born at Stockton-on-Tees, came to London. Records about his life are few but apparently he was established in Wardour Street, Soho, in 1790, and later in Broad Street off Golden Square. His published works which had and have had a very considerable influence include: *The Cabinet-Makers' and Upholsterers' Drawing Book* and *The Cabinet-Maker, Upholsterer and General Artist's Encyclopaedia* (unfinished).

SHETLAND LACE
It is produced from spun sheep's wool and worked on two knitting needles, the end of one being anchored in a hole in a special knitting belt. Mostly shawls are made with traditional geometric patterns; the results are of great fineness and the test is to pull them through a wedding ring.

SHIELD
A protective piece of armour that was used by both mounted and foot-soldiers. Shapes varied: round, triangular, straight- and curved-sided, rectangular, and in the early periods would be little more than hide over a wooden frame, then bronze and lastly steel. Other names for a shield include targe, pavis, scutum and ysgwyd.

SHIP MODELS
The best known of these are probably the beautiful and detailed works made by the French prisoners of war at the beginning of the 19th century. They largely used bone from the meat rations; the bone was made pliable for carving by first moistening it.

A prisoner of war bone model of a three-masted ship. Courtesy of Christie's

Captured silversmiths and jewellers probably helped with such as the minute guns and metal fittings. Other models have included hulls carved from a solid block or patiently built up from shaped boards. There is also the ship in the bottle, a method that began in the first half of the 19th century where the slim model is slid into the container and then by some system of draw threads the masts are raised and lastly the bottle is sealed with, in some cases, a seemingly irremovable plug. Model boats first made their appearance in the early Egyptian tombs and crop up throughout history as ritual objects, shipbuilders' ideas and toys.

SHIRAZ

A somewhat loosely-woven Persian rug with a medium-length pile.

SIDEBOARD

A plain table or chest by a wall in a dining room for supporting serving dishes and decanters. There are many versions from the different countries, some with cupboards, shelves, drawers and several tiers.

SIENA

Potteries were probably in existence in Siena, Tuscany in the 13th century. By about 1500 faïence of fine quality was being produced; notably tiles about 5 ins (1·3 cm) square bearing designs with amorini, masks, birds and dragons. Pharmacy jars and large dishes were also made.

SILVER

A white metal which works extremely well and has been popular since the time of the ancient Egyptians for jewellery, tableware and

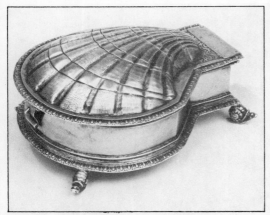

James I silver sugar box. Courtesy Phillips

Silver cake basket by George West, Dublin, 1793. Courtesy M. McAleer

Early George II Irish plain Silver Bowl. Courtesy of Frank Partridge

decorative vessels. In England, from around 1300, standards of silver and a system of hall-marking have been used. Standard silver, or sterling silver, has 925 parts of fine silver and 75 parts copper per 1000 parts. Sheffield plate which is used extensively for tableware and cutlery was invented in 1742 (*see* Sheffield plate).

SILVER GILT
Pieces of silverware covered with a very thin film of gold. This is often done as a protection against staining, particularly if it is inside a drinking cup or similar object. Until the introduction of electro-gilding in the 19th century the gold had been applied by the fire or mercurial technique. With this an amalgam of gold and mercury was applied to the silver object and then the mercury was driven off by heat.

SILVER LUSTRE
Pottery treated with platinum oxide, a method developed in the first half of the 19th century.

SINCENY
A French faïence manufactory at Aisne, Sinceny (formerly written as St Cenis) was established in 1733 by Jean Baptiste de Fayard. It was directed by Denis-Pierre Pellevé from Rouen who brought some painters with him from that centre; these included Pierre Jeannot, Philippe Vincent, Alexandre Daussy, Joseph Ghail and Joseph Lecerf. The earliest pieces were painted in blue, then in blue touched with red or green and yellow, with decorations of lambrequins, birds and butterflies and some Chinese figures. Wares included table services, figures, delicate wicker baskets, watch-stands and rococo ornaments.

SINGERIE
An ornament, particularly with the French, of a decorative and often grotesque arrangement of monkeys parading and behaving as people. It was thought up by a Monsieur Bérain, and the painter Antoine Watteau (1684–1721) elaborated on the theme with a number of satirical compositions.

SISSOO
An East Indian tree, *Dalbergia sissoo,* a dark brown and hard dense wood useful for cabinetmaking which has also been used for cannon carriages.

SIX-BACK
An American ladder-back chair with six slats which are usually slightly arched.

SIZE
A weak glue that can be used for binding colours for polychrome work, as an isolator for gesso or plaster and as a stiffener for such as linen to prepare it for buckram.

SKEAN DHU
A knife or short dagger from Scotland worn in the stocking with full Highland dress.

SKEWER
Silver skewers were introduced at the beginning of the 18th century, they generally have a shell or ring handle. They were often made in sets measuring from about 6 ins (15·2 cm) up to 15 ins (38·1 cm).

SKILLET
A 17th-century small silver vessel on three feet with a cover and a handle; it was intended for heating food. Some were made with a flat bottom.

SLAT BACK
A chair dating from the 17th century with turned posts and horizontal slats similar to a ladder-back.

SLICKENSTICK
A sturdy glass mushroom that was gently heated and used for smoothing out delicate fabrics. Its use and that of others made from stone and heated at an open fire probably date from the 17th century.

SLIP
A potter's clay watered down to the consistency of cream to coat a pot or be used for decoration.

SLIPWARE
An earthenware decorated by plain or coloured slip by brushing, trailing, spotting, combing and marbling. A method which has been used in some form from early periods.

SMALL SWORD
A light, tapering, thrusting sword once used in duelling, it dates from from the latter part of the 17th century.

SMITH, GEORGE
The English cabinetmaker who was working around 1800 to 1830 in Cavendish Square, London and later in Brewer Street, off Golden Square. He took inspiration from the early Egyptians, Greeks and Romans. His published work included a *Collection of Designs for Household Furniture and Interior Decoration* and *A Collection of Ornamental Designs after the Manner of the Antique.*

SMITH, HORACE
The American gunsmith working around the mid 19th century, at first from Connecticut and later Springfield, Massachusetts; who, in collaboration with Daniel Wesson, produced not only a fine repeating pistol but also held a patent for a metal rimfire cartridge. Later in the 20th century one of the best heavy automatics came from Smith and Wesson.

SNAPHANCE
A type of gunlock developed in Germany in about 1650, with which a trigger released the flint which was held in a cock and let it strike the steel and produce the sparks to flash the priming pan.

SNUFF-BOX
A small ornamented personal box for carrying snuff, which came in during the 17th century. The making of these has attracted many of the most skilled craftsmen. Materials have included gold, silver, brass, pewter, horn, tortoiseshell, ivory, bone, wood, papier mâché, and decorations have ranged from niello, carving, painting, enamelling and inlay to rich encrustations with precious stones.

Snuff-handkerchief, *c* 1780. Courtesy Christie's, South Kensington

Selection of Gold Snuff Boxes in the collection of the Earl of Harewood. Courtesy of Christie's

SNUFFERS
In one version or another these extinguishers date from medieval times. They were scissor-like utensils that could be used for wick-trimming as well as putting out the flame. They have been made from silver, Sheffield plate, steel, iron and brass.

SOCIABLE SEAT
A mid-19th century upholstered seat for two, constructed in plan as an 'S', the back following the line of the letter and a seat being placed in each loop.

SOCLE
A plain block slightly projecting as a base or plinth for such as a pedestal support.

SOFA
The sofa as recognised today has evolved from the French day-bed of the time of Louis XIV. It is distinct from the settee for its greater comfort.

SOFA TABLE
A small narrow table with two drawers in the apron or frieze, and drop leaves; there were often mock-drawers at the rear. It was developed in the late 18th century and it may have got its name as Sheraton stated the table was to be placed in front of the sofa.

SOFT-PASTE
An artificial porcelain composed mainly of gypsum and bone ash which was developed by European potters to imitate the hard porcelain of the East.

SOLIDUS
A gold coin of Constantine's time which replaced the Aureus, being introduced about 312.

SOUMAK
A Caucasian rug that is made with a kind of tapestry method, a flat stitch which results in a flat surface.

SOVEREIGN
English gold coin introduced by Henry VII in 1489. Under Elizabeth I it was termed a

fine sovereign to distinguish it from the pound sovereign. The present coin was issued from the time of George III.

SPANGLED GLASS
An American 19th-century glass which contained flakes of mica and which was used to make glass baskets and fancy ware.

SPÄNGLER, JEAN JACQUES
The Swiss porcelain modeller who worked at Derby around 1770.

SPARVER
The canopy or tester of a bed.

SPEED, JOHN (1552–1629)
The English cartographer who was born in Cheshire and began his working life as a tailor in London. Through progressing from a hobby of mapmaking he became one of the leading experts of his time. His main work being *Fifty-four Maps of England and Wales* which was first published between 1608 and 1610. The maps were intriguingly decorated with imaginary sea-beasts, ships and coats of arms. There are numerous copies and fraudulent examples of his work to be come across.

SPICE CHEST
An American evolution, it could be a well-made and elaborately-designed chest on legs. There would be two doors which when opened revealed a large number of small drawers.

SPIDER LEG TABLE
A revival of the gate-leg table during the latter half of the 18th century with a lighter construction. Often the legs were turned spindles.

SPIDER WORK
A lace made with the spider stitch which gave an impression of a spider's web.

SPINDLE
A thin turned member generally tapered at each end. It appears in chair backs, stretchers and legs.

SPINET
A musical instrument that had keyboard and strings closely resembling a harpsichord. It dates from around 1650. The cases are quite often converted into shallow writing desks.

18th century fruitwood spinning wheel. Courtesy of Phillips

SPINNING WHEEL
The first efficiently working example probably dates from around 1350. They have been made from oak, yew, box and beech. The treadle operation came in about the middle of the 16th century.

SPODE, JOSIAH (1733–97)
The founder of the English pottery at Stoke-on-Trent, Staffordshire in about 1770. He had previously been apprenticed to Thomas Whieldon. Josiah did much to perfect transfer-printing in under-glaze blue. He was joined by William Copeland in 1779. His son, also Josiah (1754–1827), carried on the business and introduced bone china which was a mongrel hard-paste that contained bone ash.

SPONTOON
A type of half-pike or halberd carried by sergeants and foot-soldiers during the 17th and 18th centuries.

SPOON

(Old English *spón,* a chip or splinter of wood.)
A table implement with a bowl at one end
and a stem of varying length, size and
design. Examples are preserved of spoons used
by the ancient Egyptians. These are made
from ivory, flint, slate and wood, often carved
with ritual symbols. The Greeks and Romans
made most of their spoons from bronze and
silver, generally with a spike or pointed handle.
Medieval spoons were mainly for consuming
thick viscous liquids rather than stirring and
were made from brass, latten, pewter, horn
and wood; silver spoons were a rarity. Spoons
of gold were reserved for ecclesiastical purposes,
royalty and nobles.

The early bowls were mostly fig-shaped
and then in the latter part of the 17th century
became broad and oval. Around 1725 the
shape becomes narrower and elliptical and then
changed again about 1760 to a bowl that was
wider at the back.

The types of spoon have been many:

Acorn:	15th century with an acorn at the handle tip.
Apostle:	Late 15th century, a full set is rare as it includes thirteen – Jesus with all his apostles.
Basting:	Late 17th century, long, slightly curved handle and large bowl.
Bright-cut:	Late 18th century with faceted formal decoration.
Caddy:	Late 18th century, oval or round bowled, short handled.
Diamond Point:	15th century, handle terminating in a diamond-point.
Egg spoon:	Late 18th century. There does not appear to have been a specific spoon for eggs before this.
Folding:	Early 15th century, pointing to the fact that spoons at this period were personal and often carried around, probably in a leather case or special box.
Maidenhead:	15th century with the finial in the form of a young lady's head generally with long flowing hair.
Marrow:	(*see* p 161)
Mustard:	Mid 18th century, in the shape of a miniature sauce ladle.
Puritan:	Mid 17th century, an almost round bowl with a flat stem with a stump end. It was popular with the Cromwellians because of the simple austere design.

Rat-Tail:	Late 17th century, distinctive by the tapering rib down the back of the bowl added for strength.
Seal Top:	15th to 17th century, the stem terminates in a seal, generally with incised initials.
Straining:	Late 18th century, with a pierced bowl and might be large, for gravy, or tea-spoon size for picking the motes from a poured cup of tea.
Trifid:	Late 17th century, the end of the stem is notched in two places, also termed a *pied de biche* spoon.

SPURS

A pointed device attached to the heel, or above
the heel, of a horseman. The earliest examples
were armed with a single prick. In England
the rowel spur is shown upon the first seal
of Henry III but it did not come into general
use until the 14th century. In the 15th century
spurs had very long shanks so as to be able to
reach the horse's flanks below the spreading
bards. They became subjects for the metalsmiths
art, decorated and sometimes even gilded,
which was a badge of rank for knights.
Apparently in the rare cases of ceremonious
degradation their gleaming spurs were hacked
from their heels with a cook's chopper.
Spurs reached their most exotic and cruel
state with the huge examples worn by the
Mexican cavaliers.

After the battle of Courtrai in 1302, it is
recorded that the victors hung up bundles of
gilt spurs in the churches of Courtrai and
Maastricht as trophies of an event that is still
recalled by the Flemings as the *Goudensporendag.*

SQUAB

Removable cushion from a chair, often quite
thick and firm, dates from the late 17th
century.

SQUARE PIANO

A type of piano introduced in the latter part
of the 18th century. It has an oblong case and
does not have as many octaves as a full piano.
As with the spinet it is liable to become a victim
of alteration and may emerge as a desk or a
small chest on legs or other such pieces.

STAFFORDSHIRE

The potteries begin close to the Cheshire
border at Green Lane and include places
associated with famous manufactories such as

Staffordshire figures: on the left Tom Cribb and on the right Tom Molineaux. Courtesy of Oliver Sutton Antiques

Golden Hill, Red Street, Newfield, Smithfield, Chele, Tunstall, Brown Hills, Longport, Burslem, Hotlane, Cobridge, Hanley, Shelton, Vale Pleasant, Etruria, Stoke, Fenton, Lower Lane, Lane Delph and Lane End, all within an area about ten miles across.

STAINED GLASS

That which has been stained by either the introduction of metallic oxides in the melting pot or by coating with a film of coloured glass. Other methods include the application of a silver compound in the fire, which turns the glass yellow. Then there is the covering with coloured enamels which are then fused, vitrified into the glass; with this, sgraffito work could be done before firing. In the 16th century the art of painting on glass with translucent colours was introduced.

STANDISH

See Inkstand

STARCHER

An instrument rather like a small mangle with geared rollers and a long cranked handle for stiffening up collars. Closely allied came such as goffering irons for dealing with the wavy crimped details. Other specialised irons include the hefty tailor's 'goose' that weighed up to thirty pounds and got its name from the long handle and the hatter's poker with a flattened end curved to fit the shape of a silk hat.

STEELYARD

A type of balance in which the body to be weighed is suspended from the shorter arm of a lever, which turns on a fulcrum and a counterpoise is slid along the longer arm which is graduated to indicate the weight.

STIEGEL, HEINRICH WILHELM
(1729–85)

He emigrated from Mannheim, Germany to Pennsylvania. He set up a glasshouse and brought in European craftsmen to make a flint glass that would be as good, if not better, than that from the other side of the Atlantic. Unfortunately he overspent with some of the expansions and went bankrupt. Identification of a Stiegel glass is difficult as the glasshouse used no identifying mark.

STILETTO

A 17th-century European slender stabbing weapon; the blade often had a square or triangular section to give strength and lessen the risk of breaking.

STIRRUP CUP

One with no base and generally made from silver, often with the bottom in the form of a fox's, hare's or hound's head. Besides silver they have been made in porcelain, bone, china, and glass. These cups are mentioned as early as 1681.

STOMACHER

An ornamental covering for the front of the upper body. It was worn, into this century, by ladies and, earlier, also by gentlemen. Many were made with some of the different laces.

A stirrup-cup which measures about 3 ins (7·6 cm) in diameter and is decorated with floral sprays. Courtesy China Choice, London

STONEWARE

A type of coarse potter's ware that is glazed and fired to density, temperatures rise to between 1200 and 1400°C.

STORR, PAUL (1771–1844)

The celebrated English silversmith who was apprenticed to the Swedish craftsman Andrew Fogelberg. His work was registered in 1792 and he started in partnership with William Frisbee, but this soon broke up and Storr started on his own in Air Street, off Piccadilly, London. He was a true genius of his art and Storr pieces have that quality of greatness that makes them unique. He liked to introduce fantasy into his work, serpents, dolphins joined with gadrooning, scrolls and leaf patterns provided that controlled enrichment for which he was famous.

STRASBOURG

A faïence manufactory founded and run by the Hannong family from about 1721 until 1780. Actually prior to this there was a Hannong, making stoves of green enamel, and Charles Hannong was making pipes in 1709 in the Rue du Foulon. The faïence made from 1721 to 1739 was under the direction of Charles Hannong, then that from 1740 to 1760 under Paul Hannong and that from 1761 to 1781 under Pierre Hannong. Notable is the treatment of flowers in the decoration and also the dishes with painted fruit.

STRAW WORK

The technique of ornamenting boxes, frames, small table tops and similar items with laid straw. First the straws were split and if necessary bleached and dyed and then cut to size and shape and stuck down. The practice started in the late 17th century in France and Spain. The English centre was in Bedfordshire. The French prisoners of war also decorated many items in this way.

STRETCHER

A horizontal cross-piece connecting the legs of chairs, stools and tables.

STUMP WORK

A type of elaborate high-relief embroidery that was popular in England during the 17th century. It was used not only to make panels for framing but also to decorate bookbindings and boxes.

SUGAR TONGS

First introduced around 1720, made in silver the early examples were scissor shape, the spring bow came later in about 1750.

SUNDERLAND

A number of potteries were working in County Durham in the late 18th and 19th centuries. These included the Sunderland Pottery which produced a pink metallic lustre. A favourite decoration was a ship of war with a verse underneath. A butter dish has one that bore the name 'The Northumberland, 74 guns' and underneath

> The troubled main, the wind and rain,
> My ardent passion prove;
> Lash'd to the helm, should seas
> o'erwhelm,
> I'll think on thee, my love.

Other potteries were: Newbottle, started by Mr Byers about 1755; the Garrison; the Carr's Hill set up about 1730; the Ford that made brown and white ware; and the Hylton set up around 1780.

SUNDIAL

An instrument to show the time of day by the shadow cast by a gnomon. The dials could be made from bronze, slate or cut from stone. It is likely it was the earliest of all time measuring and telling devices.

SUNG PERIOD

The great period of the arts in China, the Sung dynasty (960–1278). In particular, ceramics flourished and considerable advances

17th century English stumpwork, re-mounted on ivory silk. Courtesy of Phillips

TABLE 213

were made with techniques in glazing, painting and firing.

SUNRAY CLOCK
A design popular during the reign of Louis XIV, the so-termed 'Roi Soleil'. It appeared as a sunburst, with the clock face in the centre.

SUTHERLAND
A narrow-topped table with drop leaves evolved early in the 19th century.

SWAG
An ornamental festoon of fruit and flowers that may be carved or modelled. Drapery and ribbons are often included.

SWANSEA
The making of earthenware started in the Strand about 1750. Then around 1780 Mr Haynes took over the works and named them the Cambrian Pottery. The ware resembled the translucent whiteness of Nantgarw. Decoration used included figures, birds, flowers and landscapes.

SYMPIESOMETER
A sensitive barometer that was patented in 1818 by Adie. It worked by atmospheric pressure acting on a liquid and compressing a gas. It was convenient for use at sea but did not have the accuracy of the mercurial barometer.

TABARD
A garment with short sleeves or without that was worn over a knight's armour. It would normally be emblazoned with his coat of arms. Worn also by heralds showing the arms of their sovereign.

TABERNACLE
(From the Latin *tabernaculum*.) In Christian Art this word may have a variety of meanings: a reliquary, a repository, a triptych or a niche for an image. Originally it was a kind of temporary dwelling or movable abode, a portable sanctuary which was probably first used by the Israelites during their early wanderings.

TABERNACLE MIRROR
An American-style mirror, a vertical, rectangular wall mirror with a column each side and a cornice. The name is supposed to have been derived from the seeming resemblance to a tabernacle. Decoration above the mirror can consist of a painted panel, often on a naval theme and with small sprays of some plant form. The vogue was around 1800 to 1820.

TABLE
Basically an article of furniture with a flat top supported on legs or a central pillar. The earliest that can be truly visualised came with the early Egyptians, who had rectangular examples very similar to those of today. The Romans had a number of shapes and types including a charming round table, to be seen in a wall painting at Pompeii, with what looks like legs very close to cabriole. They also had bronze pedestal tables with carved slabs at the sides. Tables in the Middle Ages tended to be massive. Then, with the Renaissance, came the beginning of a return to grace and an aesthetic appreciation of material, form and an applicable design. The period of the great cabinetmakers and *ébénistes* brought tables of many types, exquisite carving, marquetry, inlays and decorations.

The principal table types have been:

Dining:	With the draw tables, refectory, drop leaf.
Side:	Fixed top service tables, usually against a wall.
Console:	Decorative features to fit architecturally with an interior.
Work:	Specifically for such as needlework, drawing, reading.
Game:	Board games such as chess and backgammon, or cards.
Writing:	Simple desks with a drawer or set of drawers.

George III satinwood Cheveret table. Courtesy Christie's

Dressing: For both ladies and gentlemen, accessories would include mirror, light-holding fixtures.

To these could be added special tables that do not fit into the foregoing divisions:

Cabaret: For serving such as coffee or
(*c* 1700) chocolate it had a top and a plateau.

China: Intended to hold a service of china
(*c* 1750) and this had a small gallery round the top.

Drinking: A horseshoe shape for use after
(*c* 1780) dinner; the ends of the horseshoe would face the fire and it had a fitting for a screen to shield the party from the heat.

Drum: Round library table with drawers
(*c* 1790) and mock drawers.

Haricot: One in the shape of a kidney or
(*c* 1720) bean, an occasional table.

Supper: A variety of tilting top or column
(*c* 1750) and tripod support. It had compartments for dishes.

TABLE CLOCK
One with a horizontal dial, it is intended to be placed on a table and viewed from above.

TABOURET
A low, upholstered stool for sitting on, or as a footstool; it could be square, rectangular or round.

TABRIZ
A Persian rug with a very fine weave on a cotton, linen or silk ground and a short, dense pile. The colours are very rich and strong but in perfect harmony.

TACHI
An early Japanese single-edged fighting sword that has not been used as such for a long time; but has continued as a ceremonial weapon.

TAFFETA
A light, thin silk fabric with a lustrous surface and sometimes a raised pattern. It has been used for hangings and cushion covers from the early part of the 17th century.

TALLBOY
See Highboy

TALL-CASE CLOCK
See Long-Case Clock

TAMBOUR
A flexible shutter or door moving either horizontally or vertically between straight or curved grooves. It is made of a number of thin strips of wood with a convex moulding facing outwards and glued to canvas or strong linen.

TAMBOUR CLOCK
One that is enclosed in an upright tambour-shaped case somewhat extended at each side.

TAMBOUR EMBROIDERY
A type of embroidery worked on a tambour, round frame from the Far and Middle East. Its first introduction to Europe came in Switzerland in about 1750. The patterns are

worked with a tambour needle, hooked and using cottons or silks.

TAMBOUR STITCH
One used in embroidery that results in the appearance of a chain.

TANG
The piece forming an extension of the blade and connecting with the handle in swords, daggers or table and carving knives.

T'ANG PERIOD
The flowering of Chinese Art during the years 618 to 907. Sadly, little is extant owing to its destruction during the later years of the dynasty. What knowledge there is has been gained mainly from writings and from certain examples of Japanese art that are known to have been inspired by T'ang art; as well as specimens in the field of ceramics, some of which have been retrieved from burial places, indicating the mastery of the potters. It is also known that Chinese porcelain was exported to the Middle East in the days of the T'ang dynasty and was greatly appreciated.

TANKARD
Originally a tub-like drinking vessel of hooped staves; now a tall slightly tapering cylinder with one handle and sometimes a top that could be lifted with the thumb of the drinking hand. They have been made of pewter, copper, brass, silver and for a very special person, of gold. In Germany there have been examples of silver-gilt linings inside elaborately carved outer wood cases. Ivory has also been used for outer cases.

TANTALUS
A stand or open frame that holds square decanters, which can be seen but not removed as a bar passes across the top and is secured with a lock at the side. The name probably comes from Greek mythology in which a Lydian king who divulged to mortals the secrets of the gods was punished by being plunged up to his chin in the river Hades. A tree, hung with clusters of fruit, was just above his head. Whenever he tried to drink the waters receded and whenever he reached for fruit it was drawn up out of reach.

TANZENMANN
A Swiss drinking vessel, generally made of wood. It was carved in the form of a peasant with a basket on his back. This was removable and was the cup for drinking. It was introduced during the 17th century.

Ivory Tankard, French c 1870. Courtesy of Sotheby's, Belgravia

TAPE GUIPURE
Narrow tape lace often not much more than an eighth of an inch wide, although in some places it was produced up to two inches to serve for cuffs and collars. The patterns were free flowing and nearly every bobbin-lace centre made it.

TAPER JACK
A silver device for sealing letters with wax, it involved a taper holder and a small container for the wax.

Decorated caddies and biscuit tins, early 20th century. Courtesy of Christie's, South Kensington

TAPER STICK

A small candlestick for use by smokers or as a part of a standish, or inkstand, to serve for melting sealing wax. It came into use around 1680.

TAPESTRY

A heavy handwoven textile of cloth weave, sometimes twill, and decorated with patterns and scenes, it has been used as a wall, floor and furniture covering. The earliest examples were decorated by painting, printing, embroidery or a weaving method with coloured thread. Evidence points to the fact that the early Egyptians, Babylonians, Chinese, Indians, Greeks and Romans used at least some of these techniques.

Tapestry weaving must have been active in monasteries and nunneries from the 5th century onwards, and during the time of the Emperor Charlemagne, inspectors of such productions influenced and encouraged the work. In the 11th century, guilds of weavers began and in England the weavers of London and Oxford were granted charters by Henry I. It is almost certain that some of their work would be tapestry.

The most notable tapestry weaving centres have included: Arras, Aubusson, Beauvais, Berlin, Bruges, Brussels, Cambrai, Delft, Dresden, Dublin, Exeter, Fontainebleau, Fulham, Ghent, Gisors, Gobelins, Heidelberg, Kilkenny, Lille, Madrid, Middleburg, Mortlake, Munich, Nancy, Naples, Oudenarde, Oxford, Rheims, St Amer, St Petersburg, Seville, Soho, Tournai, Turin, Valenciennes, the Vatican and Venice. These and other places were in production often for long periods and it is sad how comparatively little still survives. In many ways tapestry is frail, and damp, wear, fire and probably iconoclasm have depleted their beautiful works. From 1528 Charles V ordered all *tapissiers* to mark their works and the custom spread over Europe. But in many cases these marks have been cut out and transferred so that it can be very difficult to accurately place a tapestry. Many famous painters made designs including: the Van Eycks, Roger van der Weyden, Mantegna, Raphael, Bernard van Orley, Primaticcio, Rubens and Edward Burne Jones.

TAPPIT HEN

A drinking vessel from Scotland, generally of pewter, it is cylindrical in shape with a slight concave middle and has a side handle. It should have a lid on which is a knob that represents a crested (tappet) hen from which comes the name. It holds two Scottish pints or more.

TARGE

A shield, usually round, it implies specifically the hide and wood type with large metal bosses used by the Highland warriors.

TARSIA

A type of Italian inlay associated with Lombardy and Tuscany (*see* Intarsia).

TASSET

Armour to protect the upper thigh, it could be in the form of a short skirt and was in use from about 1450.

TASSIE, JAMES (1735–99)

A Scot who, with Henry Quin, a physician, developed a vitreous paste that would simulate gem stones. He produced an amazing number of imitations of antique gems. Rudolf Eric Raspe made out a catalogue of some 15 800 'tassies' as the clever productions were nicknamed.

TATTING

A type of knotted lace made from cotton or linen thread wound on a shuttle. Fashionable in the 19th century, but the origin is unknown.

Rare Chelsea White 'Chinaman and Serpent' Teapot and Cover modelled in the form of a seated 'magot' figure derived from the Chinese god of plenty, Pu Tai, *c* 1750. Courtesy of Sotheby Parke Bernet

TAVERN TABLE

A small table with a round, oval or rectangular top with turned legs and low set stretchers used as a service table in inns from the 18th century onward.

TAZZA

A drinking vessel with a wide, shallow bowl mounted on a pedestal pillar or stem with foot. They have been made of silver, often enamelled, and glass.

TCHICHI

A Caucasian rug with a wool foundation and fine pile. Often repeating patterns are used and held in with strong parallel broad strips.

TEA CADDIES

The first examples came at the end of the 17th century. They have been made from silver, Sheffield plate, pewter, brass, japanned tin and wood. The most popular were from wood, inlaid and decorated, the container or containers inside being lined with lead.

TEAK

A tall East Indian timber tree, *Tectona grandis*; a strong yellow-brown durable wood, particularly resistant to damp and decay. It has been much used in Eastern furniture. Its leaves yield a red dye.

TEA-POTS

The earliest silver pot dates from about 1740 and had a tapering cylindrical body with a handle at right angles to the straight spout. From this the vogue moved towards a shorter, more bulbous shape and a spout which was curved rather like a swan's neck and which was placed opposite to the handle. This has broadly remained the popular shape with varieties including an oval fluted upright and an octagonal body. Besides silver, tea-pots have been made from earthenware, stoneware, porcelain, pewter and japanned tin plate.

TEAR

A drop-shaped bubble of air enclosed in solid glass as an ornament, as with a wine glass stem.

TELESCOPE

The basic idea of using two lenses came accidentally to a spectacle maker of Middleburg in 1608. The story has it that one Hans Lippershey was holding two convex lenses some distance apart and happened to see the neighbouring church spire through them and noted how much larger it appeared. It is recorded that Galileo Galilei (1564–1642), when he received the news about Lippershey's discovery, saw it as the key he had been subconsciously looking for and after only a day's study of the idea he was to invent his telescope. From a threefold magnification he progressed to a power of 32. He made his own instruments and in fact produced hundreds that were soon in demand by astronomers all over Europe.

After the Galilean came the reflecting telescope, the earliest form being the Gregorian, designed by John Gregory of Edinburgh in 1663. After this the Cassegrainian, invented by Cassegrain in 1672 and then the Newtonian developed by Sir Isaac Newton at about the same time. Telescope-makers, men such as Christopher Lock, active around 1673, John Hadley, at the beginning of the 18th century, George Adams, appointed instrument maker to the Prince of Wales before he became George III in 1760, and James Short (1710–68) became as celebrated as clockmakers.

TELLURIAN

An apparatus which shows the causation of day and night by the rotation of the earth on its axis in relation to the sun. The machine could also demonstrate the dependence of the seasons on the sun's declination.

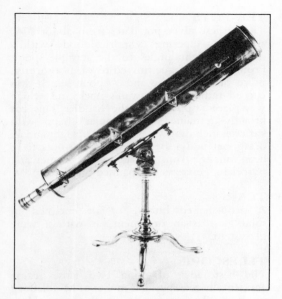

18th-century brass reflecting telescope by G. Adams, a mathematical instrument maker, Fleet Street, London. Courtesy Christie's

TENT STITCH
A short stitch used in embroidery, it is worked in even lines from left to right.

TERM
A pedestal or short pillar often carved or moulded with a decorative figure.

TERRACOTTA
A term derived from the Italian for 'baked earth'. Terracotta is unglazed and of a brownish-red colour. During the 16th and 17th centuries terracotta was often employed for architectural decoration. If the material has been properly made and thoroughly burned, it is of great permanence, lasting for centuries.

TERRY, ELI (1772–1852)
The American clockmaker working at North-burg who did much to develop the mass production of clocks. He later moved to Plymouth, New Hampshire. He is probably best recalled for the 'Terry Clock' a rectangular bracket or mantel instrument; and also for his use of wood for making the works of clocks instead of brass.

TESSERAE
The name of the small pieces of marble, glass, pottery or stone that are used to make up a mosaic.

Painted terracotta Blackamoor bust. Austrian c 1890. Courtesy of Sotheby's, Belgravia

TESTER
The canopy of a bed, including the frame and its hangings; it can also be made of wood.

THALER
A large silver coin used by various German states from the 15th century; it was first called a thaler in the 16th century.

THEODOLITE
The most important of the instruments used for surveying. It will measure both vertical and horizontal angles. In the main it consists of a telescope mounted so as to move on two graduated circles, one vertical and the other horizontal. The axes of the telescope pass through the centre of these circles. The earliest instruments based on this principle were Islamic and it is likely that the first example in Europe was Martin Waldseemüller's poli-metrum. Theodolites earlier than the first part of the 18th century used open sights. The first true theodolite as known today was made in about 1720 by Sisson.

National Telephone Company Wall Phone. American, 1920. Courtesy of Sotheby's, Belgravia

James I Silver-mounted Tigerware jug. Courtesy of Christie's

THUYAWOOD

This African tree, *Callitris quadrivalvis,* is much sought after for veneer work; it is hard with a pleasant brown colour.

TIFFANY GLASS

A glass that had various colours fused into it and was subjected to fumes from different super-heated metals. It was developed by Louis C. Tiffany (1848–1933), the leading American decorative glass designer.

TIGERWARE

A loose term applied to Rhenish mottled brown glazed stoneware from Cologne during the 16th and 17th centuries.

TILTING CHEST

A medieval piece which bore carved or other decoration of jousting scenes and the general panoply of combat and battle.

TIN BOXES

Under this heading come all those containers for food, sweets and tobacco that have been used in the 19th century and this century up to about 1930. They were marketed in an astonishing variety and often richly decorated.

TIN GLAZE

A lead glaze made opaque by the addition of ashes of tin. It could be coloured by using metallic oxides; it was and is largely used on faïence and majolica.

TIN SOLDIERS

The evolution of the warriors in miniature owes much to the skill of a Birmingham man, William Britain, a 19th-century maker of intricate toys with examples such as coolies pulling rickshaws and walking bears. He wished to expand and having seen the heavy, solid lead soldiers from Germany he worked on a method for hollow casting and in 1893 brought into being his first soldier, a life-guard. Since then his firm has progressed through the various types, uniforms and the rest involved in the battlefield. At every stage of production there has been, and is, meticulous research which has resulted in a whole scene of speciality collecting.

TOBACCO JARS
In various forms these started to make their appearance during the reign of Charles II. They have been made from silver and silver-gilt, tin-plate, horn, ceramics and some may be found in wood and even papier mâché. They have been cylindrical, square, rectangular and octagonal and in the shapes of grotesque heads, musical instruments and tombstones, and decorated with coats of arms, allegorical scenes, wheatsheaves, dolphins and sporting scenes.

TOBY JUGS
These beer jugs were introduced in the latter half of the 18th century and their development is credited to Ralph Wood (1716–72), the Staffordshire potter. Since his time they have been imitated wholesale.

TOFT FAMILY
Staffordshire potters active around 1670 to 1700. Thomas the father started the production of large earthenware dishes decorated with slip and using straightforward naïve subjects: Charles II and the oak tree; soldiers in buff jerkins with full-wigs and a sword in their hands. Other members of the family working in the same way included Thomas junior, and Ralph.

TOILET MIRROR
An item that came in late in the 17th century. The silver ones were often the work of the Huguenot refugees. The mirror could be a simple hand example or more complicated set in a stand that would allow it to tilt and swivel.

TOMPION, THOMAS (1639–1713)
The justly famous English clockmaker who is often called the father of English clockmaking. He was clockmaker to Charles II and William III. He worked from 'The Dial and Three Crowns' off Water Lane, London. In his work he was closely in touch with the inventive minds of the Reverend Edward Barlow and Dr Robert Hooke. He is credited with, amongst other advances, inventing the first watch with a balance spring.

TONDER LACE
A kind of Danish embroidery or drawnwork made in the early part of the 16th century.

TONLET
A piece of late medieval armour, one of the horizontal bands forming a short skirt.

TOPAZ
A semi-precious stone which was first given its name by the Greeks and Romans. Today it is also known by the name Chrysolite.

TORCHÈRE
An 18th-century decorative slender candlestand often with a tripod base.

TORCHON
A coarse bobbin lace made with linen thread and using geometrical patterns. It was made by the peasants in many European countries from the late 16th century.

TORTOISESHELL
The most sought after tortoiseshell came from the hawksbill and was used for inlay or marquetry in the 18th century. Before that it was made up into fan frames, snuff-boxes, card cases and ornamental combs, and also large sheets about one sixteenth of an inch thick were flattened and used to cover caskets and then decorated by sgraffito and filled and held in place by chased silver mounts.

TORTOISESHELL WARE
A Staffordshire earthenware made about 1750 with a glaze containing metallic oxides that flowed and gave a tortoiseshell-like look.

It can also be an American 19th-century glass that has streaks and swirls of dark and light-yellowish warm browns.

TOUCH BOX
A small container that would carry the lighted tinder for soldiers in action with matchlocks.

TOUCH MARK
The pewterer's engraved mark on a piece he has made.

TOUCHPIECE
A coin or medal given out by various English sovereigns up to Queen Anne to persons touched by them for the cure of the king's evil.

Russia, Order of the White Eagle,
c 1855. Courtesy of Spink

Clock in rock crystal with diamond settings by Cartier. Once in the collection of King Farouk. Courtesy of Christie's

Paperweights: top right, Baccarat rose; bottom right, St Louis posy with yellow twist ring; top left, St Louis posy with yellow flower; bottom left, St Louis dahlia on spiral cushion. Courtesy of Spink

Francis I walnut meuble en deux corps. Courtesy of Christie's

TOUCH-PLATE
A plate of pewter kept by the Pewterers' Company on which pewter makers must strike their mark. Sadly, the Great Fire destroyed the Pewterers Hall and also the old touch-plates. The custom was restarted in 1668.

TOUCHSTONE
A black siliceous stone rather like flint which was used to test the purity of gold and silver by the streak left on the stone when it was rubbed with the metal.

TOWEL HORSE
A light wooden frame introduced about 1750.

TOYS AND GAMES
These pastimes and tools of childhood have in the past ten years become a field for investment and interest for the collector. Broadly those items prior to 1939 (and even some after the Second World War) have graduated from playtime ephemera to items for care and display. All kinds of working models, steam engines, trains, clockwork boats as well, building blocks, dice games, happy family cards and the rest are looked for.

TRACERY
Lattice-like work founded on the Gothic windows that appears as decoration with furniture.

TRADE CARDS
The small advertisement and personal cards of the craftsman of former years. The earliest of these seem to appear about the middle of the 17th century. They often carry quite charming and interesting engravings as well as written material such as this:

> George Paravicini At the Blackamore's head in Bedford Street (sometimes called Half-Moon Street) Pinker Cutter & Raiser of Sattin He also Draweth all Sorts of Point Patterns, & Patternes for Beds Petticoats, Wast-coats, Quilts And all sorts of Indian Patternes for Japan or Printing.

Tradesmen whose cards might be come across include: booksellers, chronologers, girdlers, gold lace men, haberdashers, mercers and playing card makers.

TRANSFER PRINTING
A technique for decorating pottery in which designs engraved on a metal sheet or stone are transferred to the pieces by means of tissue

Wooden model of a Helter Skelter 34 ins (86 cms) high. Courtesy of Christie's, South Kensington

Paddy and Pig. German *c* 1912. Courtesy of Sotheby's, Belgravia

Wooden Noah's Ark, *c* 1875. Courtesy of Sotheby's, Belgravia

Working model of a Fairground Roundabout, 15 ins (38 cms) high. Courtesy of Christie's, South Kensington

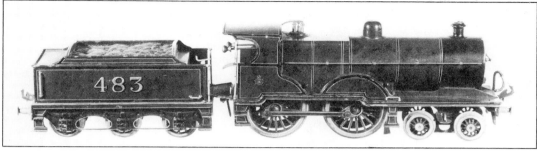

Bassett-Lowke Gauge-1 Clockwork 4+4-0 Locomotive and Tender. Courtesy of Christie's, South Kensington

Tinplate Clockwork 'Bucking Broncho' by Lehmann, patented 1881. Courtesy of Christie's, South Kensington

paper. It was gradually introduced during the second half of the 18th century.

TRAVERSE BOARD
A board having the four cardinal points of the compass marked on it, and for each point eight holes bored (one for each half hour of the watch), formerly used to record the courses made by the ship in each half hour.

TRAY
Earliest examples came with the Middle Ages and since then they have been made from not only wood but also silver, papier mâché, brass, japanned tin; shapes have been rectangular, round, oval, scallop-edged and have been with and without handles.

TREEN
A broad collective term for small objects made from wood. It is derived from the Old English *treowen*. A wealth of these domestic utensils were laboriously carved from different woods; they include: bird scarers, butter moulds and pots, knitting sheaths, boot-jacks, harvesters' kegs, watchmen's rattles, truncheons, coffee mills, candle and salt boxes, washing bats, woolwinders, corn and flour measures and spoons.

TREFOIL
An ornament which has three cusps in a circle, roughly representing a clover leaf. It was adapted from architecture for furniture.

TRENCHER
A wooden platter for serving food. Prior to these, thick slices of coarse bread received the individual portions cut from the spitted or boiled joint of meat that was served on a charger.

TRESTLE TABLE
The model of the early tables, a flat, thick board placed across trestles, horses or truss-end supports.

TRICOT STITCH
The simplest of crochet stitches, it is worked with a long hook and makes a quite plain straight pattern. It is also called idiot and railway stitch and fool's crochet.

TRICTRAC TABLE
The French table for backgammon, taking its name from the French for that game.

TRIDARN CUPBOARD
One in three sections, probably of Welsh origin and dates from about 1670.

Louis XV parquetry and kingwood bureau-plât; the centre reversing to disclose a trictrac table. Courtesy Christie's

TRIVET
A three-legged stand to hold a kettle or pan beside a fire; and also a decorated metal plate on three short legs to take a hot utensil and protect the table.

TROLLY LACE
An English bobbin lace that imitates an old Flemish style; it was worked on a net ground with the designs outlined with a heavy twisted thread.

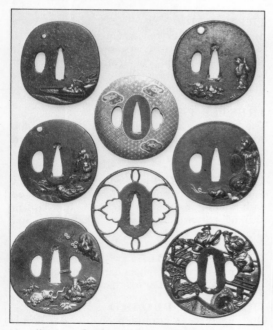

A collection of tsubas. Courtesy Christie's

TROUSSE
A case for a collection of small implements; such as that for the huntsman with his various knives or for a surgeon's instruments. In use from the 16th century.

TRUMPET LEG
A turned leg given a flare like that of a trumpet. It was used in the latter part of the 17th century.

TRUNDLE BED
A low bed that could be pushed under a higher bed. It is also termed truckle bed. First examples date from the Middle Ages.

TSUBA
The guard on a Japanese sword or knife, a metal plate often carrying fine decoration with piercing and engraving.

TUB CHAIR
A large, round easy chair with wide wings that dates from about the time of Sheraton who mentions one in his *Cabinet Dictionary*.

TUDOR ROSE
An ornament that dates from the end of the 15th century; it stood for the uniting of Henry VII of Lancaster and Elizabeth of York at the end of the War of the Roses. The flower is shown open with five formalised petals.

TULA METAL
An alloy of silver, copper and lead used in making niello. It was made at Tula in Russia.

TULIP WOOD
The timber from the *Liriodendron tulipfera* and also the Brazilian *Physocalymma floribundum*, both of which were used in cabinetwork and with age take on a pleasant warm yellow.

TULWAR
A curved sabre or scimitar that was especially a weapon of Northern India.

TUNBRIDGE WARE
A miniature inlaid technique which originated from Tunbridge Wells, Kent. Very small strips of different coloured hardwoods are used to build up the designs which may be geometrical or of flowers, small portraits or landscapes. It has been used to decorate many objects such as little boxes, caskets, tea caddies, work boxes, pencil boxes, glove boxes and toys such as the pre-Second World War yo-yo.

Above: 19th-century Tunbridge Ware. Photo by the author

Top right: Famille rose ox-head tureen, Ch'ien Lung. Courtesy of Christie's

Middle right: One of a pair of Silver Tureens by Juste Aurele Meissonnier made in 1734 for the Duke of Kingston. Courtesy of Christie's

TUREEN
A large deep vessel with a cover for serving soup, it has been made from silver and ceramics. The custom for bringing soup to the table in a large bowl or tureen dates from the latter part of the 17th century.

TURKEY WORK
A type of needlework imitating oriental carpets that have been woven with a knotted pile.

TURNER, JOHN (1738–87)
An English potter working in Staffordshire, first at Stoke and later at Lane End. He made high quality creamware, and also blue jasper ware and stoneware.

TURNING
In furniture-making it means shaping a component part whilst it is turning in a lathe.

TWIST TURNING
The giving of a spiral or twist shape to a leg for a table or chair. There were double and single twists.

TYG
A drinking mug or cup with two or more handles that was first made by English potters in the early years of the 17th century.

George III silver sauce tureen. Courtesy of Garrard

UNICORN
A Scottish gold coin current in the 15th and 16th centuries, it had a unicorn on the obverse.

UNITE
An English gold coin that was first issued by James I, the name referred to the union of England and Scotland. A version that was issued showing the king wearing a laurel wreath was called a laurel.

URBINO
The leading majolica centre in Italy, the manufacture has been carried on there since the late 15th century. Records quote the Cardinal of Carpaccio commissioning work from a potter Francesco Garducci in 1501. Ascanio del fu Guido was working in 1502; but these early works have disappeared or become attributed to others and so their true identity is lost. As the 16th century progressed it has been possible to connect painters and makers with their work; Guido Durantino was one, another was Francesco Xanto Avelli da Rovigo who painted after designs by Raphael and Orazio Fontana with several members of his family. From the middle of the century the centre came under the patronage of the Duke of Urbino.

URN
A vase of a circular form, used among ancient peoples to receive and preserve the ashes of the dead.

The urn often forms a decoration for the top of a pedestal of a balustrade or may be used as carved, moulded or painted decoration with furniture, or with interior decoration.

It can also be a closed vessel with a heating device for use with tea or coffee. They have been made from silver, Sheffield plate, copper and stoneware. Introduction was around 1750.

UTRECHT VELVET
One made from mohair or a mohair and cotton mix that had a cut pile. It was used exclusively for hangings and upholstery.

VALANCE
A short curtain, a drapery attached to the canopy of a bedstead, a window, a shelf or an altar.

VALENCIA
A Spanish ceramic centre of considerable age, Pliny mentions the manufacture of jasper red pottery there. The lustred ware was probably first made at the beginning of the 15th century. In 1517 Lucio Marineo Siculo said: 'In Spain earthenware vessels are made of various forms and although they are excellent in many parts of Spain, the most appreciated are those of Valencia, which are very well worked and well gilt and at Murcia much excellent pottery is made of the same kind, and at Morviedro and Toledo much is made which is very thick, with white, green, and yellow, with gilding, and is employed for daily use; the kind most esteemed is glazed with white.'

Valencia has been celebrated for its *azulejos* or enamelled tiles for a long time and examples of these appear in many buildings in the town.

VALENCIENNES
A bobbin lace worked on a ground with a square or diamond mesh. It is one of the most

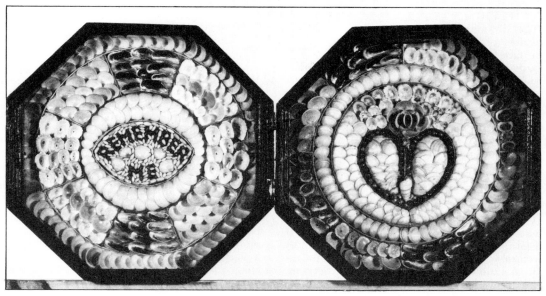

19th-century Valentine in a glazed case, worked with shells and grains of corn. Courtesy Christie's, South Kensington

complicated of this type of lace, the maker using up to three hundred bobbins at a time on the one pillow and working only a strip about 2 ins (5 cm) wide. It developed around 1725 but a similar type had been made in Flanders nearly a hundred years earlier.

VALENTINES

Although the first Valentine card was probably not sent before 1775, the custom of choosing a mate on 14 February goes back to at least the Romans who celebrated Februta Juno with boys drawing the names of girls. As time moved on the date became one for sending gifts to the chosen. In 1608 a Mr Clapton of Jesus College, Cambridge paid two shillings and sixpence for a pair of gloves for his Valentine and in 1661 Pepys tells of the Duke of York sending an £800 jewel. In the 19th century the custom came to more or less a matter of sending cards, which after the introduction of the penny post nearly always went anonymously. The cards appeared in every conceivable manner – perfumed artificial flowers, tinsels, paper lace – and often with loving verses pouring out the feelings:

Were I possessed of Fortunes store,
  I'd give it all to thee,
For thy affection still is more
  Than all the world to me.

And can you then such love repress,
A heart so true resign.
Dear maid return my tenderness,
And be my Valentine.

Artists of the calibre of such as George Cruikshank joined in the production of these light-hearted but often serious tokens. He produced a special for Lord Godrich to send to his old nanny in 1834. Francesco Bartolozzi the talented engraver was another.

VAMBRACE
Protective armour for the forearm dating from about 1220.

VEILLEUSE
A night-light, a night-lamp, a watch-light or a float-light.

VELOURS
A number of fabrics that have a pile similar to velvet.

VELVET
A rich silk fabric having a pile of erect threads. When they are uncut it is termed pile velvet and when they are cut it is called cut velvet. Early centres for manufacture include Lucca, Florence and Genoa, which were active in the 13th century.

VENEER
The decoration of furniture by using thin wafers of expensive and rare woods over a surface of cheaper woods. The basic idea goes back to the early Egyptians and the Romans and then it disappeared until the Renaissance with the use of intarsia. In England there were only a few instances of the technique before the time of Charles II. Its peak of perfection came possibly in the 18th century.

VENETIAN EMBROIDERY
A type of cut work carried out on batiste, linen or net using buttonhole and other lace stitches.

VENETIAN GLASS
Glasshouses first appeared in Venice in the 11th century, but towards the end of the 13th century they were transferred to the mainland at Murano to reduce the fire risk to the island town. Over the centuries a great many glasses have been produced, some of them examples of delicate and artistic handling of the material, such as: millefiori, latticinio, lace glass, milk glass and aventurine. The height of production was up to about 1700.

VENETIAN LACE
A needle-point lace dating from the 15th century; silks of black and white mingled with silver thread built up a distinctive material.

VENETIAN VELVET
A material in which very low relief designs were achieved by skilful cutting.

VENTAIL
The lower movable front of the helmet, the piece below the visor. It was provided to give ventilation if needed.

VERMEIL
Vermilion, ruby, ruddy or silver-gilt.

VERNIS MARTIN
A preparation of greenish varnish with gold powder (see Honey) developed by the Martin family and used during the time of Louis XV.

VERRE ÉGLOMISÉ
A technique for decorating glass from the back using gold and silver leaf and colours.

VERZELINI, GIACOMO (1522–1606)
The Venetian glassmaker who came to London and for a short time worked with Jean Carré at the Crutched Friars glasshouse. In 1575 he received the Royal Warrant from Elizabeth I and set up a glasshouse to make Venetian Glass.

VICKERS METAL
A 'safe' leadless form of pewter made by alloying tin, copper and antimony. It was developed around the end of the 18th century by a John Vickers of Sheffield.

VIENNA
A hard-paste manufactory set up in 1718 by a Dutchman, Claude Innocent du Pasquier, who brought in an expert from Meissen named Stenzel.
    The early wares were fine examples of the baroque manner and then later the quality of design became more imitative of Meissen and Sèvres and with the looser decoration of the rococo. Among the more notable productions were the exquisitely modelled figures.

VIGNETTE
A picture, landscape, portrait or design that has the edges blended, graded or softened away; a method used with decoration of some ceramics.

VILE, WILLIAM
Important cabinetmaker active in England around 1750 to 1765. He worked in partnership with John Cobb in St Martin's Lane. He was an expert carver and master with veneer.

VINAIGRETTE
Originally a small box now more often a bottle. The box would have contained a small sponge to be impregnated with aromatic vinegar; this would be held in place with a perforated inner lid. The vinaigrette was a fashion that started late in the 18th century and rose to its peak about 1830. The little boxes appeared in the shape of shells, hearts, books, purses and eggs. They were made of silver and silver-gilt.

VINE MOTIF
Formalised decorative ornament making use of vine leaves, vine stems and bunches of grapes.

VIRGINAL
A small rectangular spinet, without legs, that has just one string to each note and this is picked by a quill point when the key is struck. In fashion during the 16th and 17th centuries.

VISOR

The front upper movable piece of the helmet that can be raised to show the face. Normally these would have some small openings to allow sufficient sight and ventilation.

VITRINE

A glass-fronted showcase, sometimes with glass sides, for displaying ceramics, glass, curios and small treasures.

VITRUVIAN SCROLL

A repeating ornament of wave-like scrolls popular with designers in the 18th century.

VOIDER

A tray, basket or container of some kind used to clear scraps of food left on the dining-table either between courses or at the end of the meal. In use in some form from about 1600.

VOLANT

In armour it is a detachable piece that can be adjusted to protect the throat in jousting.

VOLUTE

A spiral scroll which forms the principal feature of the capital of the Ionic order in Greek and Roman architecture. It also appears in the Corinthian and composite orders.

It was popular with the French *ébénistes* in the time of Louis XIV and Louis XV.

VOUGE

A long-handled halberd, a weapon of the Middle Ages.

VOYEZ, JEAN (1735–1800)

A skilled silversmith and carver and also ceramic modeller who came to London from France. In 1768 he was taken on by Wedgwood as can be noted in a letter by Wedgwood dated 31 March 1768: 'I have hired a modeller for three years; the best, I am told, in London. He . . . is a perfect master of the antique style in ornaments, vases, etc etc, and works with equal facility in clay, wax, wood or stone.' Not long after the hiring Wedgwood found their man in trouble and the engagement was broken and Wedgwood was in some concern over Voyez giving away his secrets to others.

VRAI RÉSEAU

A handmade bobbin net ground that was made in strips about one inch wide and then joined together.

VULLIAMY FAMILY

Swiss clockmakers who came to London in the early part of the 18th century. Benjamin Vulliamy (1780–1854) made a number of clocks and watches for George III and became the Royal Clockmaker.

WAFER BOX

A silver, glass or porcelain box to hold the wafers used to seal letters. The wafers were thin, brittle disks made of a thin paste of very fine flour baked between 'wafer-irons' over a charcoal brazier until the paste became dry. The paste sheet was then cut into round disks with steel punches. Non-poisonous colours were sometimes added. Some wafers have been made from gelatin.

WAGON SEAT

Somewhat rough but strong double seats with slat backs and either plain board or rush seats.

An American evolution, they were intended to be used in the farmhouse and the wagon.

WAG-ON-THE-WALL

An American slang name for the dial and works of a long-case clock that was hung on a wall without a case. Sometimes the clockmaker did this whilst he was still working on the case.

WAINSCOT CHAIR

A heavy oak chair with solid panels in the back and the seat. Sometimes there was carving on the back and turned posts. They

date in England and France from the 16th and
17th centuries and were made in America
about 1700.

WAKIZASHI
The shorter of the two swords that are
carried by the Japanese samurai. In shape it is
similar to the large sword, the katana.

WALKING STICKS
Although walking sticks are nowadays seldom
seen being used, they are becoming trophies
to be sought out and in some cases arranged
in fanciful patterns on the wall as past
warlike characters have displayed their swords,
daggers, spears and firearms. Henry VIII
apparently had six to ease the passage of his
royal bulk, and one contained amongst other
things a compass and a knife. Walking sticks
have been made from canes, ebony, mahogany,
ash, beech, oak, blackthorn, furze, maple,
myrtle, narwhal; they have been covered with
leather, thin silver plate, tortoiseshell, tin,
pewter. They have also been made from glass.
Handles have come from many of the fine
ceramic houses, they have been carved, and
have carried tobacco, snuff, spirits, writing
materials, fishing rods for poachers, or a
sword. The last mentioned makes it one of the
deadliest weapons. The user threatens his foe
by raising the stick. The foe grabs the stick
and he is then wide open for a quick
withdrawal of the blade, which is likely to be
a fine Toledo épée, and an even faster lunge
back.

WALLENDORF
German porcelain manufactory in Thuringia
established in 1762 by Greiner and Haman.
Wares produced were for domestic use,
although some good copies of Meissen figures
were made but they were unmarked. The house
mark was a 'W' put on to imitate the cross
swords of Meissen.

WALL FOUNTAIN
A water holder made of pottery, copper,
pewter with a small tap which was intended
to hang on the wall over a small basin.

WALLPAPERS
The earliest examples date from the latter part
of the 16th century and their use to a degree
was started as a more economic substitute for
tapestries and other rich wall hangings. They
did not, however, become generally used until
the 18th century. Quantities of Chinese painted

papers were imported about this time and also
the printing of papers from large wood
blocks was being developed. Another introduction was the flock paper with its heavy pile
and look of a textile. Patterns ranged from
small-repeats of flowers and plants to large
landscapes and figure compositions. William
Morris's ideas contributed much to papers in
his time and have since.

WALNUT
The wood of the *Juglans regia* which has been
one of the most popular with cabinetmakers
and was much used by the English craftsmen
after the Restoration.

William and Mary walnut bureau cabinet. Courtesy
W. R. Harvey & Co.

WALSALL
An important 19th century centre for the making of leather and metal fittings for coaches and horses. There were numerous craftshops at work on brasses and all the complicated items of saddlery and the upholstering required.

WALTON, BENJAMIN
An English japanner active around 1810 to about 1845 in Wolverhampton where his works employed well over 500 craftsmen and produced an enormous amount of japanned goods and also papier mâché.

WARBURTON
A well-known family of potters of Hot Lane, Cobridge, Staffordshire, active from around 1760, makers of high-quality cream earthenware. Wages for this period are interesting to note: a man would get 5 shillings and a boy 1 shilling and 3 pence per week.

WARDROBE
In medieval times the word could signify a room or closet for the nobleman to keep his clothes. Later it came to mean a massive movable hanging cupboard often of oak.

WAR HAMMER
A heavy-headed weapon on a long stout wooden handle, generally with a spike on one side and rough blade on the other. It was principally the tool of the foot-soldier to enable him to break up his opponent's armour.

WARMING-PAN
A copper or brass lidded pan with a long handle into which live coals were put so that the instrument could be used to warm beds.

WASHSTANDS
A small table or cabinet for holding a basin and other accessories for washing. It very often had a lift-top that when it was again in place gave the stand an appearance of a night table. They could be rectangular, square, or triangular to fit in a corner. Both Hepplewhite and Sheraton made designs for these.

WASSAIL BOWL
A large bowl of silver and sometimes lignum vitae to hold the wassail liquor drunk at Christmas and on Twelfth-Night. It was made up of ale or wine flavoured with spices, and it also contained sugar, toast and roasted apples.

WATCH STANDS
Produced from the late 18th century onwards to hold a pocket watch. They were made from ceramics or wood and were often elaborately decorated being made in the appearance of groups of people round a centre object, castles and miniature grandfather clocks.

WATER CLOCK
An instrument to measure time by using a flow or fall of water, otherwise termed as a clepsydra. There were numbers of such instruments faked in Birmingham in the late 19th century.

WATERFORD
The celebrated Irish centre of glassmaking. The earliest mention of the production of flint-glass there seems to be in a Dublin Journal for 1729. This would have been at Gurteens a few miles out from the city. The main glasshouse was started in 1784 with some government aid and under the English glassmaker John Hill who had left Stourbridge, Worcestershire, with a number of skilled craftsmen to work in Waterford. Production continued with very high-class cut flint-glass wares including vases, jugs, table glass, decanters and toilet articles.

WATER LEAF
An ornament inspired by an elongated laurel leaf, and popular with Adam, Hepplewhite and Sheraton.

WATERMARKS
Marks that may be initials, names, dates, symbols, coats of arms or line patterns that are put into paper during the making. They are not always a safeguard as to authenticity because in many cases they can be quite effectively imitated or faked by the careful use of a caustic liquid.

WATKINS & SMITH
A London firm of instrument makers in production around 1750. Some of their works were complicated composite constructions that could include in one case a hygrometer, a thermometer, a barometer, a perpetual calendar and sundry scales and guides to calculations.

WAX JACK
See Taper Jack

WAYWISER
(Also odometer, pedometer, peramulator and surveyor's wheel.)

Mahogany waywiser by Alfred Joy of Chichester. Courtesy of Phillips

Basically a large wheel linked to a dial that could record the number of revolutions, and thus the rough distance between places. Probably the earliest mention of such like instruments is in the writing of Vitruvius (the author of a treatise on architecture, who appears to have served as a military engineer under Julius Caesar, in the Africa War, 46 BC) who described a gadget with cogs that could be connected to a carriage wheel and would record the number of revolutions.

WEB FOOT

A carved foot found on cabriole legs during the time of Queen Anne; it got its name from a resemblance to a webbed foot.

WEDGWOOD, JOSIAH (1730–95)

The famous British potter who established the works at Etruria, Staffordshire. Josiah was born at Burslem, the youngest of thirteen. Many members of his family had been working as potters in Staffordshire during the 17th century and played notable parts in the development of techniques. Dr Thomas Wedgwood of Burslem was one of the best of the early salt-glaze potters. By the age of ten Josiah was learning the arts of his trade to be. In 1734 he was apprenticed to an elder brother. By 1752 he was manager of Alder's pottery, Stoke-on-Trent. Two years later he was in partnership with Thomas Whieldon of Fenton then the finest master-potter in the area.

In 1759 Josiah leased the Ivy House pottery from some relatives and produced quality salt-glaze and green and yellow glazed ware. In 1762 he leased the 'Bell' works and made some of the finest white English earthenware. He produced the celebrated cream earthenware and from it a service for Queen Charlotte in 1762. Thus it became known as Queen's ware. He also received the royal appointment to the king and queen.

He then turned to the study of classical ware and translated the manner to the tastes of his time; this was particularly demonstrated with his Jasper bodies (see Jasper ware) and sensationally so with his reproduction of the famous Portland or Barberini vase in blue-black with white figures. There was also his much sought after black basalt brought in during 1769.

He married a cousin, Sarah, in 1764, and had a large family, one daughter was to become the mother of Charles Darwin. His descendants carried on the work into this century.

WEESP

The first manufactory for porcelain in Holland it was started in 1764 by the Count Gronsveldt-Diepenbrock who by some means had procured the secret of the composition of hard-paste. He produced some very fine white porcelain but the works closed in 1771. It was reopened a short time later by a consortium of Amsterdam business men led by the Rev. De Moll; shortly after, the works were moved to Loosdrecht and later to near Amsterdam.

WEISWEILER, ADAM (c 1750–1809)

The French maître-ébéniste who was born in Germany and who emigrated to France and Paris during the time of Louis XVI. He was noted for incorporating graceful caryatids in bronze as supports for desks and tables, and also embodying exquisitely painted Sèvres plaques.

WELSH DRESSER
A type of open oak dresser common in Wales. The sideboard part would have drawers and often small cupboards.

WHATNOT
A light, open set of shelves sometimes housing one or two drawers at the bottom; it was a 19th century introduction.

WHEAT EAR
An ornament of several ears of wheat that was used on some chair backs and with low-relief carving on large pieces.

WHEEL BACK
A chair with back spindles arranged in a radiating manner. An English 18th-century style.

WHEEL-LOCK
A gun-lock in which sparks could be struck from a flint, or sometimes a fragment of iron pyrites by a revolving wheel. The name also applied to a gun equipped with such a lock.

WHIELDON, THOMAS (1719–95)
The British master potter who started out at Fenton Low, Staffordshire in 1741. One of his apprentices was Josiah Spode. Later he was to partner for a time Josiah Wedgwood (*see* Wedgwood). He was particularly noted for his tortoiseshell, agate and marbled wares. It is unfortunate that he never marked any piece so that authentification is difficult.

WHITE IRON WARE
Objects made from iron coated thinly with tin. It is probable the first use of the manner was in 17th-century Scotland.

WICKER FURNITURE
Items, such as chairs, small tables, waste baskets, etc, made from osiers, reeds or rattans.

WIEDERKOMM
A tall, cylindrical German glass drinking vessel of the 16th and 17th centuries that would hold about a quart. They were generally richly decorated with enamel showing armorial bearings, and landscapes.

WILLARD BROTHERS
Amongst the leading clockmakers of America, the four brothers Benjamin, Ephraim, Simon and Aaron were born in Grafton, Massachusetts, and were active between them from about 1765 until around 1840. Benjamin the eldest, after serving his apprenticeship, returned to Grafton and set up a workshop in the family home. From there the four made several moves before finally splitting up and moving to Boston where they worked independently. Simon is probably the best remembered of the four, especially for his 'banjo' clock patented by him in 1802; he also patented a 'lighthouse' clock. Both his sons, Benjamin and Simon junior became clockmakers. Aaron was noted for the Massachusetts shelf clock, and his sons, Henry and Aaron junior, also followed in the craft and trade.

WILLOW PATTERN
A pattern pretending to be in the Chinese manner that has been credited to Thomas Turner and T. Minton, both of Caughly about 1780. It has been considerably copied and varied not only in Britain but also in Germany and France.

WILTON
Carpet making centre which had a charter granted in 1701, although there is little evidence that manufacturing began then. But it would certainly have been active when Lord Pembroke introduced the methods from Brussels in 1740 (*see* Brussels Carpet). Axminster type carpets were made there from about 1835.

WINCHESTER RIFLE
One of the best-known rifles of all, it was made by the Winchester Repeating Arms Company, Connecticut, which was established by Oliver F. Winchester in 1866. This interesting character started his working life making shirts and then became interested in firearms, and, in particular, the Volcanic Repeating Arms Company, which had some clever ideas with regard to loading and magazines. When this firm went bankrupt in 1857 Winchester bought it and formed the New Haven Arms Company which in its turn became the Winchester Repeating Arms Company.

WINDSOR
A type of chair popular in the 18th century in Britain and North America. It had a spindle back, splayed legs, with an 'H' stretcher and often a saddle seat. The first were made in

Britain, about 1700, and they appeared in Philadelphia around 1725.

WINE CISTERN

A large oval and often indeed massive vessel for holding bottles of wine in ice or cold water. The finest were made of silver and often designed around Classical ideas. Paul Storr (*see* p 212) adapted the famous Warwick vase, excavated at Tivoli and brought to Warwick Castle in 1744 by the Earl, as a wine cistern. Earlier cisterns had been made from brass, copper, pewter, bronze. Wood tub shapes, hooped with brass, had lead linings. Also called a wine cooler.

WINE LABELS

The fashion began around 1720 to have small silver or Sheffield plate labels hung round bottle or decanter necks with the type of liquor indicated. At first there were quite plain rectangles, later decorated with engraving and piercing. Labels of this type were also used for patent medicines and sauces.

WING CHAIR

A large, high-backed upholstered chair with sides to the back to shield from draughts, and to rest the head on. It was introduced around 1670.

WINGED LION

An ornamental device of the French Empire style with supports for tables and chairs. Other imaginative beasts included the winged sphinx.

WIRE

One of the most wayout collectors' items must surely be barbed wire. For some time there

Silver wine label. Courtesy M. McAleer

has been a society in America devoted to this material. The claim is that there are some 300 varieties of barbed wire that are no longer on sale and that are thus eligible as collectors' items.

WISTARBERG

A glasshouse that was founded by Caspar Wistar (*c* 1695–1752) in 1739 in Salem County, New Jersey, America. He was a Dutch emigrant, arriving in 1717. At his works he employed only other Dutch emigrants. After his death the glasshouse was run by his son Richard. The wares produced included: dishes, pitchers, lamp chimneys, bottles and window glass.

WITCH BALLS

Brightly coloured glass balls about seven inches in diameter, many of them were made at Nailsea (*see* p 168).

WOOD, ENOCH (1759–1840)

He was the son of Aaron, the gifted modeller, and was apprenticed to Josiah Wedgwood. He had inherited his father's talent and in 1781 worked a bust of John Wesley and also of the Rev. George Whitfield. In 1784 he went into partnership with his cousin, Ralph Wood, and six years later with Caldwell under the title of Wood & Caldwell; from 1879 the company was Enoch Wood & Sons. They produced enamelled earthenware figures and stoneware.

WOOD, RALPH (1715–72)

English potter working at Burslem and a talented modeller; he produced many Toby Jugs in lead-glazed earthenware and figures under such titles as the 'Vicar and Moses'.

WORCESTER

English porcelain manufactory founded in 1751 by 14 associates, including the celebrated physician and chemist Dr John Wall, who was also a painter of some talent. His time with the company is known as the Wall Period (1751–83). The manager of the pottery was William Davis. The early ware was in a fine soapstone porcelain and decorations showed an influence from Bristol and from China.

In 1783 the works were bought by Thomas Flight, and later Martin Barr was taken into partnership and with other members of the family the firm became 'Barr, Flight & Barr'. In 1862 it became the Royal Worcester Porcelain Company and as such still exists.

Worcester figure from the Shakespeare service, modelled by William Boyton Kirk, 1853. Courtesy of the Dyson Perrins Museum

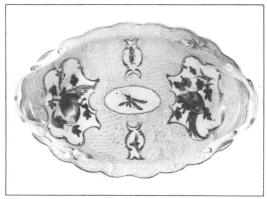

Worcester yellow-scale oval spoon tray. Courtesy of Sotheby Parke Bernet

WORK BOX

One fitted up as a sewing box with places for cottons, needles and etceteras. Earliest examples appear in the 17th century and are often covered with elaborate embroidery work.

WORK TABLE

This was introduced in the 18th century and to a degree made the work box obsolete. It had a top that lifted to disclose a well and generally two shallow drawers. It could be on a pillar support and tripod legs, and also four cabriole legs. Sheraton gives them a showing in his 'Drawing Book'. He produced the work table with a silk pouch. Some of them had highly-imaginative designs such as in the form of a globe as one made for Queen Charlotte.

WREATH

An ornament that owes its inspiration to the Romans, it appears during the Renaissance and with other revivals of the Classic manner. It might be carved, left plain or gilded, or as a bronze appliqué.

WRIGHT & MANSFIELD

Makers of reproduction 18th-century furniture and active around 1860. Their work had a very high degree of craftsmanship and with the passage of years, polishing and use it has been taken many times for genuine 18th-century furniture.

WRITHING

A decoration with glass involving a swirling ribbing or fluting on the bowl or stem.

WROTHAM

An earthenware manufactory active in Kent probably from around 1612. They were making a wide variety of wares including jugs, tygs, posset-pots, dishes and candlesticks. Most were decorated with a yellow slip, sometimes with incised or scratched patterns and raised tablets, and the whole covered with a lead glaze. Some would have inscriptions such as this one that was on a four handled tyg:
COM . GOOD . WEMAN . DRINK . OF . THE . BEST.
ION . MY . LADY . AND . ALL . THE . REST.

WROUGHT IRON

One that has a very low carbon content, often less than 1 per cent. It is tough and malleable and resistant to rust. It is not so brittle as cast iron.

X-FORM CHAIR
A folding chair with this form; the design goes back to the early Egyptians and Romans and it also appears during the Middle Ages.

X-STRETCHER
One that joins the legs of a chair or table. It was used during the time of William and Mary and in France during the reign of Louis XIV.

YARKAND
A Turkoman rug, it has a cotton foundation and a long wool or sometimes silk pile. Principally made near Kashgar.

YATAGAN
A long knife or a short sabre; it has no cross-piece and is common among Mohammedans. The blade is single edged and has a shallow double curve.

YEW
A tree of the genus *Taxus* which yields a wood with a close grain and warm reddish-brown colour, it is resistant to decay and wear. Used since the late 17th century as a veneer, it is noted for the high polish it will take.

YOMUD
A Turkoman rug with foundation and pile of wool or goats' hair. Patterns usually include diamonds but may have Caucasian latch hook variations.

YORKSHIRE CHAIR
One made in England during the 17th and 18th centuries. It was quite small with knobbed, turned legs, and with straight uprights ending at the top with scrolls and a broad carved top-rail.

YOUGHAL LACE
A type made at the Presentation Convent, Youghal, Co. Cork, in 1852. It was entirely needle made.

YOUNG, WILLIAM WESTON
A talented painter working at Swansea around 1800 to 1813, in the latter year he went to Nantgarw. He was noted for his work with plants and butterflies.

YSGWYD
An ancient British shield which resembled the oblong shape of that of the Romans.

ZAFFRE
An impure cobalt oxide used in the manufacture of smalt and also for colouring glass and ceramics.

ZEBRA WOOD
A tropical tree, *Connarus guianensis,* with a marked stripe in the wood, it has been popular for inlay and veneer work, particularly in the 18th century.

ZŌGAN
A form of Japanese inlaid metalwork.

ZOGRASCOPE
A large magnifying glass set in a frame on a stand that could be tilted for examination of drawings, prints, lace, embroidery and other detailed work.

ZOOMORPHIC DECORATION
The representing or imitating of animal forms as ornaments or patterns in designs for furniture, carving, ceramics, glass or metalwork.

ZOPHORUS
A frieze with a carved moulded relief with men or animals forming a flowing continuous pattern.

ZURICH
A Swiss porcelain manufactory established in 1763 by a few gentlemen from that city including the celebrated painter and poet Salomon Gessner, who not only prepared many designs but did some painting himself in the works. The managing director was a German named Spengler. Fine figures were modelled by another German, a political refugee by the name of Sonnenschein, who left after a few years to become the first director of the Art Academy at Berne. A distinctive feature of the porcelain is the delicate painting of the beautiful Swiss landscapes. Specimens are rare and much sought after.

A winding machine used in the wool trade to make up sample skeins or small hanks of yarn for weighing and testing. Courtesy Christie's, South Kensington

GALLERIES AND MUSEUMS

GENERAL COLLECTIONS

Specialist collections are in parentheses
(This list is only a selection from the thousands throughout the world.)

ALBANIA
Tirana
Ethnographical Museum

ALGERIA
Algiers
Musée National des Beaux Arts d'Alger

ARGENTINA
Buenos Aires
Museo de Armas de la Nación (*Arms*)
Museo Municipal 'Brigadier-General Cornelio
  de Saavedra'
Museo Nacional de Arte Decorativo
Museo Municipal de Numismática y Medal-
  listica (*Coins* and *Medals*)

AUSTRALIA
Sydney
Art Gallery of New South Wales
Museum of Applied Arts and Sciences
Melbourne
National Gallery of Victoria
Adelaide
National Gallery of South Australia

AUSTRIA
Vienna
Heeresgeschichtliches Museum (*Arms*)
Kunsthistorisches Museum
Schönbrunn Palace (*Furniture* and *Tapestries*)

Klagenfurt
Landesmuseum für Kärnten
Graz
Kulturhistorisches und Kunstgewerbemuseum
Landeszeughaus (*Arms*)

BELGIUM
Antwerp
Museum Smidt van Gelder (*Ceramics*)

Bruges
Musée de l'Hospice de la Poterie
Musée Gruuthuse
Brussels
Musée Royal de l'Armée et d'Histoire Militaire
  (*Arms*)
Musée des Beaux-Arts d'Ixelles
Mariemont
Musée et Domaine et Mariemont
Verviers
Musées Communaux: Beaux Arts (*Ceramics*)

BOLIVIA
Potosi
Museo Nacional de la Casa de Moneda de
  Potosi (*Coins*)

BRAZIL
Rio de Janeiro
Museo e Arquivo Histórico do Banco do
  Brazil (*Coins*)
Sabará
Museu do Ouro (*Gold* and *Silver*)
São Paulo
Museu Paulista (*Coins*)
Vitória
Museu Capichaba (*Arms* and *Coins*)

CANADA
New Brunswick
Beaverbrook Art Gallery
Quebec
Museum of Laval University (*Coins* and
  Scientific Instruments)
Saskatchewan
Western Development Museum

CHILE
Santiago
Museo Histórico Nacional de Chile

Hualpen
Museo de Hualpen (*Arms* and *Coins*)

CHINA
Peking
Imperial Museum
The Peking Lu Hsün's Residence
Shanghai
Shanghai Museum

COLOMBIA
Bogotá
Museo Nacional (*Arms* and *Coins*)
Museo de Arte Colonial

CUBA
Havana
Museo Nacional

CYPRUS
Nicosia
The Cyprus Museum (*Early Coins, Glass* and *Pottery*)

CZECHOSLOVAKIA
Prague
Národni Museum
Harrachov
Glass Museum (*Glass*)

DENMARK
Copenhagen
Nationalmuseet
Orlogsmuseet (*Weapons*)
Frederiksborg
Det Nationalhistoriske Museum paa Frederiksborg

EGYPT
Cairo
Coptic Museum (*Pottery* and *Glass*)
Gayer Anderson Pasha Museum (*Oriental*)

FINLAND
Helsinki
Kansallismuseo (*Coins* and *Medals*)
Turku
Turun Kaupungin Historallinen Museo

FRANCE
Paris
Musée du Louvre
Musée de l'Armée (*Arms*)
Musée des Arts Décoratifs
Musée Astronomique de l'Observatoire de Paris (*Instruments*)
Musée des Thermes et de l'Hôtel de Cluny

Musée d'Ennery (*Oriental*)
Musée Monétaire (*Coins* and *Medals*)
Musée Nissim de Camondo
Musée Céramique de Sèvres (*Ceramics*)
Angers
The Château (*Tapestries*)
Limoges
Musée Municipal (*Enamels* and *Gem Stones*)
Nice
Musée du Vieux-Logis (*Furniture*)
Tours
Musée des Beaux-Arts
Blois
The Château
Cheverny
The Château
Villandry
The Château

GERMANY
Berlin
Bode-Museum
Bremen
Focke-Museum
Brunswick
Herzog Anton Ulrich-Museum (*Ceramics, Coins* and *Lace*)
Cologne
Wallraf-Richartz-Museum
Darmstadt
Schlossmuseum (*Carriages* and *Harness*)
Dresden
Museum für Kunsthandwerk
Hamburg
Museum für Hamburgische Geschichte (*Coins*)
Hanover
Kestner-Museum (*Incunabula, Coins* and *Medals*)
Leipzig
Städtisches Museum des Kunsthandwerks Leipzig (*Ceramics, Glass* and *Textiles*)
Munich
Bayerisches Nationalmuseum
Nuremberg
Germanisches Nationalmuseum

GREAT BRITAIN
London
British Museum
Geffrye Museum
Hampton Court Palace
Iveagh Bequest, Kenwood
London Museum
Science Museum (*Instruments*)
Sir John Soane's House and Museum
Tower of London Armouries (*Arms*)
Victoria and Albert Museum

Wallace Collection
Wellington Museum (*Porcelain* and *Silver*)
Barnard Castle
The Bowes Museum
Bath
Holburne of Menstrie Museum of Art
Birmingham
City Museum and Art Gallery
Bristol
Museum and Art Gallery
Cambridge
Fitzwilliam Museum
Leeds
City Museum
Temple Newsam House
Manchester
City Art Galleries (*Costume*)
Newcastle upon Tyne
Laing Art Gallery and Museum
Oxford
Ashmolean Museum
Cardiff
National Museum of Wales
Glasgow
Art Galleries and Museum
Edinburgh
Royal Scottish Museum

GREECE
Athens
Benaki Museum

HUNGARY
Budapest
Hadtörténelmi Muzeum (*Arms*)
Magyar Nemzeti Muzeum—
Iparmüvészeti Muzeum

INDIA
Baroda
Baroda Museum and Picture Gallery
Jaipur
Central Museum (*Carpets*)
The Maharaja of Jaipur Museum (*Textiles, Carpets, Arms* and *Lacquer*)
New Delhi
National Museum of India
Bihar
Patna Museum (*Coins*)
Ajmer
Rajputana Museum (*Arms* and *Coins*)
Hyderabad
State Museum, Government of Andhra Pradesh (*Arms, Bidriware* and *Coins*)
Bombay
Victoria and Albert Museum (*Silver* and *Lacquer*)

IRAN
Shiraz
Pars Museum (*Earthenware* and *Coins*)

IRAQ
Baghdad
Arms Museum (*Arms*)

IRELAND
Dublin
National Museum

ISRAEL
Haifa
Museum of Ancient Art (*Early Textiles* and *Coins*)
Nazareth
Terra Santa Museum (*Early Coins* and *Glass*)

ITALY
Arezzo
Pinacoteca e Museo Medioevale e Moderno (*Glass, Majolica, Seals* and *Coins*)
Faenza
Museo Internazionale delle Ceramiche
Florence
Bargello
Museo degli Argenti (*Jewellery, Cameos* and *Porcelain*)
Appartamenti Monumentali (*Furniture*)
Museo Horne (*Furniture*)
Museo Stibbert (*Arms, Furniture* and *Tapestries*)
Milan
Gabinetto Numismatico Municipale (*Coins* and *Medals*)
Museo d'Arte Antica
Naples
Museo Nazionale di S. Martino
Museo e Gallerie Nazionali di Capodimonte
Perugia
Galleria Nazionale dell' Umbria (*Jewellery*)
Rome
Museo Nazionale Romano (*Coins*)
Museo di Castel S. Angelo (*Arms* and *Furniture*)
Turin
Armeria Reale (*Armour*)
Venice
Museo Archeologico (*Coins* and *Jewels*)
Museo Vetrario (*Glass*)

JAPAN
Tokyo
Kokuritsu Hakubutsukan
Nezu Art Museum
Kyōto
Yūrinkan

Ehime Prefecture
Oyamazumi Jinja Kokuhokan (*Arms* and *Mirrors*)
Hiroshima Prefecture
Itsukushima Jinja Hómotsukan (*Swords*)
Hyōgo Prefecture
Hakutsuru Bijitsukan (*Ceramics, Bronzes* and *Silver*)

LUXEMBOURG
Luxembourg
Musées de l'Etat

MEXICO
Mexico City
Museo de Arte Religioso (*Gold*)
Museo Nacional de Historia
Puebla, Pue
Museo de Arte 'José Luis Bello y González'

THE NETHERLANDS
Amsterdam
Rijksmuseum
Arnhem
Gemeentemuseum (*Ceramics, Glass* and *Silver*)
Delft
Rijksmuseum 'Huis Lambert van Meerten te Delft' (*Furniture* and *Ceramics*)
Gouda
Stedelyk Museum 'de Moriaan' (*Ceramics* and *Pipes*)
The Hague
Gemeentemuseum
Rotterdam
Historisch Museum der stad Rotterdam
Maritiem Museum 'Prins Hendrik' (*Model Ships, Globes* and *Maps*)
Museum Boymans-van Beuningen

NEW ZEALAND
Auckland
Auckland Institute and Museum

NORWAY
Oslo
Kunstindustrimuseet i Oslo
Trondheim
Nordenfjeldske Kunstindustrimuseum

PAKISTAN
Karachi
National Museum of Pakistan

PERU
Lima
Museo Arqueológico 'Rafael Larco Herrera'
Museo de Arte

POLAND
Warsaw
National Museum
Polish Army Museum
Cracow
State Collection of Art in the Wawel
Poznan
National Museum

PORTUGAL
Lisbon
Museu de Arte Sacra de S. Roque
Museu-Escola de Artes Decorativas
Museu Militar (*Arms*)
Belém
Museu Nacional dos Côches (*Coaches, Harness,* etc)

RUMANIA
Bucharest
Art Museum of the RPR
Cluj
Art Museum

SINGAPORE
Singapore
Art Museum and Exhibition Gallery

SOUTH AFRICA
Cape Town
Koopmans de Wet House

SPAIN
Madrid
Museo Arqueológico Nacional
Museo Cerralbo
Museo Municipal de Madrid
Museo Nacional de Artes Decorativas
Barcelona
Museo del Arte Escénico del Instituto del Teatro (All things of the *Theatre*)
Burgos
Museo Arqueológico de Burgos (*Enamels* and *Ivories*)
Toledo
Museo Parroquial de San Vicente (*Church Vessels* and *Carpets*)

SWEDEN
Stockholm
Nationalmuseum
Statens Historiska Museum (*Coins* and *Medals*)
Kungl. Livrustkammaren (*Arms* and *Coaches*)

SWITZERLAND
Fribourg
Musée d'Art et d'Histoire

Geneva
Musée d'Art et d'Histoire (*Coins*)
La Chaux-de-Fonds
Musée des Beaux-Arts (*Tapestries*)
St Gallen
Industrie- und Gewerbemuseum (*Embroidery* and *Textiles*)

THAILAND
Bangkok
National Museum

TUNISIA
Tunis
Musée du Bardo (*Mosaics*)

TURKEY
Istanbul
Topkapu Palace Museum
Türkiye Askeri Müzesi (*Arms*)

UNION OF SOVIET SOCIALIST REPUBLICS
Kuksovo
State Ceramic Museum
Leningrad
State Hermitage Museum
Moscow
Folk-Art Museum
USSR State Collection of Antiques (*String Instruments*) .
State Museum of Eastern Cultures

UNITED STATES OF AMERICA
Chicago
Adler Planetarium and Astronomical Museum (*Astronomical Instruments*)
Boston
Museum of Fine Arts
Brooklyn
Brooklyn Museum
Cincinnati
Art Museum
Cleveland
Museum of Art
Dearborn
Henry Ford Museum
Minneapolis
Society of Fine Arts
New York
Cooper Union Museum for the Arts of Decoration
Frick Collection
Metropolitan Museum of Art
Philadelphia
Museum of Art

URUGUAY
Montevideo
Museo Histórico Nacional

YUGOSLAVIA
Belgrade
Narodni Muzej
Ljubljana
Narodni Muzej

AUCTION ROOMS

(This is only a selection from the many establishments around the world.)

AUSTRALIA
Sydney
Associated Auctioneers Pty Ltd
Melbourne
Age Gallery. Christie, Manson & Woods
Leonard Joel

AUSTRIA
Vienna
Auktionshaus Schloss Potzneusiedel

BELGIUM
Brussels
Palais des Beaux-Arts

CANADA
Toronto
Abbey Auctions Ltd
Robert Deveau Galleries
Sotheby Parke Bernet Inc.

DENMARK
Copenhagen
Arne Bruun Rasmussen

FRANCE
Paris
Hôtel Drouot

GERMANY
Cologne
Kunsthaus am Museum
Lempertz, Kunsthaus
Hamburg
Dörling
Neumeister KG
Sotheby Parke Bernet

GREAT BRITAIN
London
Bonham's Ltd
Christie, Manson & Woods Ltd
Glendining & Co
Phillips
Sotheby Parke Bernet
Bath
Jollys Auction Rooms

HOLLAND
Amsterdam
Brandt BV
Christie's
Sotheby–Mak van Waay
The Hague
Van Maril en Bignell

IRELAND
Slane Castle
Sotheby Parke Bernet

ITALY
Rome
Christie, Manson & Woods (Italy)
Milan
Gallerie d'Arte Geri
Florence
Palazzo Internationale delle Aste ed Esposizioni,
  SpA
Sotheby Parke Bernet Italia. S.A.L.

JAPAN
Osaka
Osakaminamibijutukaikan
Tokyo
Hotel Okura. Christie, Manson & Woods

NEW ZEALAND
Auckland
Beltons Auctions Ltd.

NORWAY
Oslo
Börsums Bokauksjoner

PORTUGAL
Lisbon
Leiria & Nascimento Lda

SOUTH AFRICA
Johannesburg
Sotheby Parke Bernet, South Africa
  (Proprietory) Ltd

SPAIN
Madrid
Sotheby Parke Bernet Del Prado Calle
Subastas Madrid, Marqués de Caubas

SWEDEN
Stockholm
Bukowskis

SWITZERLAND
Lausanne
Ader Picard Tajan
Bern
Auktionhaus Dobiaschofsky
Galerie Jürg Stuker AG
Geneva
Christie's (International) SA
Lucerne
Galerie Fischer
Basle
Münzen & Medaillen AG
Zürich
Sotheby Parke Bernet AG

USA
San Francisco
Butterfield & Butterfield
New York
Christie, Manson & Woods International Inc
Phillips
Sotheby Parke Bernet
Philadelphia
Samuel T. Freeman & Co.
New Orleans
Morton's Auction Exchange
Boston
William A. Turtle & Co.

CLASSIFIED HEADINGS INDEX

COINS AND MEDALS

DECORATION AND ORNAMENT

EMBROIDERY

FURNITURE

GLASS

LACE

JEWELLERY

LEATHER

METAL WORK

MIRRORS

MISCELLANY

SCIENTIFIC INSTRUMENTS

SILVER, GOLD & SHEFFIELD PLATE

TEXTILES